The State of Islam

THE STATE OF ISLAM

Culture and Cold War Politics in Pakistan

Saadia Toor

PlutoPress
www.plutobooks.com

First published 2011 by Pluto Press
345 Archway Road, London N6 5AA

www.plutobooks.com

Distributed in the United States of America exclusively by
Palgrave Macmillan, a division of St. Martin's Press LLC,
175 Fifth Avenue, New York, NY 10010

British Library Cataloguing in Publication Data
A catalogue record for this book is available from the British Library

ISBN   978 0 7453 2991 8   Hardback
ISBN   978 0 7453 2990 1   Paperback

Library of Congress Cataloging in Publication Data applied for

This book is printed on paper suitable for recycling and made from fully managed
and sustained forest sources. Logging, pulping and manufacturing processes are
expected to conform to the environmental standards of the country of origin.

10   9   8   7   6   5   4   3   2   1

Designed and produced for Pluto Press by Chase Publishing Services Ltd
Typeset from disk by Stanford DTP Services, Northampton, England
Simultaneously printed digitally by CPI Antony Rowe, Chippenham, UK and
Edwards Bros in the United States of America

To Ammi and Abba

Contents

Acknowledgments

This book is the product of a long and rewarding journey. Along the way I have accrued debts of gratitude to several wonderful people.

This book started life as a PhD dissertation in the field of Development Sociology at Cornell University. I owe a lot to the members of my dissertation committee—Shelley Feldman, Phil McMichael and Biodun Jeyifo—for their patience and intellectual generosity. A big thank you to Phil McMichael in particular for all his help in the years since I left Cornell.

Staff members at the National Archives in Islamabad and the Punjab Public Library in Lahore went above and beyond the call of duty to help me in my research. A very special thanks is due to Ahmed Salim for giving me access to historical material I could not have found elsewhere, and to his sister for graciously hosting me for several weeks while I pored over it.

At CUNY, the course releases I received through the PSC-CUNY Women's Studies Fellowship Program, the Center for Place, Culture and Politics, the Center for the Humanities, and the Faculty Fellowship Publications Program freed up valuable time from teaching to think, research and write. Two of the chapters in this book benefited enormously from being shared with colleagues in the CUNY Faculty Fellowship Publications Program, and in the seminars on "Capitalism and Catastrophe" and "Aftermaths" at the Center for Place, Culture and Politics, and the Center for the Humanities respectively.

I have been fortunate to have had warm and supportive colleagues in the Department of Sociology, Anthropology and Social Work and in the Women's, Gender and Sexuality Studies Program at the College of Staten Island.

I am grateful for the generous help extended by Kamran Asdar Ali, David Gilmartin, David Lelyveld, David Ludden, Tayyab Mahmud, Vijay Prashad, Shahnaz Rouse and Neil Smith over the years. A very special thanks is due to Tariq Ali for reading the original book proposal and giving me valuable feedback, and to Ayesha Siddiqa for taking me under her wing and introducing me to her (now my) editor at Pluto Press, Roger van Zwanenberg.

I am indebted to Roger for seeing a book in the prospectus I had originally submitted, and for giving me the opportunity to publish with Pluto Press. The editorial and production team at Pluto has my gratitude for their hard work, patience, professionalism and good humour throughout the process of transforming the manuscript into a book.

In Ithaca, Philadelphia, Urbana-Champaign and beyond, I have been lucky enough to have the comradeship of many wonderful people: Humera Afridi, Snigdha Ali, Cindy Caron, Zahid Chaudhary, Sasha Constanza-Chock, Sandra Comstock, Iftikhar Dadi, Tulsi Dharmarajan, Indranil Dutta, Jude Fernando, Priya Gopal, Amy Guptill, Khalid Hadeed, Tanya Heurich, Farhana Ibrahim, Shakti Jaisingh, Shuchi Kapila, Sunaina Maira, Sheetal Majithia, Sarah McKibben, Monika Mehta, Sujata Moorti, Peter Morey, Carol Jinhi Park, Mindy Peden, Raj Patel, Ra Ravishankar, Cabeiri Robinson, Simona Sawhney, Magid Shihade, Dina Siddiqi, Ramkumar Sridharan, Ajantha Subramanian, Shivali Tukdeo, Meg Wesling, Chi-ming Yang, Usha Zacharias and Anna Zalik.

In New York City, I found an amazing community of people whose emotional and political support has been invaluable for me: Zohra Ahmed, Amna Akbar, Anthony Alessandrini, Aniruddha Das, Kazembe Balagun, Padmini Biswas, Tahir Butt, Miabi Chatterji, Ruchi Chaturvedi, Robindra Deb, Blair Ellis, Jayanth Eranki, Kouross Esmaili, Arvind Grover, Anjali Kamat, Sangeeta Kamat, Ronak Kapadia, Leili Kashani, Surabhi Kukke, Deepa Kumar, Jinee Lokaneeta, Aleyamma Mathew, Biju Mathew, Amanda Meade, Sangay Mishra, Tejasvi Nagaraja, Prachi Patankar, Radhika Piramal, Andy Pollock, Sekhar Ramakrishnan, Prerana Reddy, Sabina Sawhney, Ragini Shah, Silky Shah, Svati Shah, Ashley Smith, Amita Swadhin, Sue Susman, Max Uhlenbeck, Saba Waheed and Michael Washburn.

Ayaz Ahmed, Nikhil Aziz, Kate Bedford, Yukiko Hanawa, Karen Miller, Lisa Jeane Moore, Sarah Schulman and Jeanne Theoharris have provided friendship, love and support above and beyond the call of duty.

A very special thanks to Manan Ahmed, Shehla Arif, Abira Ashfaq, Sofia Checa, Saqib Khan, Zahra Malkani, Rakshi Saleem, Sahar Shafqat and Adaner Usmani of Action for a Progressive Pakistan for being such wonderful comrades in struggle. Without the community they have helped create, these past few years would have been bleak indeed.

My work with the Mazdoor Kissan Party gave me more political insight and a deeper sense of the history of the Left in Pakistan than any book I could have read. I learnt a great deal about what it means to live a life of unflinching activism from Ghulam Nabi Kalloo in the short time I knew him before his death and remain in awe of his indefatigable energy and commitment to the cause of working people. Latif Chaudhry, Parveen Kalloo, Kamoka and Bai Siddique in Faisalabad, and Amir Butt, Syed Azeem and Taimur Rahman in Lahore were my second family for two eventful years. I am also grateful for the chance to have gotten to know the wonderful Abdullah Malik before he died; memories of summer mornings spent in political discussion on his veranda remain among my most cherished.

Amanullah Kariapper and Qalandar Memon fill me with hope for the future of the Left in Pakistan, and inspire me with their energy and commitment.

Urvashi Butalia, Uma Chakravarti, Mary John, Tejaswini Niranjana and Paromita Vohra have been exemplars of trans-border feminist solidarity, and their love and intellectual support has been enormously sustaining over the years.

I would have been well and truly lost without the keen wit, sharp politics and genuine warmth of Firdaus Arshad, Neelam Hussain, Nighat Said Khan, Lala Rukh and Azra Sayeed. Rubina Saigol (Ruby) and Farzana Shameem (Farzee), in particular, have always been there with unconditional love and entertainment.

My extended family on both my father's and mother's side has given me so much love and joy over the years that I cannot even begin to thank them. I wish my Dadi could have lived to see this book in print; I know that she would have been extremely proud. I also know that my Nani is eagerly awaiting it, mostly because it means that I will finally have time to cook myself a decent meal.

I am grateful to have old friends like Tahira Jaffer, Tayyaba Jaffer, Maryam (Mimi) Khan, Amina Munir, Saira Saif and Amna Yaqin whose love has sustained me through many difficult times.

My gratitude towards Raza Mir and Farah Hasan for their warm hearts and generous spirits is unbounded; their home has been a treasured escape from the craziness of everyday life. Rupal Oza and Ashwini Rao have been the most wonderful of friends and comrades, always ready to rescue me from stress with gossip and good humor. Thanks to Sreekanth Bollam (aka Loony) for comic relief and high spirits, to Satish Kolluri for laughter and other forms of restorative medicine, to Sangeeta Rao for her open house and open heart, and to Syeda "Bibi" Fatima (aka Bibi) and "Mo" Meghji for providing excellent reasons to take the day off and paint the town red.

Thanks to Samina Omar for coming into our lives and filling it with her lovely zaniness and kind heart. Among other things, I remain amazed at the twist of fate that gave me Khadija Omar as a bonus grandmother; I can only hope this book lives up to her expectations.

As my best friend of thirty years, Arifa Noor is in a class of her own. I hope she knows just how much her quiet presence in my life has meant to me.

Samina Choonara has been friend, sister, sounding-board and more. I admire her intellectual fierceness and emotional courage more than I can say.

Shefali Chandra's keen intellect and sharp wit, her unconditional love and unflinching support have carried me through the better part of my life. She is my moral compass, my harshest critic and my fiercest defender. I have no words to describe all that she has meant to me over the past twenty years; that that should be half my life is entirely appropriate.

I feel truly blessed to have a sibling like Yasser who, along with being the best brother in the world, is also one of my closest friends and a true comrade. His sensitivity and generosity—not to mention his formidable social skills and ridiculous sense of humor—never cease to surprise and humble me.

I have no words to describe how much Ali Mir's reassuring companionship has meant over the last several years. He has been friend, comrade, editor, critic, coach and cheer-leader. Without his good humour, not to mention keen editorial eye, this book would never have seen the light of day. Dear Ali, thank you for being the generous and loving person that you are, for giving so selflessly of your time and affection, and for simply being there to hold my hand when things looked bleak.

And finally, to my father, lover of life, philosopher at large, and story-teller extraordinaire, I owe more than I can say. Thank you, Abba, for allowing me to spread my wings and expand my horizons, for never judging me or the choices I make, for teaching me that the injustices and inequities of this world are not part of the natural order of things, and that all human beings deserve a life of dignity. From your example, I learnt never to compromise on principles and to struggle for what I believed in. There can be no more precious a gift that a parent can give a child.

1
Introduction

The image on the cover of this book, a contemporary photograph of a women workers' protest against rising food prices, captures the spirit of a variety of movements that inhabit the political landscape of Pakistan today.[1] The cadence of the half-hidden sign in the front that says "*Ghareeb Bachao, Ghurbat Mukao*" ("Save the Poor, End Poverty") echoes the beat of a progressive sentiment that was at the heart of the newly de-colonized and independent nation that came into being on 14 August 1947.

Although beset with huge problems and seemingly insurmountable odds, and despite the trauma of the violence of Partition, ordinary Pakistanis at that time were hopeful of forming a society in which they would have a place and a voice. The anti-colonial movement in the subcontinent was suffused with a radicalism that had led many to believe that the departure of the British would herald an egalitarian social system. While the period following Independence was one of contestation over the political and economic soul of the nation, it was one which progressive forces believed they could help shape. This book seeks to offer an account of Pakistani history that foregrounds the important role played by these forces from the very inception of the nation-state.

Today, the Western media has no space for images such as the one on the cover, or for stories that contradict the dominant narrative of Pakistan as a fountainhead of extremism. Alternate frameworks for understanding the country and its people are conspicuously absent from both mainstream media and academic discourse. Within the historiography of the subcontinent, dominated as it is by Indianists, the establishment of Pakistan is projected as the culmination of an essentially religious movement, which destroyed the secular fabric of India.[2] The problems that Pakistan faces today—particularly the rise of religious extremism—are thus presumed to be the poisonous fruit of this flawed foundation,[3] with parallels often being drawn with Israel which is identified as the only other modern state established on the basis of religion.

This narrative obscures several important facts: first, that the ideology of Muslim nationalism which underpinned the demand for Pakistan embodied an ethnic and not a religious nationalism;[4] secondly, that unlike Israel, which was from the very beginning cast as a homeland for all Jews, Pakistan was never understood as the purported homeland for all Muslims but only those of the Indian subcontinent, and finally, that there was a progressive element to the "Pakistan Movement" which came under increasing pressure following the establishment of Pakistan because of the classes which came to constitute the ruling establishment in the new state.

A parallel line of argument posits that Pakistan's problems can be traced to a confusion over its national identity—that it was, echoing Rushdie (2000: 86), "a place insufficiently imagined." This confusion (or "insufficiency") is understood as an indication of the inherent "inauthenticity" of Pakistan's national project, and is seen as having explanatory power. There are several problems with this analytical framework. First, it assumes that there are, in fact, such things as "authentic" nations and national projects. In doing so, it *mis*-understands the very nature and purpose of nationalism, thereby participating in the naturalization of a "hugely powerful repertoire and rhetoric of rule" (Corrigan and Sayer, 1985: 197). As the legitimating ideology of the modern nation-state, nationalism is by definition a discourse of power and as such is always deeply contested. Rather than a sign of confusion and inauthenticity, the contentious debates among Pakistani intellectuals over what constituted Pakistani nationalism should be seen as reflecting the vibrant and dynamic nature of the politico-ideological field in Pakistan.

Moreover, to posit the confusions and anxieties reflected in these ideological debates as the *source* of Pakistan's past or present problems is deeply flawed. As later chapters in this book show, these confusions could be very productive from the point of view of the Left, which could (and did) propose progressive models for the Pakistani nation-state project. The problem was not ideological *confusion*, but the active attempts by the Pakistani establishment and its organic intellectuals to marginalize secular and democratic models of the nation-state which they saw as threatening to their interests.

The tendency of the Pakistani establishment to turn to Islam— and, more importantly, to Islamist forces—in order to undermine progressive politics was evident from the very beginning and created the conditions for the increasing power of the religious Right within

Pakistani society and politics. Even then, the increase in influence did not proceed in any kind of neat fashion; this is a story of contingencies, contradictions, breaks and spikes. The Ayub regime, for example, went from actively targeting the *Jama'at-i Islami* to making strategic alliances with it when faced with mass mobilization on the Left. The secular and "socialist" Bhutto contributed to this trend (and set the stage for General Zia ul Haq's efforts to Islamize Pakistan) by reaching out to the Gulf Arab states for moral and material support, and by choosing to appease the increasingly belligerent religious groups rather than strengthen his working-class base. And it's worth noting that even Zia ul Haq, a US-backed military dictator and the head of the most brutal regime in Pakistani history, met significant resistance when he tried to operationalize his Islamization project.

The institutional power behind specific ideological projects is far more significant than the inherent persuasiveness of the ideas they embody. The greater a group (or class's) institutional power, the greater its ability to spread its own message far and wide and to suppress or misrepresent alternatives. Thus, we must look to such things as the balance of power between the different social forces, the confluence of domestic and international political agendas, and the political interests embedded in the various ideological projects in order to understand why a particular set of ideas—of the nation, the state, and (crucially) Islam—seems to "win" over others at any given moment in time. In Pakistan, as in other parts of the Muslim world, the rise of Islamists as a social and political force was *engineered* both directly, by inducting them into state institutions as Zia did, and indirectly, by "cleansing" the political sphere of their only effective nemesis/counter, the Left. The story of the marginalization/decimation of the Left is thus a crucial part of the story of the Islamization of Pakistan.

Both the anticommunism of the establishment and the turn towards Islam as a means to undermine the Left had an international dimension. During the Cold War, the US establishment believed that Islam, particularly its radical variant, could provide an effective politico-ideological bulwark against communism in Muslim countries generally, and be a thorn in the side of radical nationalist regimes in the Arab-Muslim world. Saudi Arabia's crucial function in this scheme was as an exporter of a rabidly anticommunist Islamist ideology. These Cold War scenarios were playing themselves out across the Muslim world, and were not unique to Pakistan. What really set Pakistan apart, however, and decisively changed the game, was the US's proxy war in Afghanistan. It was through this war that violence in the name of Islam became legitimized, the means by which to inflict it became freely available, and the networks through which it was to be operationalized were created.

This book highlights the fact that "Islam" is far from being a monolith, even within the specific context of Pakistan. It has always been and continues to be not only invested with different meanings and associations by different actors, but also articulated with wildly different political projects, and is thereby itself a deeply contested ideological field. The book illustrates the diversity of meanings and political programs associated with "Islam" through Pakistani history—from the modernist Islam of the Muslim nationalists, to the Sunni radicalism of the *Jama'at-i Islami* to the "Islamic socialism" of Bhutto's People's Party. This diversity, along with the popular heterodox forms of Islam indigenous to Pakistan, has been steadily under attack by domestic and international forces invested in a much narrower and far more intolerant version of the "faith." The book offers an account of this contestation, and draws attention to the growing forces of radicalization and their relationship with the imperialist project, first under the sign of the Cold War and now under the Global War on Terror.

The other goal of this book is to resurrect the important role played by the Pakistani Left from the very inception of the nation-state in challenging both the establishment and the religious Right. While it is usually either ignored or dismissed as irrelevant within the mainstream discourse on Pakistan, the Left's influence on Pakistan's culture and politics has been significant and often far greater than its organizational strength would warrant. Many, if not most, of Pakistan's most well-respected writers, poets, intellectuals and journalists in the early period of its history were affiliated either with the Communist Party or the left-wing Progressive Writers Association, or with both. The fact that they were and continue to be household names bears further testimony to their importance within the cultural and political life of the new state. The most obvious example is that of Faiz Ahmed Faiz, general secretary of the All Pakistan Trade Union Federation, editor-in-chief of Progressive Papers, Ltd. (a family of left-wing periodicals), winner of the Lenin Peace Prize, and Pakistan's unofficial poet laureate.

While the Pakistani Left has been (often justly) criticized for the strategic errors which it made at various points, these mistakes must not be used to dismiss its contributions, for no other political formation embodied its progressive ideals of anti-imperialism, international solidarity and social justice, a fact that becomes distressingly clear when we look at what has come to pass for "progressive" politics in Pakistan after the decimation of the Left in the 1980s. From the very beginning, members of the Pakistani Left faced hostility, harassment and violence at the hands of the state. Faiz himself was incarcerated several times, but never left Pakistan until Zia ul Haq's regime. Within Pakistan, the absence of the Left from mainstream accounts of Pakistani history is part of a concerted and ongoing attempt at limiting the political imaginary of the Pakistani people. Outside of Pakistan, these "sanitized" accounts reinforce existing stereotypes about Pakistan and Pakistani society as hopelessly reactionary.

This book is a small attempt to disrupt the mainstream account of Pakistani history by offering an alternative narrative, one which explains Pakistan's present reality not as an inexorable unfolding of a teleology, but as the result of a complex and contingent historical process with both domestic and international dimensions. It aims to highlight resistance and struggle, and to document the important and historical role played by the Pakistani Left in the culture and politics of the country.

The remainder of this chapter, apart from offering an overview of the book, provides a brief outline of the history of the demand for Pakistan. It lays out the context against which many of the issues that came to inflect the Pakistani nation-state project need to be understood, particularly the development of a Muslim identity beginning in the late nineteenth century and its expression as Muslim nationalism. Most importantly, it highlights the contingencies and contradictions that lay behind the establishment of Pakistan as a separate nation-state.

Almost immediately following independence, the Pakistani establishment realized that East Bengal, with more than half of the population of the new state, and a history of radical politics, posed a potent threat to its corporate interests. In fact, East Bengal embodied almost all the contradictions and tensions which defined the nation-state project at this time: the question of what constituted Pakistani culture, the place of non-Muslim (particularly Hindu) minorities within the nation-state, the essentially non-representative nature of the Muslim League government, and the emerging authoritarianism within the state. Undermining East Bengal and countering its demographic majority thus became the singular focus of the ruling establishment at this time. The opportunistic and contradictory ways in which the Muslim League government deployed "Islam" in order to accomplish this task in this early and formative period of Pakistan's history are the focus of Chapter 2.

During this same period, an acrimonious debate erupted in West Pakistan between members of the influential and left-wing Progressive Writers Association (PWA) and a group of liberal anti-communist intellectuals who pointedly identified themselves as "nationalists." Chapter 3 highlights the important role played by the cultural Left in Pakistan in terms of countering the reactionary politics of the establishment and its organic intellectuals, while holding out an alternative, people-centered model of the nation-state.

The story of the cultural Cold War as it unfolded in Pakistan under the martial-law regime of Ayub Khan is continued in Chapter 4. Ayub Khan sought to legitimize his rule by casting himself in the role of the great modernizer. While economic modernization (that is, "development") was to proceed along the trajectory laid out by the Harvard Advisory Group, the project of social and cultural modernization involved the co-optation of liberal anti-communist intellectuals. Eventually, the contradictions of the economic model of "functional inequality" along with the deeply repressive nature of the regime led to a massive outpouring of dissent, and the consolidation of a left-wing mass movement. As the popularity of the Left became clear, liberal anti-communist intellectuals joined forces with the religious Right in what proved to be an unsuccessful attempt to stem the tide of history.

Chapter 5 charts the dramatic turn-around from the rise of a new revolutionary and mass-based left-wing politics in the late 1960s to Zia's military theocracy. The Bhutto regime, which linked these two dramatically different periods of Pakistani history, was characterized by contradictory politics in which "socialism" and "anti-imperialism" were officially extolled while the organized Left was systematically repressed. This laid the groundwork for the counter-revolution of General Zia ul Haq, who came to power through a military coup. Zia's Islamization project sought to "purge" Pakistan of the viruses of secularism and socialism, and managed to transform Pakistani culture and politics in significant ways, despite the substantive and broad-based resistance from democratic forces. The chapter highlights the important role played by feminist poets in articulating a critique of the regime's retrogressive project.

Often regarded as a "lost decade," the 1990s were, in fact, a crucial period in terms of the consolidation of a number of processes which had been set in motion during the Zia regime, such as neoliberalism, violent sectarianism and the dramatic erosion of the rights of minorities and women. Chapter 6 focuses on two cases which turned into moments of national crisis and thereby highlighted the complexity of the ideological terrain at this time: the shocking honor killing of Samia Sarwar, murdered by her family in her lawyer's office for trying to obtain a divorce, and the story of Saima Waheed, a young woman who had married against her family's wishes. Both cases generated a widespread discourse on national culture and identity, "Islam" and "the West," and the status and rights of Pakistani (Muslim) women. Among other things, these cases highlight the opportunistic ways in which "Islam" is deployed by those in power—pressed into service when useful, ignored when inconvenient.

The book ends with a discussion of Pakistan today, focusing in particular on the fall-out of the Global War on Terror. While it has become commonplace to point out that Islamic militancy is shrinking the space for progressive politics (and even progressive culture), the nature and internal contradictions of this progressive politics have not been the focus of much analysis. The Epilogue argues that the decimation of the Pakistani Left in the 1980s left a vacuum within Pakistani politics which liberals—with their aversion for mass-based politics and their predilection for technocratic solutions—were unable to fill, and that the present bellicosity of the religious Right is at least partly the fruit of this failure.

Just as the anti-communism of the Cold War enabled the marginalization—via ideological warfare as well as through the use of repressive tactics such as censorship, arrests, disappearances, torture and assassinations—of certain political imaginings threatening to the establishment, the ideological circulation of the Islamic terrorist as the new enemy of freedom and democracy that underpins the War on Terror has similarly enabled the emergence of a reactionary liberal politics within Pakistan. The Epilogue sketches out some of the contours of this politics, and ends by arguing that the only true source of hope for Pakistan lies, as it always did, in the struggles of its working classes.

INDIAN MUSLIMS AND THE POLITICS OF REPRESENTATION

In order to follow the trajectory outlined above, we need to first come to terms with the process through with Pakistan was established, and its roots in a Muslim self-consciousness that began to develop in the nineteenth century. This self-consciousness was itself the product of British colonial politics, which were based on an understanding of Indian society as structured primarily around religious cleavages. British colonialism thus identified religious communities as the basic units of Indian society; in time, this "communal" framework came to structure Indians' own self-understanding (Pandey, 1990). The everyday experiences of Indians were mediated through a British administrative and political system which placed them first and foremost as members of a religious community (Shaikh, 1989). Significantly, Muslim nationalism—and what Francis Robinson (1974) refers to as Muslim *separatism*—had its roots in the Muslim-minority regions of India (specifically the United Provinces), where the fear of Hindu majoritarianism began to assert itself as soon as soon as a (limited) political space started to open up. This fear was affirmed by the rise of a militant Hindu nationalism which explicitly challenged—indeed rejected—the very idea of a syncretic Hindu-Muslim (that is, *Hindustani*) cultural history, by branding Muslims as invaders, and therefore outsiders. This was exemplified by the successful efforts of Hindu nationalists to split the Hindustani language, a prized product of the shared, syncretic culture of North India, into a *Hindu* Hindi and a *Muslim* Urdu in the late nineteenth century (King, 1994; Kumar, 1990; Rai, 1984).

The fact that Muslim intellectuals chose to articulate their claims to political and cultural representation from the nineteenth century onwards within the quintessentially modern framework of nationalism is noteworthy. Muhammad Iqbal, the iconic Muslim poet, philosopher and statesman of the late nineteenth/early twentieth century mused that Muslims were "the only Indian people who can fitly be described as a nation in the modern sense of the word"; the Hindus "though ahead of us in almost all respects" had "not yet been able to achieve the kind of homogeneity which is necessary for a nation, and which Islam has given you as a free gift" (Iqbal, 1930). In an exchange with Gandhi in September 1944, Jinnah similarly argued that Indian Muslims were not a *minority*, but a *nation*. Gandhi had dismissed Muslim nationalist claims in the following words (the racial logic of the argument is particularly noteworthy): "I find no parallel in history for a body of converts and their descendants claiming to be a nation apart from the parent stock. If India was one nation before the advent of Islam, it must remain one in spite of the change of faith of a very large body of her children" (Puckle, 1945: 320).

To which Jinnah had famously replied:

We are a nation of a hundred million, and, what is more, we are a nation with our own distinctive culture and civilization, language and literature, art and architecture, name and nomenclature, sense of value and proportion, legal laws and moral codes, customs and calendar, history and tradition, aptitude and ambitions; in short, we have our own distinctive outlook on life and of life. By all canons of international law we are a nation. (Ibid.)

Significantly, Muslim religious scholars or *ulema* in colonial India rejected this modern political and cultural identity, and the demand for Pakistan which was premised upon it, on the grounds that nationalism as a political concept was incompatible with Islam because a nation-state's exclusive claim on the emotional and political allegiances of its members undermined the solidarity of the global Muslim community, or *ummat*.[5]

It is important to underline the fact that Islam as religious ideology played no role in Muslim League politics prior to Independence and even the "rare attempts to place 'Islamic ideology' on the agenda of the Muslim League were firmly scotched by the leadership" (Alavi, 2002: 4520).[6] Jinnah was a staunch secularist who disagreed with the inclusion of religion in politics, and for this reason mistrusted what he saw as Gandhi's irresponsible mixing of the two.[7] He had categorically rejected demands made by the *ulema* that the Muslim League address the issue of Islamic law in the proposed state thus: "Whose Shariah? Hanafis? Hanbalis? Sha'afis? Malikis? Ja'afris? I don't want to get involved. The moment I enter the field, the ulama will take over for they claim to be the experts and I certainly don't propose to hand the field over to [them] … I am aware of their criticism but I don't propose to fall into their trap" (Iqbal, 1986: 25).

In response, Syed Abu Ala Maududi, founder of the proto-fascist religious party the *Jama'at-i Islami*, denounced the League's secular agenda and tried to dissuade Muslims from voting for it in the elections of 1945 (Nasr, 1994: 114). These facts become even more significant in light of the way in which the Muslim League leadership, starting with Prime Minister Liaquat Ali Khan, began to deploy Islam for political exigency almost immediately following Jinnah's death in September 1948. In fact, Khan did not just invoke Islam, which would have been problematic enough in the context of a secular nation-state, he also solicited the support of the various extremist Islamic groups which had begun to make their presence felt in Pakistan. By so doing, he opened the doors to their ubiquitous and continuing influence in Pakistani politics (Samad, 1995).

Until the mid-1930s, Indian Muslim intellectuals had understood themselves as having two separate identities—Muslim and Indian—which they did not see as mutually exclusive or antagonistic. At the Round Table Conference in London in 1930, for example, Mohammad Ali, a leading Muslim political figure, had famously defined himself as belonging to "two circles of equal size, but which are not concentric. One is India and the other is the Muslim World" (Barlas, 1995: 177). At the same time, in his famous presidential address to the Allahabad session of the All India Muslim League in 1930, Muhammad Iqbal argued that India's religious, cultural, linguistic and racial diversity meant that any attempt to apply "the principle of European democracy" in India had to be premised on a recognition of this diversity. It followed from this, then, that the "Muslim demand for the creation of a Muslim India within India" was "perfectly justified"; in fact, he argued that the "life of Islam as a cultural force" within what was "the greatest Muslim country in the world" (that is, India) depended "largely ... on its centralization in a specified territory" (Iqbal, 1930). These were clearly far from separatist sentiments.

By the latter half of the 1930s, the increasing communalization of Indian politics and society further strengthened Iqbal's sense (expressed within this same address) that a unitary system of government as proposed by the Congress would compromise the corporate interests of the Indian Muslim community. However, even at this time, the idea of a separate state was not proposed as the solution to this problem. Barlas (1995: 176-7) notes that "if there was a flaw in Muslim nationalist discourse, it was not the inability of the Muslim nationalists ... to develop loyalty to a territorially defined ... [state], but their continuing sense of commitment to the Indian state."

MUSLIM NATIONALISM IN THE POLITICAL ARENA

The Muslim League was the political organization which came to mediate political claims for representation on behalf of Indian Muslims. Founded in Dhaka in 1906, the League was originally a party representing the interests of the Muslim gentry of the United Provinces of India with the support of their counterparts in Bengal, the Muslim aristocracy or *ashraf*, and was not much of a force in all-India politics (Robinson, 1974). At this point, all that was meant by "separatism" was the idea that Muslim interests stood apart from those of other Indians, specifically Hindus, and so deserved independent representation. This original League succumbed to a lack of support and internal disagreements among its members and was revived in a different mold in 1936 by Jinnah upon his return from a self-imposed exile in Britain.

The changes in the arena of Indian politics during the early twentieth century—from the institutionalization of community-based representation to dyarchy ("shared" government) to the Government of India Act of 1935—contributed to a re-organization of the League as a party with a claim towards the political and moral leadership of all Indian Muslims. The new Muslim League—led by a small number of liberals such as Jinnah and Liaquat Ali Khan, who were characterized by their western education, professional vocation and secular outlook—represented a very different class of Muslims. This was the class which Hamza Alavi (2002: 4515) defined as the "salariat," comprised of individuals increasingly tied by jobs to the colonial bureaucratic apparatus and defined by their western education and "Anglo-vernacular culture" which they shared with members of the emerging professions such as lawyers and doctors.[8] Members of this professional class generally had what Aijaz Ahmad (2000: 122) calls a "composite" view of Indian social life, but the increasingly communalized space of politics in the years leading up to Partition made them acutely aware of the potential problems of living as a minority in an independent India.

The new configurations of Indian politics from the late 1930s onwards required that political parties aiming for hegemony be mass-based (Jalal, 1994; Barlas, 1995). The League needed to gain the support of the various Muslim factional and regional interests as well as popularize its agenda among the vast number of middle and lower-middle-class Muslims, both urban and rural.

The 1930s also saw the beginning of a wave of revolutionary fervor and activity which characterized the subcontinent into the 1940s; anti-colonial and socialist feelings were high, and a period of mass unrest among the working classes had begun. By this period, "socialism"—variously and often broadly defined—had become, along with "anti-imperialism," part and parcel of mainstream nationalist discourse in India. This was due, in no small measure, to the work of the All India Progressive Writers Association (AIPWA, or simply PWA), a Marxist literary organization associated with (but not an official front of) the Communist Party of India (CPI). The latter's cross-class "United Front" strategy, broadly defined by anti-imperialism and anti-feudalism, was replicated in the cultural-literary field through cultural organizations such as the AIPWA and the Indian People's Theatre Association.[9]

It was not surprising then that the Muslim League turned its attention at this time to the economic welfare of ordinary Muslims. As early as 1937, Muhammad Iqbal, in a letter to Jinnah, had expressed his conviction that the League could not hope to win the support of the majority of Indian Muslims if it continued to ignore economic issues, which for a significant part of the community amounted to a question of survival. The hegemony of the socialist vision among the ordinary Muslims which the League was trying to attract also explains Jinnah's use of the ambiguous yet effective phrase "Islamic socialism" to describe the League's economic vision.[10] The idea of Pakistan, besides being presented as a homeland for Indian Muslims which would guarantee them a free and sovereign cultural and political life, also came to represent a utopia in terms of economic opportunity and material benefits. It was clear to the intermediate classes of the urban areas that their interests lay in supporting a Muslim state. Advertisements in the newspapers urged Muslim businessmen to invest in the future of "their" state by contributing to the League fund and, of course, by supporting it in the elections. This economic nationalism did not translate into any coherent economic or social plan, however, even for the middle classes which were allegedly the League's stronghold (Barlas, 1995), but in its vague form it could be offered as a panacea for all Indian Muslims, and was accepted as such by significant portions of the mercantile, entrepreneurial and salariat classes (Alavi, 1988).

Jinnah's main concern was to establish the Muslim League as the "sole spokesman" of Indian Muslims, that is, the only party which could claim to represent them; without this, he had no political leverage vis-à-vis the Indian National Congress (INC). The British decision to withdraw from India and the subsequent compressed timetable for the transfer of power turned this into a race against time. As a result, Jinnah concentrated on winning over the dominant classes; the compromises the League ultimately made, therefore, were not to subaltern interests, but to various elite ones. Hitherto, the League's electoral performance in Muslim-majority areas had suffered because of the fact that the rural vote was controlled by landlords (Alavi, 1988). In the Punjab, one of the two largest Muslim-majority provinces of India, these landed magnates were members of the Unionist Party, a cross-communal alliance of Punjabi landlords. Viewing their interests very much in class terms, they were not interested in the Muslim League or the idea of Muslim nationalism. However, by the early 1940s, the INC's commitment to land reforms started to become clear, and Unionists wanted to ensure that the Congress would not come to power in the Punjab and Sindh (Alavi, 2002). An alliance with the League now began to look attractive to them in so far as a national League leadership could ensure "that the post-Independence government [in the Punjab] would not be in the hands of the Congress Party ... but rather a party that was dependent on them and ... which would ensure their survival as a class" (Alavi, 1988: 100). Despite the fact that they now needed the League as much as it needed them, they managed to extract a deal which promised them *carte blanche* in return for their (howsoever nominal) acceptance of the Muslim League label.[11] As a result, instead of "deliver[ing] the landowners into the hands of the Muslim League," the alliance "delivered the League" into theirs (ibid.: 100).

While Jinnah disliked the Unionists, the turn of affairs did not worry him unduly at this time since "Pakistan" was still not understood as a separate, sovereign state but rather a set of zones or states within a federated Union (ibid.); it was only after Independence that their inclusion into the League became deeply problematic, compromising an already threadbare Muslim League agenda. One stark example was the about-turn in the League's position on the rights of the rural poor, especially the landless. The original manifesto of the Punjab Muslim League—drafted in 1944 by Daniyal Latifi, a communist—was fairly radical, promising, among other things, substantive land reform. Following Independence, the Muslim League government in the Punjab made it a crime for a tenant to read this manifesto "in public or private"; the punishment for a tenant caught in the act was immediate eviction by his local landlord (Ali, 1970: 40).

A "MAIMED, MUTILATED AND MOTH-EATEN PAKISTAN"[12]

Along with labeling the Pakistan movement as an anti-secular force, many Indian historians tend to see Partition and the establishment of Pakistan as a result of Jinnah's personal ambition and/or intransigence. In fact, Jinnah always was and remained a staunch secularist till the end. He started his political life as a member of the Indian National Congress, joining the Muslim League only in 1913, at the behest of a new and more radical leadership which saw the future of Indian politics lying in Hindu-Muslim (and thereby

Congress-League) unity, and had identified Jinnah as the best man to bring it about.[13] Jinnah delivered on this promise, even at the expense of alienating some of his Muslim League colleagues, until such a time that it became impossible to do so, not because his own ambitions got the better of him, but because the priorities of the INC began to change (Alavi, 2002).

By the mid-1930s, a contradiction began to emerge between the Congress's secular nationalist stance and the slippage between "India" and "Hindu" that was encouraged by Gandhi's deployment of a religious, and specifically Hindu political vocabulary, and also by the increasing influence of militant Hindu nationalists within the INC. This was exemplified in the choice of *Vande Matram* ("Hail to the Mother[land]") as the party slogan, despite its explicitly anti-Muslim connotations.[14] The final nail in the coffin of Congress-League solidarity was the INC's refusal to share power with the League after the elections of 1937, despite a prior agreement. This produced a distrust of the INC and affirmed the sense that Muslim interests would not be safe within an independent India. It was against this sense of disillusionment that the idea of a separate homeland for Indian Muslims first began to circulate, and was finally formally voiced at the 1940 session of the All India Muslim League in Lahore. The "Lahore Resolution," as it came to be called, is written into official national historiography as the originary moment of the demand for an independent Pakistani state, but in actual fact it proposed the formation of more than one Muslim state within a loose federation (Alavi, 2002). This was the basis of Jinnah's "Fourteen Points," a plan of sharing power after the withdrawal of the British, which was framed around the perceived need to protect Muslim-minority interests in a Union through a structure that had a weak center. The INC refused to accept this proposal.

Between 1946 and 1947, Indian politics reached a stalemate, with no compromise forthcoming between the Muslim League and the Congress. "Pakistan" had to be continuously "re-imagined" by the League to fit the various options fought out between the League, the Congress and the British over the political map of the subcontinent (Samad, 1995). In the elections of 1946, the Muslim League won decisive victories in Punjab and Bengal. In 1947, Mountbatten was sent as India's last viceroy, tasked with striking a bargain between the League and the Congress. The result of these negotiations was unprecedented. Jinnah was forced to accept a separate country comprising the Muslim-majority states that had been part of the Pakistan plan, or nothing at all. However, even these states were not to be handed over in their entirety. In response to the demands of militant nationalist groups, the INC made the partition of Bengal and Punjab along communal lines a precondition for conceding Pakistan (Chatterji, 1994; Gilmartin, 1988; Talbot, 1998). Among the biggest losses was that of Calcutta, Bengal's magnificent cosmopolitan metropolis, and the center of Bengali culture, politics and history. The nation-state which finally emerged in August 1947 was thus the fruit of many historical contingencies and political exigencies.

The resulting Partition of the subcontinent into India and Pakistan was marked by the outbreak of severe communal violence, which helped fuel the epic migrations in both directions across the newly delineated boundary. However, Partition did not produce a neat communal division of the population of the Indian subcontinent. The idea of Pakistan as an independent, separate state was of such recent vintage that the vast majority of the population was either unaware of it or did not see it as affecting it in any significant way. Complicating matters still further was the fact that the precise nature of the boundary between the two new states was not determined until the very last minute, and so people in the divided provinces of Punjab and Bengal did not know until after the fact whether their village was part of Pakistan or India.[15] Even many of those who were forced to migrate thought of the division as temporary, and left behind keys and valuables in the safe-keeping of their neighbors. Many Muslims, including some of Jinnah's own associates such as Ismail Khan and the Nawab of Chhatari, ultimately could not "tear themselves apart from their social milieu and cultural moorings" and decided to stay in India (Hasan, 1993: 26), while many Hindus stayed on in both West Pakistan and East Bengal for the same reason.

COMMUNISM AND MUSLIM NATIONALISM

While the 1930s and 1940s were crucial in the development of anti-colonial nationalist politics in India, they were just as significant for the Indian Left. In 1934, the Communist Party of India (CPI) was banned by the colonial state for the "subversive" nature of its activities. However, the Seventh Comintern Congress, held in 1937, encouraged communist parties in colonized societies to form and participate in united fronts with nationalist and other anti-imperialist forces (Haithcox, 1971).[16] As a result, Indian communists joined broad coalitions, and helped popularize socialist ideas within the mainstream of the nationalist movement.[17] Ties between the CPI and the Muslim League began to grow in the early 1940s. In part, this was because both the CPI and the Muslim League both happened to be pursuing a "loyalist" line *vis-à-vis* the British in World War II (Ali, 1983).[18] However, the real basis for this relationship was the CPI's support for Muslim nationalism at this time. In 1942, the CPI adopted the controversial "Adhikari thesis" named after the member of the CPI who articulated it in pamphlets like "Pakistan and Indian National Unity" (Adhikari, 1943), which acknowledged Muslims as a nation(ality) and therefore recognized their right to self-determination.[19] From 1942 to 1947, the CPI line was one of Hindu-Muslim unity, the denunciation of communal violence and communalism, and the demand that Congress leaders be released from jail. The CPI appointed itself an "honest broker" between the League and the INC during the war years, and declared the League an anti-imperialist patriotic party. Tariq Ali (1983: 55) quotes Sajjad Zaheer, member of the Central Committee of the CPI (also a founder-member of the All India Progressive Writers Association and later the first secretary general of the Communist Party of Pakistan) as saying: "The task of every patriot is to welcome and help this democratic growth which at long last is taking place among the Muslims of the Punjab. The last stronghold of the imperialist bureaucracy [that is, Punjab] is invaded by the League. Let us help the people of the Punjab to capture it."

The Muslim cadres of the CPI were instructed to join the League to organize a Left pressure group within it, and to support its "progressive" elements, much as the communists in the Congress Socialist Party had done.

Thus there was a socialist strand within the Pakistan movement which may have been overwhelmed by the vested interests of the feudal and comprador elements that came to dominate the Muslim League after Independence, but was not completely erased. Often couched within a religious idiom, this socialist vision looked to "[t]he more radically religious interpretation of Islam" rather than the "glorious peaks of Muslim civilization" for its inspiration; it saw in it and in the "pristine revelation of the Prophet ... social revolution, the overthrow of the oppressive exploitative powers, the end of the contempt and pride of the rich in favour of egalitarian and human social principles" (Metcalf, 2004: 220).

It is usually argued that the vagueness of the League's agenda, economic and otherwise, reflected the League's actual class priorities, and enabled the ideological and political entrenchment of the Right in the aftermath of Independence. However, it can just as fruitfully be argued that this very vagueness, combined with the liberatory and emancipatory rhetoric of anti-colonial nationalism, also left it open for strategic deployment by the Left in its demands for a more democratic, more egalitarian and more inclusive national polity. It is not often acknowledged or remembered that "even at its inception, Pakistan was not merely a sanctuary for Muslim landed, merchant, and professional groups in search of their own interests but also was a focus for radical social aspirations, a vision that has had the potential of periodic reassertion" (ibid.: 221).

It was these "radical social aspirations" which the Left drew on in its articulation of an alternative nationalism and nation-state project. After Independence, these aspirations proved to be a thorn in the side of the Pakistani establishment, which was composed of an alliance of the main propertied classes and the military-bureaucratic oligarchy. While the objective interests of these classes did not overlap entirely, they were clearly in opposition to those of the vast majority of disenfranchised Pakistanis comprised of the urban and rural proletariat, peasants, and certain sections of the urban petit bourgeoisie (Alavi, 1990). The history of Pakistan is a history of the clash between these two irreconcilable sets of interests.

2
Consolidating the Nation-State: East Bengal and the Politics of National Culture

... let me make it very clear to you that the state language of Pakistan is going to be Urdu and no other language. Any one who tries to mislead you is really the enemy of Pakistan. Without one state language, no nation can remain tied up solidly together and function. Look at the history of other countries. Therefore, so far as the state language is concerned, Pakistan's language shall be Urdu. (Muhammad Ali Jinnah, Speech in Dhaka, March 21, 1948)

Soon after Independence in August 1947, Pakistan's eastern province was rocked with protests over the central government's decision to make Urdu the sole national language of the new state. Language activists in East Bengal demanded that the Bengali language (or Bangla) deserved to, at the very least, share this status with Urdu. After all, they argued, Bangla had a long and distinguished history which matched that of Urdu, and Bengalis constituted a majority of the Pakistani population. The central government's response was far from conciliatory, as is evident from the epigraph to this chapter, an excerpt of a speech given by Muhammad Ali Jinnah (head of state and the "father of the nation") to students of Dhaka University on his first visit to the province in the wake of the initial agitations. This categorical refusal of the members of the Pakistani establishment to address the grievances of its Bengali population engendered a 5-year-long language movement which culminated in the police firing upon a peaceful demonstration in Dhaka, the capital of East Bengal, on February 21, 1952. Several demonstrators, many of whom were university students, were killed in this tragic confrontation which subsequently became memorialized in East Bengal as *Ekushey*.[1]

Jinnah's words point to a contemporary discourse of the nation in which the integrity, and indeed authenticity, of a nation-state were dependent on the existence of a bounded and unitary national culture, of which language was a crucial part. The (West) Pakistani ruling establishment's interest in consolidating power clashed repeatedly with East Bengali demands for inclusion in the nation-state. From the point of view of an increasingly authoritarian ruling elite, these demands to democratize the space of national politics and culture— represented by such interconnected issues as the national language controversy, the demand for a federal state structure, and the critique of the idea of Pakistan as an "Islamic" state—made East Bengal into a problem which required neutralization. This was effected through the deployment of two convergent discourses. In one, East Bengal was constructed as a veritable hotbed of seditious elements such as Hindus and communists who were bent on destroying Pakistan; in the other, East Bengali culture was projected as one that was hopelessly under the influence of Hinduism and therefore not Pakistani enough. As we shall see, both these discourses were mutually reinforcing, and together sought to undermine East Bengali demands for equal representation in the nation-state.

THE CONTRADICTIONS OF INDEPENDENCE

After August 1947, the Muslims of the subcontinent finally had a separate, sovereign state to call their own. Yet, ironically, the Partition, far from being a simple affair of splitting the Muslim from the non-Muslim, actually under-scored the impossibility of such a division. While the scale of the migration in both directions across the new border—Muslims in one direction, non-Muslims in the other—was unprecedented, it is also true that many Muslims in the new Indian state did not migrate to Pakistan for a variety of reasons, while many non-Muslim residents of the areas that came to comprise Pakistan, stayed on; this was especially the case in East Bengal. The majority of these non-Muslims, now technically citizens of Pakistan, were Hindu.

Jalal astutely asserts that although "[frontiers] of states have rarely matched the complex contours of multiple identities ... nowhere have the nation-state's ineluctable rules of citizenship generated more confusion and chaos than in a subcontinent dissected by the arbitrary lines of 1947" (Jalal, 1995: 247). But the confusion and chaos was not simply due to the drawing of arbitrary lines, although that certainly contributed to it—it was generated by the very establishment of Pakistan as a separate nation-state. The "national community" in whose name Pakistan had been demanded was that of the Muslims of the subcontinent, but the actually existing nation-state of Pakistan did not contain the entirety of this Muslim nation within its borders. Even more confounding was the fact that the nation-state demanded and created in the name of a "Muslim nation," and premised on the idea that Hindus and Muslims constituted two separate nations and so could not be expected to be part of the same nation-state, now had to contend with the reality of Hindu Pakistanis. The very existence of these Hindu citizens therefore posed a dilemma: their equal representation in the nation-state had to be ensured if Pakistan was to be true to its aspirations and claims of being a modern state, but in order to do so, extant ideas about what constituted the "nation" which corresponded to the "state" of Pakistan would have to be revisited and revised.

Since Pakistan had not really been imagined as a separate nation-state, the issue of non-Muslims within the polity had not received too much attention. Under a confederated state structure, the rights of Muslims in the Muslim-minority areas were to be guaranteed by the "reciprocal hostages theory": "the idea that the fate of non-Muslims in the Muslim majority zone would be a guarantee for their protection in the other zone in which they were a minority'" (Alavi, 1988: 104).

Once it became clear that Pakistan was to be a separate nation-state, however, Jinnah made sure to clarify that it was to be a secular-democratic one. In a press conference on July 13, 1947 (almost exactly a month before Partition and Independence), he "assured the minorities in the Pakistan Dominion that they would have protection with regard to their religious faith, life, property and culture. They would, in all respects, be citizens of Pakistan without any discrimination and, no doubt along with it they would have the obligation of citizenship" (*Pakistan Times*, July 14, 1947).

In his first address to the Constituent Assembly on August 11, 1947, Jinnah once more underscored this secular vision of the Pakistani nation state:

> You are free. You are free to go to your temples, you are free to go to your mosques or to any other place of worship in this State of Pakistan. You may belong to any religion or caste or creed – that has nothing to do with the business of the State ... Now, I think we should keep that in front of us as our ideal and you will find that in the course of time Hindus will cease to be Hindus and Muslims will cease to be Muslims, not in the religious sense, because that is the personal faith of each individual, but in the political sense, as citizens of the state. (Jinnah, 1976: 9)

He also gave voice to the minority issue, recognizing the tensions it could potentially cause: "In this division it was impossible to avoid the question of minorities being in one Dominion or the other ... Now if we want to make this great State of Pakistan happy and prosperous we should wholly and solely concentrate on the well-being of the people, and especially of the masses and the poor" (ibid.: 8).

On October 21, 1947, the Food Minister Ghazanfar Ali Khan gave his assurances that the rights of minorities would be respected should they choose to stay in Pakistan. Replying to an assurance of loyalty to the Pakistan State given by a section of the non-Muslims in the city of Rawalpindi, the Food Minister said:

> It does not become of a modern democratic State to nourish misgivings and suspicions about a minority community within its boundaries on grounds of mere religious differences ... for our part, we have no demands on the minorities to prove their bona fides to the State, but have repeatedly declared that all nationals of Pakistan, irrespective of any cult or creed, will be equal partners in all spheres of activity. We shall not doubt their loyalty unless it was proved otherwise by their action. (*Pakistan Times*, October 21, 1947)[2]

Jinnah exhorted the Muslims of Pakistan to "bury the hatchet" and accept everyone who lived within the territorial bounds of Pakistan as an equal citizen "with equal rights, privileges and obligations" (Jinnah, 1976: 8), because the future of the new state depended on it. But burying the hatchet became difficult to contemplate in the aftermath of the brutal communal violence of Partition, and other cultural and political developments within India only seemed to validate the Muslim League's predictions regarding the vulnerability of Indian Muslims under Hindu majority rule. The accommodation of non-Muslims into the nation-state was to be far more fraught an enterprise than Jinnah imagined. Jinnah's secular-democratic vision of Pakistan was also going to face severe challenges from within his own establishment: the fact that some members of the Constituent Assembly tried to prevent Jinnah's speech from being made public was a sign of things to come.

The confusion generated by Partition was neatly expressed by the *Pakistan Times* a mere four-and-a-half months after the creation of Pakistan. Noting that "the Muslims of Pakistan are greatly bewildered when they are told by their leaders that all the inhabitants of Pakistan form one nation and that the Muslims of India are not of that nationality but are the nationals of India," the *Times* also identified the source of this confusion—the "basic fallacy" that was the "presumption that the Hindus and/or the Muslims are a regular nation (jointly or separately) in the modern sense of the term" (December 28, 1947). In essence, the *Pakistan Times* was proposing that the "two-nation theory" could not (or could no longer) be accepted as a viable political idea.

These confusions and contradictions had implications for the Muslim League, and therefore for the ruling classes whose interests the Muslim League represented. In fact, as early as July 1947, Mr. Suhrawardy (the former premier of Bengal) had asserted the need for a nationalist organization in Pakistan with both Muslim and non-Muslim members. At the time, Jinnah had responded with misgivings about whether the Muslim masses were ready for such an organization. Suhrawardy had in turn expressed the hope that

> ... this situation is not unalterable ... I am sure that if they are informed of the actual state of affairs, Muslims will see the criminal folly of excluding non-Muslims from an organisation like the Muslim League, which is to have an important role in formulating the principles of government in the Dominion. The exclusion of the non-Muslims will mean that they will have no voice in influencing the shape of Pakistan to come. It would also mean a denial of their political rights and their subjection to the worst form of discrimination, democratic principles being thrown to the winds and a fascist rule being perpetuated. (*Pakistan Times*, July 25, 1947)

However, many provincial Ministers expressed the opinion that "Muslims must not be divided now in the face of the danger which surrounds Pakistan and that the Muslim League must be maintained as a communal organisation." This raised several questions for Suhrawardy on the future status of minorities in a Pakistan ruled by the League and hostage to its politics. "How", he asked, "does the entry of non-Muslims into the League divide Muslims and how does its conversion into a Nationalist League endangers [*sic*] and jeopardise Pakistan?" (ibid.).[3]

Suhrawardy's idea of a National League was based on the sense that the actually existing nature of the new nation-state, as well as Jinnah's pronouncements on Hindus being equal citizens of the state meant that the "two-nation theory" had run its course and could no longer be used as Pakistan's *de facto* nationalist ideology. However, the Muslim League's claim to legitimacy as the ruling party of Pakistan was based on its claim to being the representative of the Muslim nation. Doing away with the "two-nation theory," and disbanding the Muslim League in favor of a "National League" was not an idea that the ruling establishment was about to embrace, given the greater democratization and secularization of politics that such an initiative would likely engender.

Partition also produced cultural anxieties. As an influential Pakistani scholar argued, August 14, 1947 marked the achievement of merely a "political nationhood" for Pakistan; the project of cultural nationalism remained incomplete since "[c]ulturally ... [Pakistan] was not yet a nation" (Ahmad, 1965: 35). The newly formed nation-state saw the need to cut "adrift from the Hindu cultural residue of India in order to isolate and establish the new nation's cultural identity" as its most pressing problem (ibid.). No cultural overlap between the two states could be conceded, because according to the dictates of cultural nationalism, that was precisely what distinguished one nation from another (Handler, 1988). Thus a shared culture with India would not only undermine (retrospectively) the very *raison d'être* of the demand for Pakistan, but also throw Pakistan's status as a legitimate nation-state into question.

Partition had cast a wrench into the neat division between Hindu and Muslim culture and civilization that had been contained within the "two-nation theory." The clearest manifestations of the Indo-Muslim culture and history (such as the Taj Mahal, Fatehpur Sikri, Delhi's Jama Masjid, and so on) on whose basis claims to Muslim nationhood had so persuasively been made over the preceding decades, had not fallen within the newly constituted borders of the state of Pakistan. Under these circumstances, the Urdu language became imbued with even more meaning as the one aspect of Indo-Muslim culture which was not at the mercy of arbitrary borders. The proposal that Bangla be considered Pakistan's second national language therefore posed a challenge to the very idea of a shared Muslim nationhood, premised on a unitary (national) culture of which the Urdu language was understood to be a crucial part. In the eyes of Muslim nationalists in East and West Pakistan, Urdu was the "natural" choice as the national language of Pakistan because of its prior status as the "lingua franca" of Indian Muslims, and because of the recent history of language politics in colonial India,[4] not to mention its embattled status as a minority language in post-

Independence India where it metonymically stood for the embattled members of the Muslim nation that had been "left behind."

Pakistan's unique status as a "parenthetical" state,[5] made up as it was of two geographically non-contiguous "wings" separated by 1,200 miles of hostile Indian territory, only compounded the expected complexities of post-colonial nation-statehood. The national language controversy transformed the insecurities generated by this geographical non-contiguity into an anxiety over a possible *cultural* non-contiguity between the two wings, which would undercut Pakistan's claims to nationhood. The assertion of cultural differences which were seen to underlie Bengali demands appeared to subvert the very basis of Muslim nationalism, that is, the idea that all (Indian) Muslims shared a common culture and history, which was distinct from that of the Hindus. East Bengal and the issue of language rights thus became a sign of the crisis of the nation-state.

These contradictions were cause for serious anxiety on the part of nationalist intellectuals, but also for the Muslim League whose legitimacy was premised on its representation of a "national community"—the Muslims of the subcontinent—which did not map on to the demographic and cultural reality of the state created in its name. In these circumstances, how could the Muslim League lay claim to being the ruling party of Pakistan?

The concerns of neophyte statehood complemented and compounded these cultural and political anxieties. The imperative was to establish a functioning state as soon as possible, to establish internal social order, and to defend the new nation-state from possible attacks from its neighbors[6]—all in the face of severe resource limitations.[7]

In this climate of national insecurity, all demands for regional or provincial rights, especially those couched in cultural terms such as the language controversy, were framed by the Muslim League establishment as a direct challenge to the very legitimacy of the Pakistani nation-state. It was hardly surprising then that Muslim League politicians and the organic intellectuals of the ruling class attacked Bengali demands for equal political and cultural representation in the new nation-state as unpatriotic and even seditious. The Muslim League, after all, derived moral authority from its claim to represent "the Muslim nation"; a crisis in the definition of this nation would be nothing less than a crisis of legitimation for the ruling party.

The politics of this period, cultural and otherwise, can thus best be framed as a struggle for control over the very terms of the nation-state, understood as a structure of power (Corrigan and Sayer, 1985).

THE TROUBLE WITH EAST BENGAL

The united province of Bengal had played a crucial role in the Muslim nationalist movement. The Muslim League was established in Dhaka[8] in 1906, and the Muslim League leadership included many prominent Bengalis. However, the West Pakistani ruling elite, made up largely of Punjabis and Urdu-speaking *Muhajireen,*[9] had no intention of sharing power at the national level with their Bengali counterparts. As far as the Muslim League's ruling clique was concerned, East Bengal posed a potent political threat. It was demographically Pakistan's majority province with over 50 per cent of Pakistan's total population, which meant that within a truly democratic set-up, East Bengal would dominate national politics. East Bengal also had a history of political awareness and activism and had seen a gradual rise in grassroots militancy and political consciousness after the establishment of Pakistan which threatened the class interests of the ruling elite.[10] Moreover, East Bengal was home to the majority of the new nation-state's Hindu population, many of whom were active and vocal members of the official Opposition and not content with being subsumed into the category of "*dhimmis.*"[11] The Muslim League thus tried its best to contain East Bengal and deny it its rightful representation in the nation-state, both at the symbolic level (in the "imagined community" of the nation) and at the level of the state (that is, political representation, recruitment into the bureaucracy and the military, and access to economic resources). As the Muslim League progressively lost legitimacy in the aftermath of independence, limiting, neutralizing, containing and ultimately actively undermining East Bengal's influence in national politics became the major preoccupation of the (West) Pakistani ruling class.[12]

From the perspective of the (West) Pakistani nationalist intelligentsia, East Bengal appeared to embody all the tensions of the nationalist project: it had a sizable minority of Hindus, Bengali language and culture was irredeemably and inordinately influenced by Hinduism, and by demanding that Bangla be given the status of a second national language, Bengalis had effectively shown their disdain for the idea of a shared Pakistani culture.

This narrative dovetailed neatly with the political imperatives of the state, in particular with the ruling Muslim League party. As a result, East Bengal was increasingly constructed in the popular (West Pakistani) imagination as a "problem" province—the place where all subversion against the nation-state was located, and therefore the place which had to be constantly policed, both literally and figuratively.

"MUSLIM" URDU VERSUS "HINDU" BANGLA

The language controversy began in the aftermath of the first National Education Conference held in November 1947, where the issue of the medium of instruction, and therefore the "national" language, had naturally come up. Urdu was proposed as a candidate based on its past status as the accepted lingua franca of Indian Muslims, but the Bengali contingent's strong objections meant that the conference only "recommended," with strong qualifications, that Urdu be accepted as the national language of Pakistan,[13] and even the decision to use it as a medium of education was left to the discretion of provincial governments (Bukhari, 1985: 554).

However, this conference was by no means the first time the issue of the place of Bangla—and by extension, of Bengalis—in the new nation-state had come up. In October, a State Language Action Committee had been formed in Dhaka which had taken strong exception to the symbolic marginalization of East Bengal from the national imaginary, evidenced by the fact that Bangla did not feature on many of the artefacts of the state from the newly issued postage stamps and coins to the official forms of the Government of Pakistan (Islam, 1994); Bangla had also been removed from the list of approved subjects issued by the Pakistan Public Service Commission (Umar, 2004).

Despite the qualified recommendations of the Education Conference, the federal Minister of Education continued to make several public statements in which he categorically argued that Urdu should be the national language of Pakistan (Umar, 2004). It was in the context of these slights, and the growing sense in East Bengal that it was being relegated to the status of an internal colony[14] that the recommendations of the conference caused a furor in East Bengal. On December 5, the Language Committee organized a street demonstration against the conference. In a sign of the times to come, the state retaliated by invoking Section 144 of the Government of India Act 1935, which prohibited public assembly. Having just emerged from an anti-colonial struggle in which civil disobedience, in particular the flouting of Section 144, had been a crucial aspect of the nationalist struggle, members of the Language Committee decided to ignore the prohibition and assemble anyway, resulting in a confrontation with the police which served to harden Bengali attitudes against the Muslim League government.

The Urdu–Bangla controversy was, unsurprisingly, overdetermined by the politics of class, region, religion and ethnicity. While it certainly acquired a regional (East Pakistan versus West Pakistan) dynamic towards the end of the five years during which it raged, it was primarily a clash between the middle-class Bengalis who were seeking equal representation in the nation-state and an increasingly fascist ruling party at the center dominated by not just the (predominantly Punjabi and *Muhajir*) West Pakistani ruling elite but also the Bengali *ashraf*. Urdu was a crucial part of the *habitus* of these three factions of the ruling class at the center. The clash between the Bangla-speaking middle class, which Rounaq Jahan (1972: 38) calls the "vernacular elite," and the old Urdu-speaking Bengali aristocracy, the *ashraf*, indexed the ongoing class struggle *within* East Bengal (Jahan, 1972; Rahman, 1996). The Bengali *ashraf* considered themselves part of an all-India Muslim aristocracy bound together by a shared Indo-Persianate high culture and "foreign" ancestry (a racialized discourse of difference which was augmented by British racial classifications), which set them apart from the Bengali Muslim *hoi polloi*. These attitudes, and the actions taken by the leaders of the East Bengal Muslim League government, only served to intensify the identification of Urdu as a language of the elite, and as a symbol of centralized authority.

The national language issue in Pakistan at this time was also refracted through the cultural politics of the previous half-century or so in colonial India, specifically the Hindi–Urdu controversy, which had resulted in the breaking up of the shared and syncretic literary tradition represented by a single language (Urdu/Hindustani) into (Muslim) Urdu and (Hindu) Hindi under pressure from Hindu nationalist forces. The "Hindi, Hindu, Hindustan" slogan of the Hindi movement (validated by Gandhi) implicitly and explicitly associated Urdu with Indian Muslims. The Hindi movement was seen as a precursor of the likely fate that awaited Muslims in India following the end of British rule. The preservation of Urdu consequently became part of the Muslim nationalist program (Fatehpuri, 1987; King, 1994; Rai, 1984). The language controversy in Pakistan was further exacerbated by contemporary news reports regarding the declining status of Urdu in post-Independence India, where Hindi had been declared the national language, a decision which had generated its own share of controversy across the border. If Hindi was now Hindustan's national language (in keeping with the "Hindi, Hindu, Hindustan" slogan), then Urdu had to be Pakistan's. For Muslim nationalists in Pakistan, Urdu's fate in India also represented the precarious status of Indian Muslims in Independent India, retroactively justifying their fears of living under a Hindu majority, and solidifying the idea that Pakistan was Urdu's "home," where it would be protected and preserved as a repository of Indo-Muslim culture and history.

In contrast, Urdu's partisans saw in Bangla's script and vocabulary the corrupting influence of Sanskrit, and thereby Hinduism; this was in keeping with their general attitude towards East Bengalis' culture which they considered far too in thrall to "Hindu" culture, from its focus on classical dance to their appreciation of the songs of Rabindranath Tagore.[15] Even after the tragedy of *Ekushey*, the *Civil and Military Gazette* asserted that Bangla could not be the state language of Pakistan because it was "mainly based on Sanskrit, the language of the Vedas" which rendered it unthinkable as the language of "a state brought into being for the establishment of Islamic values."[16] The implication and the effect of this discourse was the designation of Bengali culture and therefore Bengalis themselves as not Muslim enough, and by implication, not Pakistani enough, thereby justifying their relegation to the margins of the national project. All demands by Bengalis for equal representation in the nation-state, and in later years for greater political autonomy from the center, were mediated through this powerful discourse of exclusion, which served to justify various forms and levels of state repression against them, up to and including the military action in East Pakistan in 1971.[17]

In February 1948, Khwaja Nazimuddin, the premier of East Bengal at this time (later, prime minister of Pakistan) and a representative of the Bengali *ashraf* class, responded thus to a proposal that Bangla be considered one of the official languages of the Constituent Assembly of Pakistan:

There is only one state of Pakistan and that can have only one language and that can only be Urdu. This means that the language of the Central Government and the language used for communication with the provinces will be Urdu, when it is decided to replace the English language by the national language ... Urdu has already been virtually recognised as the language of the Muslim nation since before the Partition of India, and it cannot be substituted by any other language now. (*Dawn*, February 26, 1948)[18]

However, despite these categorical statements in favor of Urdu as the only national language, the increase in political agitation in East Bengal forced the government of Pakistan to belatedly declare Bangla the second national language, but with a proviso that it be "reformed." In 1949, it set up the East Bengal Language Committee whose mandate was to examine "the question of the standardisation, simplification and reform of the Bengali language current in East Bengal" so that it could better "fulfil its role" as a national language and to suggest ways in which the Bengali language could be brought "into harmony and accord with the genius and culture of the people of East Bengal in particular and of Pakistan in general" (Report of the East Bengal Language Committee (EBLC), 1949: 2). The committee had been asked to look into the issue of a change in script which could help popularize Bengali in other parts of Pakistan, and also help it shed its "Sanskritic" past. Among the committee's recommendations was the suggestion that the Arabic script be adopted for Bangla in order to make it more of an "Islamic" language:[19]

It is a historical fact that languages grow with the growth of the nation and develop in accordance with their cultural background. Pakistan has been achieved with the sole purpose of enabling the Muslims to revive and develop their culture and traditions. East Pakistan being the major area of the new State, the language of this area should grow according to Muslim ideology ... Adoption of the Arabic script is the first pre-requisite for the above purpose ... Persian and Urdu are the two best illustrations of the importance of the script and its effects on the cultural development of language. (Ibid.: 35)

The committee also proposed that the reform of Bangla along these lines was crucial in order to distinguish it from the language of *West* Bengal, arguing that "in the interest of the State and the Nation a difference in language of two Bengals to a certain extent has been a necessity" (ibid.: 27). It noted that West Bengal was "proceeding towards colloquialism in light literature with the support of the masses; and Sanskritisation in high literature under the Government and University patronage" (ibid.: 27–8), and concluded that the use of colloquial forms of Bangla and existing standardized forms which had an "unwarranted tendency to use words of Sanskritic language in profusion" should be discouraged since it would undermine the important effort to distinguish between the languages of the two Bengals, which itself was mandated by the tenets of the "two-nation theory."

Dissident members of the committee questioned the assumptions implicit in this recommendation, arguing that "the idea, that Bengali language is not in harmony with the genius and culture of Pakistan ... is born of a very incorrect information [*sic*] that Bengali is the language of the non-Muslims, saturated with un-Islamic ideas only." Instead of a change in the Bangla script, they recommended a "shaking off of the present attitude and notion of those who look askance at Bengali" (ibid.: 35).[20]

Defenders of Bengali argued that the change in script would spell disaster for the people of East Bengal who would

> ... at once be cut off from their cultural heritage of literature, enshrined in Bengali characters. Not to speak of the contribution of any other literati, even poets and literati like Ahmad Saghir ... of the past, and Rabindra-nath [Tagore], Nazrul [Islam] ... of the present age, will at once become unreadable and unintelligible to us. It will be a huge task beyond the capacity of the limited resources of the Government to transcribe even a small part of our past and present literary heritage. We, therefore, do not like to reduce ourselves to a nation of fools at least for two generations, if not more. (Ibid.: 25)

Of course, from the point of view of the state and the nationalist intelligentsia, cutting East Bengalis off from their (Hindu) past was precisely the point. The change in script would have killed two birds with one stone: not only would it have helped the new nation-state assert its unique and bounded cultural identity, but by reducing East Bengal to "a nation of fools" it would hopefully also seriously undermine the threat that the latter posed to the center.[21]

In conclusion, the committee noted that "nowhere in India and Pakistan" had there been such a precedence to "reform a language in all its aspects, viz., alphabet, spelling system, vocabulary, grammar." Most importantly, this reform, when implemented would not only have "narrowed down the scope for easy entrance of Sanskritic influence in respect of thoughts, ideas and vocabulary, but also have struck at the root of the existing Sanskritic aristocracy of the land by bringing it down to the level of the man in the street." Simultaneously, the "gates of the language" would have been "flung wide open for the ushering in the language and in the country of Islamic ideology and culture, so dear to the vast majority of the sons and daughters of the soil" (ibid.: 12).

In East Bengal, the atmosphere around the issue was so charged that the contents of this report were ultimately not made public, even though the committee did not agree to the proposed changeover to the Urdu script, and actually recommended a reform of the Urdu language and script as well, in order to facilitate its learning by non-Urdu speakers. However, fears that the Urdu script would be imposed on Bangla were strong enough that it became a significant issue in the East Bengal Legislative Assembly (Rahman, 1996).[22]

In February 1952, Khwaja Nazimuddin asserted once again that Urdu alone would be the state language of Pakistan. To make matters worse, the government of East Bengal responded to the peaceful procession of Bengali students who wished to protest against this pronouncement, with violence of an unprecedented nature, resulting in the *Ekushey* tragedy. The provincial government then proceeded to declare that the law-and-order situation was out of control and imposed a curfew on Dhaka. The *Pakistan Times* (March 6, 1952) noted that not "content with having provoked the people to anger by a series of harsh acts and having precipitated a major crisis," and instead of trying to ease the situation, the East Bengal government acted "in a negative way, to keep up an atmosphere of unrest and agitation." This irrational behavior on the part of the East Bengal government prompted the *Times* to speculate that the government's action, which had originally appeared to be a response to the agitation over the language issue, was perhaps actually about something else.

This momentous event served to stiffen Bengali attitudes towards the government, and generated symbols such as the "*Shaheed Minar*" ("Martyrs' Minaret"), which was erected to commemorate the "language martyrs," and around which the movement for the secession of East Bengal later coalesced.

THE STATE OF THE MUSLIM LEAGUE

For its part, the Muslim League saw the demands of the Language Committee as a challenge to a unitary idea of the nation on which its claim to legitimacy was based. The League had asserted its right to be the "sole spokesman" (Jalal, 1994) of Indian Muslims in the decade prior to Independence, a right which was understood to have been validated by the results of the 1940 elections (in which it won a majority of the Muslim vote), and which was the basis of the League forming the government in Pakistan immediately after independence. However, the mandate was merely provisional and was meant to last only until the new sovereign state held its first national elections. It soon became clear, however, that the Muslim League leadership had no intention of allowing its hold over power in the new state to be challenged by the electorate. This disinclination manifested itself in an authoritarianism that only increased as it steadily lost popular support.

The League's loss of legitimacy was also directly connected with its failure to deliver on its promise of economic welfare for ordinary Muslims, reflected in its hostility towards any efforts at redistribution after Independence. The Pakistani state that emerged in August 1947 was dominated by an alliance of the main propertied classes—the small bourgeois class, the landlords and the military-bureaucratic oligarchy (Alavi, 1973, 1990; Gardezi, 1973). The objective interests of these classes didn't always overlap neatly, but conflicts between them represented non-antagonistic contradictions; their real conflict was with the disenfranchised majority of Pakistanis, comprised of the urban and rural proletariat, peasants and certain sections of the urban petit bourgeoisie. Colonial history and their shared interests thus bound them in a neocolonial relationship with metropolitan capital and the metropolitan bourgeois classes, and pitted them against the majority of Pakistan's population. The shift in the priorities of the League in the immediate aftermath of Independence can be seen in the purges of its leftist and other independent-minded members, such as Mian Iftikharuddin (who resigned as minister of rehabilitation and refugees in protest soon after Independence), and Hussain Shaheed Suhrawardy, a prominent Bengali statesman-politician.

Even *Dawn*, the unofficial Muslim League newspaper, was forced to acknowledge that, by not delivering on its promises, the League was losing its legitimacy, and delivering Pakistan into the hands of its detractors:

> If the Muslim League cannot give to the masses what they need and what is theirs by right, along with the ideology they value, it will be encouraging them to accept the same thing from others minus perhaps the ideology. Those who are today shy of facing opposition in the reactionary front are really building up a more

formidable front against them in the future ... A distinction will have to be made between the deathless devotion of the patriotic millions and the dubious support of the propertied few. (*Dawn*, January 5, 1952)

The Muslim League's reactionary and anti-democratic politics were also reflected in Liaquat Ali Khan's decision to woo the forces of the religious right. Following Jinnah's death in September 1948, Liaquat Ali Khan increasingly began to invoke Islam and solicit the support of the various extremist Islamic groups which had begun to make their presence felt in Pakistan as a way to widen his base and address the crisis of legitimacy facing the Muslim League. By so doing, he opened the doors to their ubiquitous and continuing influence in Pakistani politics (Samad, 1995: 133).

The Objectives Resolution passed by the Constituent Assembly in March 1949 as the foundation of the future Constitution, reflected this rightward shift. Its reference to Islam as the "Religion of State" and its commitment to enshrine '"the principles of democracy, freedom, equality, tolerance and social justice as enunciated by Islam" (Constituent Assembly Debates, 12 March, 1949) immediately provoked a strong reaction in secular circles.[23] Although the resolution did not offer any explicit explanation of this wording (and perhaps because it did not do so), its inclusion as well as references to the desirability of using the *shariah*[24] as the basis for law-making was seen as evidence of a drift towards a "theocratic" state which was a complete negation of Jinnah's vision of a secular and democratic welfare-state which was reflected in his inaugural address to the Constituent Assembly.[25]

A ruling party this averse to secular-democratic principles could not be expected to see the language movement as anything other than a challenge to be quashed. The prevailing view in West Pakistan of the language movement (popularized by the government) was that it was an example of the "virus of provincialism" that threatened Pakistani unity. Thus, both in 1947–48, and in 1952, "provincialism" became a major trope in the discourse on the Bangla issue. Jinnah used the word repeatedly during his visit to East Bengal. In the course of a single editorial in the *Dawn*, it was referred to as the "Enemy Number One," a "blight," an "excrescence" and a "canker," as well as "the worse [*sic*] enemy of all that this country stands for," and it was the "bounden duty of every true Pakistani" to eliminate it wherever it manifested itself (*Dawn*, January 2, 1952).

The same editorial suggested that the type of nationalism which characterized Pakistan was unique in the modern world. It had no place for issues of "geography, race, caste and colour," which it supposedly transcended. This unique nature of Pakistani nationalism and its purported superiority over other forms was testified to by how its ideology "[welded] together territories as distant as the western and eastern wings of this country." According to *Dawn*, the real threat to the nation lay not from external dangers, which in fact actually helped to *strengthen* national unity; it was "the internal danger which, through whispering, instigation and insinuation, and 'mutual belittlement' can break the collective will more than the enemy's big guns and battalions" (ibid.).

Bengali demands for representation in the nation-state were thus cast as an example of the kind of "sectionalism" that most endangered Pakistan. East Bengal was constructed as the *enfant terrible* in nationalist discourse, and compared unfavorably with the other provinces of Pakistan. In response to the disaffection expressed by Bengalis to the recommendations of the November 1947 Education Conference, *Dawn* declared that "we do not hear of a Punjabi-Urdu controversy, a Pushtu-Urdu controversy or a Sindhi-Urdu controversy. Why must there be a Bengali-Urdu controversy?" (*Dawn*, December 16, 1947). Such bewilderment was, of course, disingenuous; as Tariq Rahman (1996) points out, the reason for this disparity was that Bangla had a middle class that was invested in its development and use as a literary and every-day language in a way that was not true at this time of Punjabi, Pushtu, or Sindhi.

There was a clear anxiety among the West Pakistani state establishment and intellectuals alike that acceding to the Bengali demand would open the floodgates to centrifugal forces. Patras Bukhari[26] had encapsulated this fear back in his own response to the 1947 agitation: "Sindh and Punjab have *done their duty* by supporting Urdu ... there is the danger that in the future if not Sindhi, then Pushto might claim that, in the interests of preserving cultural diversity and ethnic autonomy within national unity, I should be given more importance vis-a-vis the educational development of Pakistan" (Burkhari, 1985: 557, emphasis added).

It is clear that the issue here is not, or at least not *simply*, that giving Bangla its due would create conditions for other "languages" to demand their "rights." Language rights in this discourse are clearly a metaphor for greater provincial (political) representation, and perhaps even challenges to central authority. A ruling clique invested in a highly centralized form of state because of the consolidation of power which that allowed, and a nationalist intelligentsia which was invested in a unitary idea of the nation could only see such democratic demands as open challenges to the state and to the mythic nation respectively, challenges which were therefore framed as nothing less than seditious.

The national language controversy thus stood at the nexus of most, if not all, of the crises and challenges faced by the Muslim League at this time, while also exposing the non-democratic character of its leadership. Having squandered the moral authority it had built up prior to Independence as a result of the classes whose interests it now represented, the Muslim League proceeded to respond to all challenges by resorting to repression. It is telling (but hardly unique among post-colonial states) that this repression was effected through quintessentially *colonial* instruments of power—Safety Acts, Security Bills, Press and Publications Ordinances and declarations of Emergency. The use of these instruments and of state repression of legitimate democratic dissent was in turn legitimized through a discourse of sedition in which East Bengal figured prominently.

Following the tragic events of February 21, the nationalist press in West Pakistan and the rhetoric of the central government in the Constituent Assembly became rife with references to "subversive elements" at work in East Bengal. These "subversive elements," it was claimed, were none other than the "one community [which was] foremost in the defiance of the order under Section 144," the community whose members had "instigated the local Muslim youth against the Muslim refugees from Bharat [that is, India]" (*Dawn*, February 23, 1952). While *Dawn*'s language is oblique—referring, for example, to a "number of *non-Muslim foreigners*" who had "been arrested while distributing inflammatory leaflets"—it is hard to miss the fact that the absent referent in its discourse are Hindu Bengalis. Even the leftist *Pakistan Times* quoted the *Civil and Military Gazette*'s editorial which claimed that "misguided students were exploited by political self-seekers for their own nefarious ends" and noted that "[according] to reports, among those arrested were many Hindus distributing anti-Urdu literature." This helped lend credence to the claim that there were "obviously powerful elements at work in that wing of Pakistan, who see in the adoption of Urdu the end of their hopes and the frustration of their designs" (*Pakistan Times*, February 29, 1952), thus painting the language movement as nothing more nor less than an attempt to destabilize Pakistan. At the same time, the adoption of Urdu as the sole national language of Pakistan was pitched as crucial to thwarting the efforts of fifth columnists.

Dawn claimed that East Bengal was targeted by such elements "because they believe that if they can disrupt that part of Pakistan first, then half their nefarious battle will be won" (*Dawn*, February 23, 1952). The implication of this discourse was that East Bengal was the weakest link in the national security chain, and that this had everything to do with the substantial presence of Hindus. Raj Kumar Chakraverty, a Hindu member of the Congress from East Bengal, justifiably complained that "whenever there is trouble in Pakistan, it is attributed by the people to 'the enemies of the State' and, by insinuations, the Hindus are regarded as these enemies" (General Budget Discussion, Constituent Assembly Debates, March 17, 1952). Another Hindu member from East Bengal echoed these concerns, pointing out that "it has become a fashion ... to put blame and to question the loyalty of Hindus in Pakistan" (Bhabesh Chandra Nandy, Discussion on Finance Bill, Constituent Assembly (Legislature) Reports, March 29, 1952).

In fact, the level of paranoia generated around the issue reached incredible heights, sometimes verging on the ridiculous. Wild allegations of men having come across from West Bengal "dressed in a different way" to incite the demonstrators and "spoil the peace of East Bengal" were aired in the Constituent Assembly[27] and thereafter in the press.[28] The discourse of alterity was clearly at work in the reference to the supposedly "different" sartorial style of the alleged West Bengali infiltrators (meant to imply that they were Hindu).

This chain of signification (dressed "differently" = Hindu = Indian) also relied on and reinforced the idea that to be a Hindu was not to be Pakistani. Shri Dhirendra Nath Dutta (Opposition member) complained to the Speaker of the House about the level of mistrust of Bengali Hindus: "If we put on Loongi, poor Muslim clothes in Eastern Bengal, it is said we disguise ourselves. If we put on Dhoti then it is said that we have come from West Bengal. There is such a sense of mistrust and this has been engineered under the Government of Pakistan" (Discussion on Finance Bill, CAD, March 29, 1952).

East Bengal thus came to be constructed as a troubled province which was home to all manner of seditious elements, from Hindus to Communists, with the language issue as proof-positive of their nefarious plans. This was the only way in which West Pakistanis could make sense of the language controversy because surely authentic East Bengali Pakistanis had no reason to challenge the "unity in the cultural and linguistic fields" (Chughtai, letter to *Pakistan Times*, March 5, 1952), which was the prerequisite to "the unity and solidarity of our nation" (Mukhtar, letter to *Pakistan Times*, March 5, 1952). The headline for *Dawn*'s lead story on February 23, two days after the *Ekushey* tragedy, declared that "[a]ll Pakistan will grieve and our enemies will derive comfort and cheer from the tragic happenings at Dacca."

This discourse of East Bengal as, in turn, a vulnerable and a malignant/seditious place was extremely useful for the state, since it justified the use of its repressive powers there. The official line of the Muslim League government was that the action taken in East Bengal was tragic but had been necessary in order to preserve law and order. The nationalist press in West Pakistan concurred. By presenting the incident as the result of the "conflict between their [the students'] convictions on the one hand, and the principle that law and order be maintained on the other," *Dawn* managed to recast the government's actions almost as a necessary public service. The young demonstrators who had been killed by police fire had "no doubt … sacrificed their young lives for a cause they passionately believed in … and acted in their own light as true Pakistanis" (*Dawn*, February 23, 1952). However, in the final analysis they had "regrettably violated law and order, obviously under the wicked instigation of … enemies of our country … [who] … exploited their youthful emotion to … throw East Pakistan into a turmoil" (*Dawn*, February 26, 1952). Therefore, "however much one might regret the firing due to the incidents, it must be clear even to the blindest that it would have been suicidal folly for the Government to have allowed these subversive elements to go unchecked" (ibid.). Ultimately, despite the generally sympathetic tone in which it talked about the "misguided students," *Dawn* held *them*, and not the state, responsible for the tragedy: they should have known "that … subversive elements had chosen East Pakistan as the base"; they should have realised "how dangerous it was to play with the emotionally inflammable question of language in such an inherently explosive situation" (*Dawn*, February 23, 1952).

In concluding its editorial comments on the Dacca incident, *Dawn* absolved the state of all responsibility for the violence it had inflicted, supporting its claim that the demands of law and order took precedent over democratic and civil rights:

The immediate attention of the Provincial and Central Governments should turn to the existence of this secret network of enemy agents (responsible for instigating the language issue) who are actively assisted by their local supporters. The language issue is only one of the weapons in their armory. Their real objective is a much bigger and more ambitious one. Therein lies the real danger to East Pakistan. *Before that danger, the tragedy of police firing pales into comparative insignificance.* (*Dawn*, February 26, 1952; emphasis added)

The "tragedy of police firing" may have "paled into comparative insignificance" for the editors of *Dawn*; based far away from Dhaka as they were, they may not have realized the intensity of emotion that the government's actions had incited in East Bengal. But perhaps a look in their own columns would have helped. On February 25, Zeb-un-Nissa Hamidullah, a regular columnist for *Dawn*, had written a strong indictment: "I speak as a Bengali today. Always in the past the Pakistani has been uppermost, the Bengali mattered least of all. But today I and millions of other Bengalis feel we must raise our voice and cry: 'Is this what we should expect from Pakistan?'" (*Dawn*, February 25, 1952)

Hamidullah was not a student under the sway of enemy agents; she was a well-known Karachi socialite—cosmopolitan, English-speaking and urbane. In effect, she was a member of what Jahan defines as the "national elite" (Jahan, 1972: 28). Her recuperation of a Bengali identity at this time testifies to the extent of the damage done to the possibility of a national consensus on issues of culture and identity by the government's actions. In her own words, "death does not kill a cause; frequently it creates a cause and brings to it adherents who might otherwise never have taken sides" (*Dawn*, February 25, 1952). The incident resulted in producing a heightened sense of Bengali-ness:

For most of us, I am speaking of the average intellectual Bengali, the question of the State language was never a controversial one. We accepted the fact that a nation, to be united in the true sense of the term, must have a single State language. Urdu was the obvious choice and all of us accepted it ... I want to forget that I am a Bengali again and become only a Pakistani, so do millions of others. Will the Government make it possible? (Ibid.)

The government action resulted in a flurry of letters to the *Pakistan Times* in support of the language movement.[29] One writer expressed it thus:

> It passes the comprehension of a reasonable and tolerant individual why Urdu alone is being adopted as the official or State language in the face of opposition by about 45 million of our Pakistani brethren ... No language, however sweet, simple or popular can acquire a national status unless it is a genuine lingua franca and is accepted voluntarily as such by the majority of the population. (*Pakistan Times*, March 7, 1952)

The manner in which the language issue was handled, combined with other grievances against the center, reinforced the construction of a Bengali political/cultural/ethnic identity in which the status of the Bengali language came to stand for the place of Bengalis in the political and cultural framework of Pakistan. The East Bengal Legislative Assembly's passing of a hasty resolution in which it recommended that the Constituent Assembly adopt Bangla as a second national language could not undo the damage.

It is worth noting that during this very period—while Muslim League politicians and members of the nationalist intelligentsia loudly and hotly upheld Urdu's right to be Pakistan's sole national language—the *Anjuman-i Taraqqi-i Urdu* (Association for the Progress of Urdu) had been slipping into bankruptcy, due primarily to lack of aid from the Pakistan government.[30] In fact, the *Pakistan Times* (March 4, 1952) noted it as "scandalous" that "such a useful institution, with a long record of service and so intimately associated in the public mind with the progress of Urdu, should face extinction in the only State that has virtually adopted Urdu as its language." We need look no further than this fact to prove that for the West Pakistani establishment and its organic intellectuals, the imperative to undermine the Bangla movement was about something other than an emotional investment in Urdu or Muslim culture.

PRODUCING THE LAW-AND-ORDER SOCIETY

Under Jinnah in the 1930s and 1940s, the Muslim League had been turned into a highly centralized, vertically integrated structure. Jinnah did not want to risk having the League fall prey to the competing interests within, as soon as Pakistan was established. By accepting the title of governor general he ensured his control over centrifugal elements, but in so doing, he retained an office which was extremely powerful yet not democratically elected. In addition, he abandoned the federal option for the Pakistani state with its framework of weak center and strong provinces. Instead, he asked his second-in-command, Liaquat Ali Khan, to draw up a plan for a highly integrated state along the pattern of Britain's Whitehall. This was reinforced by the unification of the civil services within a centralized structure headed by the secretary general and rendered autonomous of ministers. The Planning Committee, also chaired by the secretary general, worked as a shadow cabinet where all pertinent decisions were made and then passed on to the cabinet. There were no Bengalis at this level of administration (Samad, 1995; Barlas, 1995).

As in all decolonizing states, institutional continuity was crucial in the immediate aftermath of independence; the colonial state apparatus therefore continued to provide the basis for the new state. Of these colonial hangovers, the civil service and the Government of India Act of 1935 in particular proved very useful for a state elite which was not interested in understanding ordinary Pakistanis as *citizens* with rights that the state was obliged to respect, but instead as *subjects* to rule over (Mamdani, 1996). The Act of 1935 had been a last-ditch effort by a fading colonial power to enforce its rule; it thus gave the governor general as well as the governors of each province immense executive powers. This weighed power heavily in favor of the bureaucracy over elected representatives (Jalal, 1994; Noman, 1988), a power which was reinforced by the military and civil bureaucracy's disdain of politicians. The Government of India Act (1935) functioned as the *de facto* constitution for Pakistan until an actual one was finalized, and the fact that the Constituent Assembly failed to come up with an acceptable Constitution more than five years after Independence suited the Muslim League eminently. The Press Laws Ordinance also compromised democratic procedure by allowing the state to impose bans on newspapers if it decided that their material was inflammatory.

In fact, from 1949 onwards, the bureaucracy was increasingly Pakistan's shadow government. As Opposition members Mian Iftikharuddin and Sri Sris Chandra Chattopadhyaya pointed out, most of the Muslim League's ministers, especially those in charge of defense and internal affairs, had been in civil service under the British and so were administrators rather than politicians (Constituent Assembly Debates, April 22, 1952). This was reflected, among other things, in a progressively more centralized and authoritarian form of state. Iftikhar Malik notes that "as a 'viceregal system', the bureaucracy has constantly overstepped, bypassed, dismissed and denigrated the mass verdict by simply opting for authoritarianism." Civil service officers were socialized to believe that they "belonged to a privileged group which had a major responsibility for the future governing of Pakistan" and as officers schooled in accordance with Lord Macaulay's dream, they were "trained to hold political leaders in contempt" (Malik, 1997: 60–61). In 1949, for example, the Public Representative Officers (Disqualification) Act, which had been part of the Government of India Act of 1935, was used to dismiss troublesome politicians.

Both the corporate interests of the classes represented in the state (Alavi, 1982), as well as their colonial training thus mitigated against the idea of accountability to ordinary citizens (Malik, 1997), and taught the bureaucrats to view with instant hostility even legitimate democratic demands made through legitimate democratic means. Sardar Asadullah Jan, an Opposition member from the North West Frontier Province (NWFP)[31] noted that for the bureaucracy "the citizen is not the bearer of public rights; he is only a tax-payer, whose only function is that he must obey the orders of the bureaucracy" (Speech against Security Bill, Constituent Assembly Debates, April 24, 1952). Under such a regime, the Opposition's call for the right to personal and civil liberties did not have much hope of creating an impact. The Opposition could just as well have asked what the goal of the government of Pakistan was: "the freedom and happiness of the individuals who compose it ... or that of the State?" (Asadullah Khan and Khalilur Rahman, Constituent Assembly Debates, April 24, 1952). In the case of East Bengal and the language controversy, the issue was exacerbated by the highly derogatory attitude of non-Bengali members of state institutions towards Bengalis and by the fact that there were no Bengalis in the higher echelons of the civil service or the military.

The Muslim League repeatedly used the pretext of various real and imagined crises to justify suspending civil rights, including the holding of elections, by the simple expedient of declaring an Emergency. Under an Emergency, power shifted to another colonial hangover, the governor general, who could dismiss political representatives at will. Mian Iftikharuddin took to referring to the Muslim League government as the "Executive Committee", neither representative of, nor accountable to, the people. Crises are, of course, never in short supply in newly independent decolonizing states, and they can be eminently useful for states when it comes to consolidating power (Hall, 1979). The language controversy, especially in 1952, was one such "useful" crisis in that it provided the central government with the justification it needed to increase the extra-judicial powers of the executive, citing emergency conditions, resulting in the passing of various Safety Ordinances and Security Bills (sardonically referred to by the Opposition as "Insecurity" Bills), which themselves had been important tools in the arsenal of British colonial government.

One of the Bills tabled at the session of the Constituent Assembly immediately following the events of *Ekushey*, for example, was a Central Public Safety Ordinance, similar in scope to the provincial one which allowed for "preventive detention," censorship of newspapers and the arbitrary imposition of Section 144 which banned public assembly. Mushtaq Ahmad Gurmani (Constituent Assembly Debates, April 18, 1952), the interior minister and a prime example of a bureaucrat-turned-politician, defended the need for such measures:

> ... a newly established State necessarily has problems of ... great magnitude and complexity. The first essential condition for the solution of these problems is the firm establishment of an administrative machinery adequately empowered, capable of ensuring the stability of the State and the maintenance of law and order ... every effort must be made not only to build up a sound administrative structure, but also to make certain that the hands of the Executive are ... strengthened ... in all spheres ... .

The Opposition was quick in pointing out that this Bill, as well as others like it, were a carry-over from the colonial period. Gurmani himself defended the Bill by showing historical precedence: "Similar measures were passed and enforced in all big towns in India previous to Partition" (Constituent Assembly Debates, April 18, 1952). Sri Kamini Kumar Dutta, another Opposition member, warned that the government was beholden to the Constitution when passing and enacting laws; the caveat, of course, was that there was no Constitution as yet,[32] and the Government of India Act of 1935 fully endorsed such executive, summary powers.

Speaking against the Security Bill, Raj Kumar Chakraverty (Constituent Assembly Debates, April 21, 1952), another Hindu member of the Opposition from East Bengal, pointed out the existence of an unfortunate "misconception ... among ... the executive officers of this country who have been trained in the old bureaucratic ways" that to "say anything against an officer or the Government" was tantamount to sedition.

In response to the allegation that these "safety" laws were a means of squashing legitimate political dissent and were direct descendants of the repressive laws of the British government prior to Partition, Gurmani had this to say:

> Well! These laws were certainly enacted by a foreign Government, but what was the purpose of those laws? Let that be clearly understood. Those laws were to suppress the movements for liberation of the country. Those laws were to suppress the movement for the overthrow of a foreign rule. The safety and security of the State in those days meant the safety and security of the interests which ruled the country. (Constituent Assembly Debates, April 18, 1952)

The implication, of course, was that the state now embodied the national popular will and so the very fact that these laws, repressive or not, were being enacted by a Pakistani government and not a foreign one was reason enough to justify them: "Today those [foreign] interests do not exist. Today these powers, in a modified form, are sought for what purposes? For safeguarding and protecting the freedom of Pakistan; for maintaining the security of the State; for ensuring the defence of the country" (ibid.).

Mian Iftikharuddin pointed out the obvious irony in the fact that the very set of laws which the British government had imposed on Indians and the flouting of which became synonymous with the demand for independence, were now being re-imposed on "free citizens" of Pakistan in their "best interest" (Debate on the Restriction and Detention (Second Amendment) Bill, Constituent Assembly Debates, November 14, 1952).

The provisions of the Safety Acts and the Security Bill gave an unelected executive the right to compromise the personal and civil liberties of the nation-state's citizens through summary trials and denial of habeas corpus. The Opposition expressed concern that the Act would be used for political purposes—as indeed the Provincial Public Safety Act had been in East Bengal—and that the denial of a person's fundamental rights was a matter of grave concern for a purportedly democratic country. The fact that the wording of the Act was vague in terms of what counted as a threat also drew heavy criticism from the Opposition in the Assembly, to no avail. "I fail to understand", said Sris Chandra Chattopadhyaya, a Hindu

Opposition member from East Bengal "who is not connected with subversive movement [sic] according to [this] definition ... With this vague term 'subversive action', anything will be subversive ... There is no definition of 'subversive movement'. Therefore, I oppose this" (Discussion on the Security Bill, Constituent Assembly (Legislature) Debates, April 22, 1952). Sris Chattopadhyaya's speech made clear the implications of taking a stand for any democratic demand in the face of such legislation:

> If we say that we are against two-nation theory; we want all citizens of Pakistan to be one—all Pakistanis, you will say this is against our basic conception of the State and its theory. Therefore this is a subversive movement and you will be liable to arrest. Who will protect me? I may say; "Do not make two nations; make one nation, irrespective of caste, creed and colour". Do not divide the people into Pakistani and non-Pakistani, like Muslim and non-Muslim. You will say: Subversive movement!

Hindu Opposition members from East Bengal such as Chakraverty and Chattopadhyaya were among the most vocal proponents of a pluralist *national* culture and a federalist *state* structure, both of which the Muslim League understood as anathema to its bid to stay in power. East Bengal was also the locus of the strongest opposition to attempts by the Muslim League to define Pakistan as an Islamic state—a strategy that it had resorted to in order to hold on to its increasingly elusive moral authority. The fact that some of its most strident critics were Hindu Opposition members from East Bengal thus provided the League with a happy coincidence because it could pitch the language controversy as a "Hindu conspiracy" to undermine Pakistan, while effectively neutralizing some of the most vocal voices of Opposition in the Constituent Assembly by the mere fact of their religious identity and support for Bangla.

After Hindus, communists were the fifth columnists of choice in the discourse of the state and its organic intellectuals.[33] In fact, where the loyalty of Hindus could only be obliquely questioned, communists were openly declared enemies of the state. This was in part a testimony to the fact that they were a perpetual thorn in the side of the Pakistani establishment. In East Pakistan, they were important players on the political and cultural front, including the language movement. In West Pakistan, they were stronger on the cultural front than the political but even then, their support of

Bengali demands, among other things, was seen by their liberal nationalist detractors as evidence of their treachery.[34]

The debates from the Constituent Assembly show how productive the discourse of subversion was, for it allowed the state to frame both individual liberty and the will of the "public" as threatening, thereby enabling the construction of "a law and order society" (Hall, 1979). Hence we have Mushtaq Ahmed Gurmani (Constituent Assembly Debates, March 27, 1952) arguing during a debate on the Central Safety Ordinance that "Freedom is freedom only when it is consistent with law and with discipline" and that "individual freedom and civil liberty are dependent on the [sic] national freedom and national security. Individual freedom ... [and] civil liberty is only possible, if the country is free. If you ensure the security of the country, it is only then that you can enjoy individual freedom" (Gurmani, Constituent Assembly Debates, April 24, 1952).

Thus, ran the argument, the imperatives of security were a *precondition* for the guarantee of civil liberties and, under the current state of Emergency, were critical to the integrity of the state. A similar tension was embedded in Jinnah's response to the language controversy in 1947–48. In his address to the people of East Bengal, published in *Dawn* under the heading "Quaid-i-Azam pays glowing tribute to sterling character of East Bengal's people" he had declared: "I would like now to offer a word of advice to the people of this province. I notice a regrettable tendency on the part of a certain section of the people to regard their newly won freedom not as liberty with the great opportunities it opened up and the heavy responsibilities it imposed, but as license" (*Dawn*, March 29, 1948).

"ONE UNIT" AND THE POLITICS OF PARITY

Bangla was finally declared Pakistan's second national language in 1952, in the aftermath of the tragic events of *Ekushey*. However, the (West) Pakistani establishment's efforts at containing East Bengal did not end with the resolution (however fraught) of the language controversy. East Bengal's demographic majority had been a thorn in the side of the West Pakistani establishment from the very beginning. In 1949, the first version of the Basic Principles Committee Report (the draft of the Constitution) submitted under the Constituent Assembly had proposed a legislature designed to "transform East Bengal's numerical majority of the population into a minority of seats" (Callard, 1957: 92). The result of the provincial elections in

East Bengal in 1954, reluctantly called by the Muslim League under severe pressure from the Opposition, frightened the establishment. The Muslim League was routed out of power by the United Front, a coalition of opposition parties which included the Awami League, the Krishak Sramik Party, the Ganantari Dal, the Nizam-i-Islam Party and the Youth League. The central government's reaction was, predictably, to immediately impose Governor's Rule in the province.

The likely provisions of the emerging constitution—a federal system with proportional representation for all provinces—posed another potential threat to the ruling clique at the centre, because under this system East Bengal would emerge as the majority province. The establishment responded by pushing for the consolidation of all the provinces of West Pakistan into a single administrative-political unit, the so-called "One Unit." Under the One Unit framework, the two "wings" of Pakistan would become two equal political-administrative units, with constitutional parity. The One Unit proposal was designed to both reduce what would have been East Bengal's demographic advantage under the emerging federal scheme and also neutralize any possibility of the smaller provinces of West Pakistan building alliances with East Bengal against the Punjab.

Significantly, the case for One Unit was made on the grounds that each of Pakistan's two wings—to be officially renamed East and West Pakistan—had their own unique history and culture. Needless to say, this was a complete contradiction of the earlier state discourse of the inviolability of Pakistan's unitary and shared national culture. The debates over One Unit in the Constituent Assembly are fascinating for the glimpse they give us of the ways in which (national) culture becomes the battleground for contests over power in the modern nation-state, and how different delineations of national culture enable/justify different political projects.

Significantly, the historical and cultural arguments presented by Mian Mumtaz Daultana (the chief minister of Punjab) on behalf of the government and in favor of the unification of West Pakistan's provinces into One Unit were almost identical to those that had been put forth by leftist intellectuals as part of their efforts to articulate a progressive Pakistani nationalism which, unlike official nationalism, did not posit "Islam" as the basis of the nation-state. In order to do so, they had pointed to the fact that the area that was now West Pakistan had a long history of cultural and political unity, starting from the time of the ancient civilizations of Mohenjodaro and Harappa. Daultana's aim was to argue that "the integration of West Pakistan is a natural culmination, a natural fruition, a natural realization" of a long historical process rather than a cynical political move on the part of a self-serving ruling elite; that "as far as the memory of mankind can go, the history of the area of West Pakistan has been one" (Mian Mumtaz Daultana, *Constituent Assembly of Pakistan Debates* (CAD), 1955: 337). From this illustrious beginning to the present time

> ... we have faced the world as one unity. Sir, we have always fought together the same enemies; we have faced the same problems; we have made identical adjustments; we have answered the same challenges with the same responses, from time immemorial ... In fact the unity of our valley of the Indus gave the first concept of unity to the entire peninsula of Hindusthan. Sir, ours was the first unity that an outsider could perceive in the multifarious diversity of the Indo-Pakistan sub-continent, and it is from our land, the land of the "Sindhu" that the word "Hindu" and the word "India" has been derived. It was our unity that created the conception of unity for the peoples of India. From the very beginning, from the days of Mohenjodaro to the days of our last glorious conflict for freedom against the British, we have always, invariably, acted as one people. We are not, Sir, a congeries [*sic*] of conflicts; we, Sir, are a pattern of unison. (Ibid.: 339)

Thus Daultana didn't just make the case for the historic unity of *West Pakistan*—he actually went further and asserted that it was this region's unity that had actually inspired the idea of a *unified India*. Before the members of the Constituent Assembly could begin to digest this explicit pride in a pre-Islamic history and what appeared to be the validation of the idea of a unified India coming from a Muslim League representative, Daultana added to their confusion by proudly adding that West Pakistan was also the crucible of *Hinduism*:

> It is West Pakistan which gave to the entire Hindu religion its first great mystic vision, the *Rig Veda*. When these first spiritual stirrings decayed and lost direction in a morass of ritual and superstition and the time ripened for the teaching of Gotham[35] [*sic*] to come upon the world, we took them to heart, not through the imposition of Asoka but during the glorious age of our own Kaniska. (Ibid.: 340)

It is hard to understate the significance of a Muslim League politician making glowing references to the shared pre-Islamic—and specifically *Hindu*—history of West Pakistan. We must pause here to recall the crux of the same government's official discourse on the Bangla–Urdu crisis: that the basis for Pakistan was *Islamic* culture and civilization and that Bangla's "Hindu" roots disqualified it from ever being considered a national language of Pakistan.

Daultana's historical narrative finally got to Islam, but only after a detour through the influence of the Greeks:

> ... in the final fulfillment of our existence, in the final development and culmination of our thought, when our ears heard the noble message of Islam, we accepted it, not with hesitation, not through conflict, but all the areas of West Pakistan accepted it as if at one moment of illumination, within the first century of the advent of Islam. And once having accepted Islam, despite the various conflicts that have taken place, despite the innumerable vissititudes [*sic*] and tribulations to which this area, being at the very hub of world civilizations, has been subjected we, Sir, have always held to it steadfastly, we have never resiled [*sic*] from it, we have never compromised it. This indeed is the great and noble heritage of which today we are proud. Therefore, Sir, in culture and spirit and mind we have always, not today, from the very beginning of time been one indissoluble integrated unity. (Ibid.)

This was an incredible statement to be coming from the representative of a government which had hitherto been crying foul at the slightest mention of provincial rights, not to mention a rather grandiose speech on behalf of what was, essentially, a bureaucratic proposal.

Daultana's argument, focused as it was on proving that West Pakistan was (and had been from time immemorial) a single historical, political and cultural unit, did not address the issue of what bound East and West Pakistan together. In fact, it essentially threw the issue of East Pakistan into limbo, for if West Pakistan formed an "indissoluble integrated unity" in "culture and spirit and mind," then where did that leave East Pakistan? Since the Muslim League's official line with regard to this issue had hitherto been that the basis of unity between Pakistan's two wings was Islam and Islam alone, it was not surprising that the very idea of a member of the same government extolling West Pakistan's pre-Islamic and Hindu heritage would come as a shock to many members of the Constituent Assembly. As one Bengali member put it: "Your existence may have resulted from that culture [that is, the Indus Valley civilization], but I wonder where does East Pakistan stand after the exposition of this theory? Is this talk of unity between East and West Pakistan all empty? ... What would then bind East and West Pakistan?" (Noor-ur-Rahman, *Dawn*, August 27, 1955, cited in Malik, 1963: 267).

Moreover, East Bengalis could not help but feel their regional, cultural and historical traditions slighted by Daultana's claim of the antiquity of West Pakistan. Noor-ur-Rahman continued his critique by saying that "we have our own history and heroes. Raja Ram Mohan Roy was one of them.[36] We all, Hindus and Moslems, are proud of his great deeds."[37] Daultana's arguments thus had the effect of widening the gap between East and West Pakistan.

Significantly, Daultana's case for One Unit, based as it was on *West* Pakistan's cultural unity, negated the hitherto sacrosanct establishment position that any mention of the cultural difference between East and West Pakistan—such as, for example, by championing the cause of Bangla—was tantamount to undermining the glue which held East and West Pakistan together, which was "Islam." The latter argument had proved convenient when the need of the day was to negate the legitimacy of East Bengali demands for the recognition of Bangla, and thereby for equal representation in the nation-state. However, as soon as the need of the hour changed, even the purportedly sacrosanct "two-nation theory" and the primacy of "Islam" as the national glue could be (and were) summarily discarded. Daultana's arguments thus laid bare the expediency behind the Muslim League's approach to nationalism.

Interestingly, Daultana's speech on behalf of One Unit was an almost verbatim restatement of extant arguments made by leftist intellectuals who were invested in defining a non-religious basis for Pakistani nationalism. In his response to Daultana on the floor of the Assembly, Iftikharuddin (*CAD*, 1955: 608) sarcastically pointed out that his "brilliant friend from the Punjab" was "guilty of plagiarism by stealing all the arguments that I have been giving for the last four years." This was particularly astonishing, continued Iftikharuddin, given Daultana's past record which included, among other things, signing both versions of the Basic Principles Committee Report.[38] How could one explain this paradox of a Muslim League politician (for whom the "two-nation theory" was supposedly sacrosanct) arguing that the true basis for a people's identity was not religion but a shared cultural and political history? And, perhaps more importantly, how could a progressive blueprint for Pakistani culture proposed by leftists lend itself to being so easily appropriated for reactionary ends? The answer lay in the fact that while these ideas about the importance of a shared *cultural* past could underwrite the demand for a "more lasting ... [and] far more democratic" (ibid.: 609) *federated* state structure when proposed by the Left (and East Bengalis), they could just as easily be articulated to a completely *different* political project such as a forced and "unitary" consolidation of West Pakistan.[39] The lesson here is that cultural projects are rarely progressive or reactionary in and of themselves— what ultimately determines their political effect is the political project they are harnessed to.

Perhaps the most amazing part of Daultana's argument came when he argued that the One Unit proposal should not be construed as a Punjabi conspiracy, because something called "the Punjab" simply didn't exist:

> Sir, the Punjab which we fear so much is not an ethnic entity. It is also not a linguistic entity ... Again, Sir, Punjab is not a complex of distinct and desparate [*sic*] historical experience ... Therefore, Sir, what is the Punjab? This Punjab is a term of convenience. This Punjab is in effect a geographical expression ... The moment the boundaries of the Punjab cease to exist, there remains no entity that you can distinguish as the Punjab. (Ibid.: 345)

Moreover, argued Daultana, for "those who hate the Punjabi; those who find that the Punjabis represent something perverse in the life of the nation" the One Unit proposal was actually a boon because what better way to undermine it than to "take away the boundaries of the Punjab" (ibid.).[40]

Iftikharuddin felt it necessary to address the reification of the "Punjab" and "Bengal" which Daultana's discourse both relied upon and reinforced. Far from being a monolith, declared Iftikharuddin, the people of the Punjab (and of West Pakistan as a whole) were in fact an entity separate from the Punjabi/West Pakistani ruling elite. Thus the political intrigues of the West Pakistani establishment should not, under any circumstances, be associated with the people of West Pakistan; if their past treatment at the hands of the ruling elite was anything to go by, no benefit was to accrue to them as a result of this latest "initiative." Iftikharuddin reminded the House that, in crucial ways, the people of West Pakistan were *more* deprived and suffered greater repression at the hands of the West Pakistani establishment even than those of East Bengal:

Sir, my Bengali friends ... will pardon me when I say that they have completely misunderstood and unconsciously misrepresented to themselves, the position of the present leadership *vis-à-vis* the people of the Punjab. They have confused in a most dangerous manner the present clique which rules over us with the people of Punjab. People of Punjab have no enmity, have never had any enmity with the people of other provinces ... Please do not mix the present leadership with the people of the Punjab. In fact, nobody has been a great [*sic*] enemy of the people of Punjab than the present ruling group. Nowhere have civil liberties been denied in the way that they are denied to us in the Punjab ... They adopt special repressive methods to maintain their present power there. If they lose Punjab as their base they will be nowhere. (Ibid.: 633–4)

In the end, of course, it was not the outcome of these debates that decided the matter of the unification of West Pakistan. The civil-military bureaucracy (which was always the real base of power in Pakistan) demonstrated its disdain for the democratic process and constitutional niceties by dissolving the Cabinet and disbanding the Constituent Assembly in October 1954 before the debate on the One Unit Bill was concluded. A state of emergency was declared, and the announcement that the provinces of West Pakistan were to be merged into one administrative unit by executive order followed soon after.

It was clear even at the time that the consolidation of West Pakistan was not about culture, history, or geography but about changing the political landscape of Pakistan *per se* and constraining the political imagination of ordinary Pakistanis. Moreover, the One Unit Bill was not just concerned with the actual administrative consolidation of the territory of West Pakistan as was evident from its full title: "The Establishment of West Pakistan Bill: The Bill to Provide for the Establishment of the Province of West Pakistan by Integrating Provinces and States and for other Purposes Connected Therewith." Indeed, among the "other purposes" of One Unit was the counterposing of this new province of West Pakistan to the officially renamed province of East Pakistan within a system of parity, thus effectively neutralizing any danger of East Bengal's dominance under a truly federal system.

3
Post-Partition Literary Politics: The Progressives versus the Nationalists

Voh intezaar tha jiska, yeh voh sahar to nahiñ. (This is not the dawn we were waiting for.)
Faiz Ahmed Faiz, leftist Pakistani poet, on the
moment of decolonization/Independence/Partition.

The immediate post-Independence period in Pakistan, characterized as it was by a volatile mixture of nationalist euphoria and national insecurity, posed both an opportunity and a challenge to the Left, which was seeking to articulate an alternative nationalism and nation-state project based on its vision of a progressive society. The classes in control of the state, concerned about the increasingly unruly populace, were determined to expel socialism/communism from the realm of legitimate politics. In order to do so, the ground had to first be cleared by the ideological construction of communists as enemies of the Pakistani nation-state.

Independence and Partition wrought many changes on the cultural and political landscape of the subcontinent, one of which was that Urdu writers and poets were divided by the new borders between India and Pakistan. While this division of the Urdu literary community failed to rupture its shared secular character (Ahmad, 1993), and even though this community was reconstituted within the constraints of the new political context—that is, writers from both sides continued to publish in each other's magazines, take part in important intellectual debates, and so on—new and significant ideological divides emerged.

One of the most pitched political/ideological battles of the post-independence period was conducted between two literary camps—the left-wing members of the Progressive Writers Association (PWA) and their liberal anti-communist detractors—and was understood by both to be about the very soul of the new nation-state. Far from being peripheral to national politics and issues of state, the polemical debates between these two camps were a crucial part of the ideological struggle within Pakistan at this time. At the discursive level, these coalesced around a struggle between the definitions and visions of both "nation" and "state." The anti-communist liberal intelligentsia were to become part of the larger project of relegating the socialist vision—an important feature of the anti-colonial nationalist struggle in Indian politics prior to Independence—to the margins of the political imaginary of ordinary Pakistanis. The political and ideological battle between these two factions of the hitherto hegemonic progressive literary movement exemplified the political stakes within Pakistan in this period.

THE PROGRESSIVE WRITERS ASSOCIATION

The establishment of the All Pakistan Progressive Writers Association (APPWA) was the result of the division of the All India Progressive Writers Association (AIPWA) in the wake of Partition/Independence. AIPWA itself had its organizational and programmatic antecedents in a collection of short stories titled *Angaray* ["The Embers"] that was published in 1932 by a group of young writers—Sajjad Zaheer, Mahmud uz Zafar, Rashid Jahan and Ahmed Ali—who represented a new generation of youth in explicit rebellion against the old feudal order.[1]

The stories in *Angaray* focused on a critique of traditional Indian society, and were written with the aim of stirring debate over its moribund aspects. The collection caused a sensation, as it was meant to do—after all, its iconic story ended with its protagonist, a religious figure, having a wet dream while lying on top of a Quran—leading to its proscription by the government of the United Provinces under pressure from conservative and religious quarters. *Angaray* left no sacred cows intact, attacking the prevailing familial and sexual mores, the decadence and hypocrisy of contemporary social and religious life, and religious orthodoxy in general with equal gusto. The collection left its mark on modern Urdu literature and its impact was to reverberate for many years. The themes of youthful rebellion and revolt against the old order were signs of things to come, and heralded a new age in Indian political and cultural life.[2]

In the mid-1930s, a group of young Marxist Indian students and aspiring writers studying in Oxford laid the groundwork for what became the All India Progressive Writers Association. Among them were Sajjad Zaheer of the *Angaray* group, M.D. Taseer who would go on to become the primary ideologue of the anti-communist front, and Mulk Raj Anand who later became one of the most influential literary figures in the subcontinent. Deeply moved by the contemporary political events in Germany, and inspired[3] by the first

International Congress for the Defence of Culture[4] held in Paris in 1935, these writers decided to form a literary association.[5] The exact date of the Oxford meeting which launched the Indian Progressive Writers Association appears to be under dispute, but the final form of the manifesto which they produced was first published by the *Left Review* in February 1935. Realizing that an association like this, which aimed to produce politically and socially engaged literature, could not be effective unless it had roots in India, a mimeographed copy of the manifesto was sent to Munshi Premchand, a leading figure in the contemporary social reform movement within Urdu and Hindi literature, who published a Hindi translation in his journal *Hans* in October 1935.

The manifesto began by declaring that radical changes were taking place in Indian life, with old ideas and values crumbling in the wake of a new society. It called for a socially engaged literature which reflected the changes taking place and could assist in putting the country on a constructive and progressive path. Indian literature, it claimed, had become stagnant and ineffective because it had run away from the realities of the age instead of facing them. It took refuge in devotionalism, classicism and asceticism; there was a surfeit of emotion and a paucity of reason and reflection. The declared aim of the Association was to wrest "our" literature away from the monopolistic control of "priests, pundits and other conservatives" and bring it nearer to the people through constructive social criticism and a faithful reflection of people's everyday realities and issues so as to better understand and ultimately change Indian society.

One of the major changes in the Hindi version of the manifesto was the addition of the following:

> All those things which take us toward confusion, dissension, and blind imitation is [*sic*] conservative; also, all that which engenders in us a critical capacity, which induces us to test our dear traditions on the touchstone of our reason and perception, which makes us healthy and produces among us the strength of unity and integration, that is what we call Progressive. (Cited in Coppola, 1974: 8)

Coppola notes, correctly, that this was an attempt to articulate a definition of "Progressive" which could accommodate a wide spectrum of views and attract as many people as possible. These changes from the original version reflected the difficulties and challenges of organizing writers in India around a common platform in order to establish a United Front within the cultural-literary sphere.[6]

From its very inception, AIPWA had a core group of committed communists,[7] but its larger membership was not limited to writers of any particular political persuasion. In fact, the Association was consciously opened to include writers who shared the organization's basic commitments to anti-imperialism and *taraqqi-pasandi*, or progressivism (literally translated, the term means "love of progress"). At this particular moment in colonial India, *taraqqi-pasandi* signified a constructively critical approach to traditional Indian society, a rejection of old and reactionary customs and traditions, and an investment in the building of a new and modern society. The AIPWA thus functioned as an umbrella under which progressive writers of all stripes could comfortably place themselves. It understood its mission to be that of constructing a United Front of writers *against* imperialism and reactionary social tendencies, and *for* a life-affirming art.

Never before had writers across India been mobilized around a single platform so effectively, and no previous Indian movement or literary school[8] had so redefined the terms of the writer's creative output and literature's engagement with its society and times. By the time of Independence in 1947, the progressive vision embodied by AIPWA[9]—with its twin constituent elements of socialism and anti-imperialism—had become the leading force within the literary-cultural sphere in India, such that *taraqqi-pasandi* in Urdu literature soon came to be considered synonymous with the association. Scholars, even those critical of the PWA, agree that it was the "strongest and most proximate shaping force" in India from its very inception such that "Urdu writers ... who did not subscribe to the broad consensus were relegated to the fringes of the writing-community" (Ahmad, 1993: 28).[10]

It was precisely this important place which the PWA occupied within the Urdu literary community and its legacy of socialist and anti-imperialist ideas that proved to be threatening to the establishment in Pakistan soon after Independence.

THE NEW "NATIONAL QUESTION"

In the post-Independence period, both the Indian and Pakistani states turned against the very same radical movements that had been so instrumental in the success of the anti-colonial struggle. The Indian state, led by the Indian National Congress, which had come to power on the basis of a rising tide of radical mass politics and which professed "socialism" to be one of its goals for independent India, brutally suppressed the communist-led peasant uprisings in Telangana and the north-eastern provinces, while the ruling Muslim League party of Pakistan began to bare its authoritarian teeth against its own progressives. In turn, the communists of both countries became more strident in their criticism of the state. Echoing the Zhdanovist line in the Soviet Union, a faction led by B.T. Ranadive mounted a "coup" within the Communist Party of India (CPI), declaring the ruling class(es) of both India and Pakistan reactionary, and calling for abandoning the more general anti-imperialist politics which had characterized the old United Front strategies of the World War II era in favor of an explicitly anti-capitalist line (Coppola, 1975).

This new turn in CPI policy was reflected in the analyses and activities of the Progressive Writers Association on both sides of the border. A new manifesto (henceforth "the Manifesto") was issued which declared that while the United Front might have been a necessary strategy in the period leading up to Independence, following it now in the new political context would be tantamount to a betrayal of the people. The Manifesto also declared that all intellectuals (specifically writers) *had* to take sides in this new political battlefield between the people and the ruling elite; neutrality was not an option.

This new Manifesto found expression in the rhetoric and tactics of the Progressive writers even before the formal establishment of the All Pakistan Progressive Writers Association (APPWA) in November 1949. Until then, the Progressives worked through institutions such as the local PWA chapters in Lahore and Karachi, as well as through newspapers and Urdu literary magazines,[11] in particular *Savera*, *Naqush*, *Sang-i Meel* and *Adab-i Latif*.[12] The more radical and outspoken members of the PWA at this time—Sibte Hasan, Hajra Masroor, Ahmad Nadeem Qasmi, Abdullah Malik, Arif Abdul Mateen, Zaheer Kashmiri, Mumtaz Hussain, Khadija Mastoor, among others—came to be known as the "*Savera* group" after the magazine of the same name.[13]

The political economy within which reconfigurations of class and nation took place in Pakistan were clearly reflected in the new alignments within the literary-cultural sphere as well. Intellectuals and writers such as M.D. Taseer (a member of the original Oxford group that started the PWA), Samad Shaheen, Mumtaz Shireen, and Akhtar Hussain Raipuri—all members of the PWA and therefore part of the progressive consensus of the anti-colonial period—abandoned the association within the new political context, with some going on to becoming the association's most articulate and die-hard *liberal* critics. The focus here on the *liberal* front against communism in this period is important for a couple of reasons. First, while there was an anti-communism espoused by the religious right as well, the Islamists were not yet a significant political and social force within civil society in Pakistan at this time. Secondly, the affinity of this liberal front with the international liberal front against communism in the cultural Cold War during this period was neither coincidental nor, as we shall see, irrelevant to the trajectory of Pakistani politics.[14]

Many of the members of this liberal front, such as Muhammad Hassan Askari,[15] Samad Shaheen and Mumtaz Shireen, were *muhajir*[16] and had a lot invested in the idea of Pakistan both emotionally and materially,[17] and so took their role in nation-building very seriously. As Intizar Hussain (1997), a young writer at the time and part of Askari's circle, notes in his autobiography, Partition changed Askari fundamentally from a proponent of "art for art's sake" to someone who devoted his considerable energies and talents to the task of nation-building, putting forth the need for identifying and constructing a uniquely *Pakistani* literature, a demand which later came to constitute a major node in the ideological battle with the Progressive writers.

Despite the fact that the liberal anti-communist intellectuals continued to subscribe to many of the key values of "progressivism," the stand-off between them and the Progressives was fundamentally antagonistic in nature. The latter were vocal carriers of a hegemonic socialist and anti-imperialist tradition within the Urdu literary community which dominated the intellectual space within West Pakistan (Hussain, 1997). The liberal writers thought of themselves, first and foremost, as patriots who were committed to putting their considerable energies and talents in the service of their new nation-state. Crucially, they defined this project of nation-building as being *incompatible* with the socialism and anti-imperialism of the Progressives, and strongly identified the nation with the state, and both with the Muslim League *government*. Not only were they reluctant to criticize the Muslim League despite its increasingly authoritarian character, but they swore loyalty to it, demanding that others do the same or risk being labeled fifth columnists. It is in these moments that the relationship between their politics and the interests of the ruling establishment overlapped most neatly.

Whether or not we understand this as a conscious complicity with the establishment,[18] what is clear is that their anti-communist zeal served the purposes of the state, essentially turning them into organic intellectuals of the Pakistani ruling class.[19]

The establishment and its organic intellectuals set out to accomplish the task of marginalizing the Progressives by seeking to discredit their communist/socialist vision with the help of Cold War propaganda. In addition, the fact that the Communist Party of India, with which the PWA had been affiliated, had withdrawn its initial support for the Pakistan movement just before Independence, was used to label the Progressives as enemies of the Pakistani nation-state. The consolidation of the ideological front was backed up by the coercive power of the state which was increasingly directed against Progressive publications and members of the PWA. Meetings of the association were regularly disrupted, their publications proscribed, and several of their members jailed. The climax of these repressive measures came with the arrest and trial of Faiz Ahmed Faiz and Sajjad Zaheer in the Rawalpindi Conspiracy Case in 1951 along with some senior and junior officers of the Pakistan Army,[20] who were charged with conspiring to overthrow the government. The multi-pronged assault on the PWA helped prepare the ground for the ultimate banning of the Communist Party of Pakistan and its various fronts in 1954, just in time for Pakistan to cement its Cold War alliance with the United States through the signing of the Mutual Defence and Assistance Pact.

THE PROGRESSIVES THROW DOWN THE GAUNTLET

The editorial of the first issue of *Naqush*—the unofficial literary journal of the Pakistani PWA—published towards the end of 1947 began by congratulating its readership on the establishment of Pakistan, but also cautioned that formal independence was not enough by itself to ensure the ideals, hopes and dreams that were associated with and promised by the Pakistan movement. In order to prevent slavery from reasserting itself under new guises, it was imperative that the country be set on the path of progress. According to the editors, literature had to have a distinct purpose, and therefore:

> We have decided that we will not publish any literature which is unable to make us aware of the true meaning of freedom; which reflects the heartbeat not of our millions of labouring people,

but of a few reactionaries, capitalists and feudal landlords; a literature which focuses on an unreal romanticism while ignoring the rapidly changing and evolving needs and demands of the present and which descends like an opiate fever on the awakened minds of the people. (*Naqush* 1, 1948)

This sentiment was in tune with the radical left turn taken by the Communist Party of India and found immediate expression in the writings of the Progressives right after Partition. Since the Communist Party of Pakistan hadn't yet been formed (it would be established during the Second CPI Congress in 1948), the PWA took on even more significance as the only organized platform for ideological work available to Pakistani communists.

With the ascendancy of the Ranadive faction, the old United Front policy was declared collaborationist and was abandoned in favor of an explicitly anti-capitalist line.[21] Among other things, this new line became less tolerant of ambiguity and indirection in literary style. The Progressives declared that while the United Front might have been a necessary strategy during the period leading up to independence, continuing to follow it under the changed post-colonial political context would be a betrayal of the Pakistani people.[22] These changes ultimately meant a re-negotiation of the very definition of *taraqqi-pasandi*.[23]

The new Manifesto found expression in the rhetoric and tactics of the Progressive writers even before it was publicly released during the formal establishment of the APPWA in November 1949. The Progressive critique of the Pakistani state, and its call for a literature of revolution—this time an explicitly *socialist* revolution—was articulated in meetings of local chapters of the association in cities such as Lahore and Karachi.

The sentiments expressed in the first issue of *Naqush* were echoed in the Manifesto, which declared:

We wish to remove the contradictions that exist between our social system and the needs of ordinary people because these contradictions are responsible for the fact that our society and along with it our art and culture have stopped developing in a progressive direction ... Life can be pure of misfortunes and difficulties, and more beautiful and healthy. That is, we can truly be free. This is only possible if we break down the existing capitalist and feudal system and establish a people's democratic system (under the leadership of the working class) based on a socialist economy. (APPWA Manifesto, 1949)

This distinction between formal versus substantive independence/ freedom was to become a key element in the Progressives' critique of the ruling establishment. Far from wrenching Pakistan free of the "vice" of the capitalist system, argued the Manifesto, the ruling clique had entrenched it squarely within its worst manifestation yet: (neo)imperialism. By remaining in the Sterling Bloc,[24] Pakistan was "tied to Anglo-American imperialist interest," and "Anglo-American capital [was] invited in to loot our national wealth." Additionally, the relationship with Anglo-American interests meant that in every case where a popular struggle existed which was aimed against "treacherous rulers and Anglo-American imperialists," the Pakistani government "sided with the imperialist forces," which was in itself a matter of national shame. Control of Pakistan's army and other key institutions remained in the hands of British generals. The feudal system also remained in place, wreaking havoc in the countryside and pulling "rural life ... into the vice of the capitalist system"; only, instead of serving colonial interests as it had before independence, it was now tied to the new imperialism. The Manifesto also argued that the entrenchment of the capitalist system was the reason for the "economic decline and cultural deterioration" in which the country found itself so soon after Independence.

Criticizing the government's arrest and detention of democratic political activists and intellectuals under colonial Safety Laws, the Manifesto decried these actions as an effort by an insecure ruling class to "police our voices and our pens." However, it emphasized that the "battle for true freedom" continued despite "all these difficulties." Pakistan was, in fact, in a "new phase of the war of independence," and literature itself was divided between two tendencies, one which supported the status quo, and the other which opposed it in the interests of ordinary Pakistanis:

On one side are the writers and artists who raise their voice against the oppression and tyranny of Pakistan's ruling clique— who support those who are struggling for true freedom, peace, democracy and socialism, who carry forward the democratic traditions of the old literature ... On the other side are those writers who serve to translate the designs of the ruling class; hide its oppression and tyranny, oppose democratic thoughts and democratic movements and prevent the democratic traditions of the old literature from surfacing and spread discouragement, apathy and mental confusion through their writings. (APPWA Manifesto, 1949)

According to the Manifesto, there were "many types of reactionary writers found in Pakistan"[25]: the ones who believed in "art for art's sake," the ones who advocated "Pakistani literature" and the ones who were in favor of an "Islamic literature." Those who pushed "literature for the sake of literature" remained unconcerned with whether "a thought was good or bad, beneficial or harmful," but focused instead on "how that thought, regardless of how poisonous it may be, was expressed." The claim of these writers, that "by staying away from social and political issues" they were practicing "pure literature," was patently false because "in a classed society, no literature, art or knowledge can remain free of the impact of the class struggle, nor remain above it, because it is itself a social act." Thus "all those who popularise the idea of literature for the sake of literature today are the paid propagandists of Pakistan's ruling class and support its social and cultural policy with the same intensity as other reactionary writers."

The exhortation to produce a "pure literature" free of politics was of course the hallmark of the position taken by the progressives' liberal detractors. However, this claim highlighted a basic contradiction within this discourse, because an "art for art's sake" position did not sit well with the liberals' other cherished belief: that Pakistani writers had a responsibility towards their nation. This rather glaring contradiction was papered over by the claim that for a writer to be socially conscious was one thing, but bringing politics into the space of the literary and the esthetic was crass at best, and dangerous at worst.

In an open letter to Shorish Kashmiri, published in the conservative weekly *Chatan* (June 27, 1949), for example, M.D. Taseer declared that his problem with those who drag communism into literature was that they tried to bury the writer's personality, that "Art for the sake of the Party" was an even more dangerous principle for literature than "Art for Art's sake." There was a time and a place for a literature of agitation, argued Taseer, but cautioned Pakistani writers that if they became "too political," they would be in danger of losing their cherished individuality and autonomy. He pleaded with Pakistani writers to avoid being distracted by the communists' "sloganeering," and instead turn towards higher, and more important tasks: " … literature is the highway of life, politics is beneath us; literature is eternal, sloganeering is mere wind-blowing. The Pakistani writer is the enemy of hypocrisy, despotism, lack of accomplishment and atheism, and is a passionate lover of Truth, humanity, skillfulness, and god-worship" (Taseer 1949: 296).

For the Progressives, however, "literature [was not just] ... a mirror of life but the means by which to change and improve it," while "the ideologies of literature-for-life and literature-for-struggle and literature-for-revolution were ... the foundation-stones of our movement ... ."[26] When Progressives looked at the new society, they saw "progressive and reactionary tendencies confronting each other with greater clarity and intensity." Under these conditions, writers were required to take sides with the "workers, peasants, writers, intellectuals, journalists, students, office clerks and other oppressed classes" who were engaged in a struggle "to replace the capitalist and feudal system with a democratic and socialist system" (APPWA Manifesto, 1949).[27] According to Abdullah Malik (1967: 661), a prominent journalist and PWA member, the Progressives had "indicated their position by raising their voice high against the oppressions of the Pakistani establishment" and stood in opposition to those writers "who represented only the aims and desires of the Pakistani rulers, whitewashing their tyranny and injustice, and inculcating complacency and pessimism in the minds of the people."

To be a fence-sitter under these circumstances was, according to the Progressives, tantamount to being on the side of tyranny against justice. In fact, the Manifesto implied that those writers that declared themselves to be "neutral" were the worst manifestation of the forces of reaction, because neutrality was the guise under which they "attempted to cover up the anti-people attitude of the reactionary writers and their own cowardice and cunning."

The Manifesto declared that there could be "no compromise" with such writers who were nothing less than "the paid propagandists of capitalists and feudal landlords" and thereby "enemies of the people." As Malik (1949: 222) declared in the pages of the *Azadi Number* ("Independence Issue") of *Naqush*, the standoff between the progressive and the reactionary tendencies within the literary fold was "not a conflict between two literary views but a struggle between life and death" in which there could be "no spectators and no neutrality." In a widely circulated pamphlet titled *Mustaqbil Hamara Hai* ("The future is ours"), he wrote:

In our writings we will clearly expose how the political and social policy of Pakistani rulers is destroying our cultural and literary traditions; how it is depriving the working classes of Pakistan of the benefits of knowledge and literature, and how it is snatching away our freedom of expression through Safety Acts and Ordinances. We announce that we will teach people to hate the capitalist system. We will make our literature the translator and herald of the democratic struggles—large or small—of the people of Pakistan. (Malik, 1949)

THE DISCOURSE OF LOYALTY

Muhammad Hasan Askari (2001) was the first to explicitly question the loyalty of the Progressives to the state, in a provocatively titled 1948 essay *Adeeb aur riyaasat se vafaadaari ka mas'ala: Taraqqi-pasandoñ pe kari tanqeed* ("Writers and the issue of loyalty to the state: A strong criticism of the Progressives"). Among other things, he read the Progressives' support of the demands of the East Bengali Language Committee as a conspiracy to undermine Pakistan's very existence. Commenting on the first conference of writers and journalists in Pakistan organized by the PWA in which a resolution supporting democratic movements within Pakistan was passed, Askari (2001: 65) sarcastically editorialized thus:

> ... we owe the language riots, and the inciting of students to organise around the issue of language, to this 'love for democracy'. Well, from this we have learnt that the Progressives are not men of words alone. At least when it comes to anti-Muslim feeling,[28] they are also men of action. And the biggest service they can render Sardar Patel[29] is to distract and seduce the youth and students, the weak writers ... by feeding them abstractions such as 'humanism', 'democracy', etc. in order to use them against their own nation.

This was an extraordinary statement in that Askari managed to articulate discursively Bangla not just with "non-Muslim" but with "*anti*-Muslim," labeled the demands of the Bangla movement as a "service to Sardar Patel" (that is, India) and rejected the quintessentially *liberal* values of "democracy," "humanism" and "pacifism" as not just canards, but as politically suspect in and of themselves. Just in case his readers missed his point, he went on to quote Auden, saying that "every successful writer is a fascist—humanism and democracy is touted by unsuccessful writers."

Askari agreed in principle that a writer should be free of external constraints on his thinking and writing, especially those imposed by the state for "this was not, after all, Russia." But if loyalty and lack thereof were not at issue where great writers are concerned, "*disloyalty*" (which he understood as rebellion against authority) could only be legitimate if it occurred in response to a major crisis. Yet even this principled and contextual expression of disloyalty, according to Askari, did not justify rebellion as a "constant state." His reference here was to the Progressives, who in his opinion, were stuck in a state of delayed adolescence, relishing rebellion for the sake of rebellion. It hardly behooved the Progressives to critique the Pakistani state's policies with regard to writers, he argued, since

> ... in communist Russia ... [the idea that writers have a right to dissent] has always been considered a sign of reaction. The Russian government explicitly declares that gentlemen, this is not the time for neutrality and humanism. Right now we have to strengthen the foundations of our state and protect it from the attacks of capitalist states. Right now you should help us in this work ... . (Ibid.: 67)

Askari then questioned why the same principles were not applied to Pakistan, itself a new nation-state:

> One fails to understand on what basis these people can tell Pakistan's writers not to sympathise with their nation. Why is that which is acceptable in Russia not acceptable in Pakistan? Does Pakistan not need to strengthen its foundations? Is Pakistan not besieged by its enemies? Are the activities of Fifth columnists in Pakistan not at the level at which even the Quaid-e Azam[30] was forced to name communists?[31] Has the Muslim nation not had to endure hardships? Do we not have to construct our country and our nation? Can the Muslim masses not demand of their writers that they share in their sorrows and pain? (Ibid.: 67–8)

Askari thus draws a line dividing the Pakistani communists from the Pakistani nation and state,[32] hinting darkly that, unlike patriotic "Muslim"/"Pakistani" writers such as himself, the communist was unable to "sympathize" with, or respond to, the needs of the nation because he was essentially a fifth columnist. Askari's use of the term "Muslim nation" as a *synonym* for Pakistan is notable, a slide that was not minor in its implications.

"If the Muslim nation was ... reactionary, if Pakistan was based on oppression and cruelty and the murder of justice," continued Askari, "we would have agreed that writers should indeed not be loyal to such a nation," but in fact "up till now Pakistan has only been the victim of injustice" (ibid.: 68). In a canny reversal, Askari proceeded to deploy the Progressives' own arguments about the impossibility of remaining neutral under conditions of oppression, except that where the Progressives saw the Pakistani state as the oppressor and the Pakistani people as the oppressed, Askari considered the "Muslim" nation-state to be the victim which was under siege from internal and external enemies.

Askari argues that the Progressives were out to destabilize Pakistan through their subversive political and cultural activities, and that defeating them—even throwing them literally and figuratively outside of the nation-state—was the duty of every loyal Pakistani. According to him, the burden of proving their patriotism lay with the Progressives themselves: "you need to convince us that you are in fact one of us and that your life and death are connected to the nation."

In an important piece titled *Ishtiraakiyoñ ke adabi aur ilmi nazariye* ("The literary and intellectual ideology of communists"), the other major liberal ideologue, M.D. Taseer, listed what he saw as the defining characteristics of the communists. To begin with, "they" considered the establishment of Pakistan to have been a mistake because according to them "its basis—Muslim culture—was wrong" because, according to Stalin's definition, "a shared religion could not be the basis of unity." Secondly, "they" thought that "the use of Urdu as a medium of instruction was wrong" because Stalin insisted that "the mother tongue should be the medium of instruction in elementary school," and "they" did not consider Urdu "our mother tongue" (Taseer, 1949: 293).

In another essay, "The future of culture in Pakistan," Taseer (1948) began his overview of the literary landscape of Pakistan, with a critique of the "Leftists." The creation of India and Pakistan, he said, had divided the Bengali and Urdu writers. Both states were in need of explicit expressions of loyalty, and the issue of Kashmir had made matters even more crucial. However, the PWA, "which had been taken over by the communists," had only one purpose today: to destroy the unity of Pakistani writers. This they did by actively fomenting confusion and chaos among the writers in order to render them useless to their nation. The only solution for the survival of Urdu and Bengali literature—and, by implication, for

Pakistani society—was for writers to set new, clear literary goals. While stating that he did not "claim to make laws for anyone, especially creative artists," Taseer nevertheless proposed a set of questions which could potentially "help to rid us of this mental confusion" and thereby clear the way for the kind of creative work that was the need of the moment:

1. Are you proud to be a Pakistani? Are you completely certain of Pakistan's future eminence?
2. What kind of democratic constitution do you prefer for Pakistan—Turkey's, America's, Britain's, Russia's?
3. In your opinion, which should have more freedom and rights under the constitution: the provinces or the centre?
4. What should Pakistan's policy be with regard to Kashmir, Hyderabad, India, Anglo-America, Islamic countries?
5. Which do you support—capitalism, complete socialism [that is, communism] or the British Labour Party's gradualism? (Ibid.: 28)

According to Taseer, the actual answers were immaterial to the exercise, the point of which was simply to help writers "clarify" their point of view on various contemporary issues of importance. In fact, the "survey" was Taseer's way of baiting the Progressives[33] and elicited the following response from the Progressive critic Zaheer Kashmiri (1948):

Dr. Taseer [has] requested our 'opinion' on a 'circular'. [He] thought that Pakistan's Progressive Writers would respond negatively [to his questions] and thus their movement would succumb [to the pressure of] public opinion which would be against it, and would die of its own accord. We were fully aware of the above-mentioned circular and Dr. Taseer's intentions, and so thought it best not to respond to the letter. As a result, Dr. Taseer's poisoned arrow, instead of striking us through the heart, was lost in thin air.

Towards the end of the essay, Taseer turned to the issue of loyalty to the state, laying out the conditions under which states may demand loyalty from writers and under which conditions "disloyalty" would be justified. In order to ensure that his position didn't appear too close to the "Russian" position on literary matters, Taseer (1948: 31) addressed this question of loyalty to the state in *moral* terms:

"The state grants the individual and the group the possibility of freedom, security and permanence," but there are times when it fails to do so, in which case "rebellion becomes morally justified." However, this justification is not unconditional; it depends on the sincerity of the writer. And when evaluating the legitimacy of a rebellion, it is not enough to simply take the writer's word with regard to their sincerity. Instead, "the state has the moral right to verify this sincerity," and "in order to gain the moral right to rebel," writers would first have to "establish their loyalty." In other words, it is the state that has the moral right to determine whether the dissent is "sincere."

Ultimately, however, Taseer did not feel that even this qualified right of rebellion should be held to apply in the case of Pakistan at the moment. A young country, proclaimed Taseer (1948: 31), is vulnerable, and national independence must not be taken as an excuse to indulge in "irresponsible behaviour"; instead, "our loyalty to it should be unconditional" (ibid.). While this might seem to be a strange position for a liberal like Taseer, who like his ideological partner Askari, was against the government's proscription of literary journals, it echoed the contingent application of liberal principles that are familiar to students of the cultural Cold War and the politics of the anti-communist Left.

The threats, veiled and otherwise, against those seen as dissidents, and the idea that "freedom" must not be equated with "license" were uncannily similar to the state discourse at this time, with Taseer and Askari's position dovetailing neatly with that of the establishment: Pakistan was going through a state of Emergency, and to demand civil liberties in this context would only destabilize it. Askari lamented that, if anything, the government was too *lenient* with seditious elements, allowing their leaders the freedom to enter the country from across the border, and move around in Pakistan, "inaugurating conferences" and "organising strikes."[34] He claimed that the government's silence had now reached the level of neglect, suggesting, in effect, that the state should instead be using its repressive powers against the Progressives.

These themes were echoed by Samad Shaheen (c. 1948), another member of the liberal anti-communist front, in an early editorial of *Naya Daur* soon after its reincarnation in Karachi:[35]

Pakistan is being constructed from scratch. Along with this, we have to lay the foundation of a new literature … loyalty to the state should always remain paramount in our literature. Our

literature should be infused with religious ideas like Milton's
Paradise Lost or Goethe's *Faust*. Our literature should reflect
the cultures of different areas of Pakistan's different regions like
that of Walter Scott ... Our literature should hate communism
because, after all, Arthur Koestler and Andre Gide aren't talking
nonsense when they say that the counter-revolutionaries are in
charge in Russia ... .[36]

This passage succinctly summarizes the themes common to liberal
anti-communist discourse: that loyalty to the state should be
paramount for writers, and that communism was incompatible
with "Pakistani literature" (and hence Pakistan itself); also part
of the pattern was the invocation of members of the pantheon of
the "Atlantic consensus" of the Anglo-American and European
anti-communist Left, such as Koestler and Gide (here), as well
as Auden, Stephen Spender and George Orwell (elsewhere) as
authoritative critics of the Soviet Union.

In *The Future of Culture in Pakistan*, Taseer (1948: 29) issued a
call for war against two forces which he saw as attacking Pakistan
from within: communists and religious obscurantists:

We welcome Pakistan because it has granted us our selfhood
[*khudi*].[37] All those forces which are against Pakistan are our
enemies, are the enemies of our art. We will battle these enemies,
and reactionary forces which wish to strangle our freedom and
independence, with whatever effective weapons we have at our
disposal. We will fight this battle not just with sloganeering and
proclamations but with our creative weapons.

The Progressives responded by denouncing the "so-called 'Pakistani
writers'" for spreading "the most vile and poisonous sort of
nationalism" in order to "exploit the patriotism of the Pakistani
workers for the selfish politics of the ruling class" (APPWA
Manifesto, 1949). Instead of facing up to the challenges posed
by the realities of the post-Independence period, these nationalist
intellectuals, charged the Manifesto, ignored the "real Pakistan
which lay gasping on the ground; a Pakistan where there was
poverty and unemployment, and Life was reducing to crawling on
its hands and knees while an open season was declared for Death."
Instead of focusing on the plight of the people, they constructed "a
bright and majestic Pakistan" through their "word-smithery" as a
way to distract attention away from the true picture. When they

... raise the slogan of "Pakistani literature" they do not mean that literature which refers to the desires and troubles of 95% of Pakistan's people—they actually mean that literature in which the so-called "national services" of the ruling class are extolled, i.e., their oppression and tyranny is veiled ... When these writers of a fascist mentality claim to be loyal to Pakistan, they mean loyalty to Pakistan's capitalists, landlords, nawabs and other anti-democratic elements, not loyalty to Pakistan's workers and their struggle. (Ibid.)

Zaheer Babar (1949: 73) pointed out how odd it was that Independence should have been accompanied by a radical shift in the priorities of intellectuals such that writing about "peasants and workers" was now considered "boring" or even contradictory to the interests of "Pakistan" and "Islam." No one, aside from the Progressives (least of all the "Pakistani writers"), bothered to ask to what extent Independence had changed the lives of these workers and peasants in whose name and on whose behalf it had purportedly been demanded. If anything,

The people are still eagerly awaiting that freedom which will brighten their huts, that will give them their rightful return for their labour, which will release them from the exploitation of a handful of feudal landlords. We are not opposed to illuminated palaces, but the problem is that in our society every palace is surrounded by a great number of hovels which are at best lit by clay lamps ... Pakistan would not exist without these people ... it is because of them that the fields are lush and there is activity in the factories. It was for their cultural development and social welfare that a separate country was demanded. Pakistan loses its meaning if dissociated from these seven crore[38] people.

While the Progressives always couched their arguments within a discourse of patriotism, a fact which is easily established by a glance at their published statements, there was a key difference between their patriotic discourse and that of the "nationalist" intelligentsia. The Progressives tended to speak in terms of *awam* ("the people") while the nationalists preferred the term *qaum* ("nation"). The choice between these two terms was not a semantic one. It represented a world of difference between two political philosophies and two incommensurable sets of interests. As Zaheer Kashmiri (1948) put it in his critique of the call for a new "Pakistani" literature, "for

Samad Shaheen the biggest reality is Pakistan but for the Progressive Writers the biggest reality are the Pakistani people."[39]

For the Progressives, the central issue was this: what was "the nation" in whose name loyalty was being demanded and whose interests the state purportedly served. Were religious minorities, Bengalis and the working classes part of this "national community"? The charge of "disloyalty" could thus cut both ways, depending on to whom "loyalty" was understood to be owed. To the "95% of Pakistanis," or the "ruling class which exploits them"? To "Pakistan," or "the Pakistani people"?

LITERATURE, PARTITION AND "NATION-BUILDING"

The controversy over the Progressive approach to literature was initially set off by certain literary works, particularly poems, published in various magazines in the aftermath of Partition. These poems and stories all reflect the somber mood of the time, and articulate the generally held feelings of disillusionment and loss (Hussain, 1997).

The euphoria of attaining Independence for India and Pakistan had been tempered to a great degree by the trauma of a partition which not only resulted in the largest exchange of populations in modern times but was also accompanied by communal violence[40] on an unprecedented scale.[41] The general intellectual mood was thus one of confusion and even bitterness at the irony of Fate which had granted Independence at such a heavy price.

Faiz Ahmad Faiz's[42] poem *Subh-e Aazaadi* ("Freedom's Dawn"[43]) is perhaps the best example of this genre, but there were many others such as Josh Malihabadi's *Utho Ke Nau-bahaar Hai* ("Awaken! The New Spring is Here") published in *Savera* (1948, number 3/4):[44]

Shagufta barg-haai gul ki teh meiñ nok-e khaar hai
Khizaañ kahenge phir kise agar yehi bahaar hai
Yeh inqilaab ka muzhda hai inqilaab nahiñ
Yeh aftaab ka partau hai, aftaab nahiñ

Under the fresh petals of the rose there lies the sharp point of a thorn,
If this be Spring, what will Autumn be like?
These are merely the tidings of the revolution, not the revolution itself,
This is but the reflection of the sun, not the sun itself.

Ahmad Nadeem Qasmi's *Tulu* ("Dawn") appeared in the same issue:

> *Muheeb raat ka aaghaaz kitna rangeeñ tha*
> *Muheeb raat ka anjaam jaane kya ho ga*

> The beginning of this abominable night was so beautiful,
> Who knows how it will end?

These sentiments were not confined to the Progressives alone. Hafeez Hoshiarpuri, not a Marxist by any means, wrote:

> *Maiñ apne haal ko maazi se kyooñ kahooñ behtar*
> *Agar voh haasil-i gham tha to yeh gham-i haasil*

> Why should I declare my present to be better than my past?
> If that was the result of grief than this is the grief of attainment[45]

The difference, of course, was that the Progressive critique was simultaneously a clarion call to continue the revolutionary struggle until such a time as "true" independence and national sovereignty was achieved. Faiz's poem, for instance, ended with "*Chale chalo ke voh manzil abhi nahin ayee*" ("Keep going, for that destination has not yet been reached") (*Naya Adab*, c. 1948: 193). The tone of Faiz's poem, and the ambiguity of the word "destination" didn't raise the ire of the anti-Progressives,[46] but others such as Sardar Jafri's *Khoon ki Lakeer* ("The Line of Blood") were strongly criticized for implying that Partition had been the result of a political exigency. Jafri (1948: 218) had written:

> *Yeh kaun zaalim hai jis ne qaanoon ke dahakte huay qalam se*
> *Vatan ke seene pe khoon-i na-haq ki ik gehri lakeer khenchi*

> Who is the oppressor that, with the burning pen of law
> has drawn a deep line of blood through the country's chest?

The Progressives, in turn, were openly and strongly critical of poets[47] who wrote (no doubt in retaliation) in praise of Partition. When Samad Shaheen and Askari talked of delineating the boundaries of a new "Pakistani literature," the Progressives sought to affirm the one-ness of the old Urdu literary community that spanned the borders and its shared Indo-Islamic heritage. Here, for example, is an excerpt from Ahmed Riyaz's poem *Adab ki Jaageer* ("Literary heritage/inheritance") (*Naya Adab*, c. 1948: 56; emphasis added[48]):

> *Subh-e aazadi-i nau phoot chuki hai lekin,*
> *Maazi-o-haal ki raahoñ meiñ andhera hai vohi,*
> *Hum na kafir haiñ na momin haiñ na haiñ 'arsh-nashiñ,*
> *Qaht-o-aflaas ke thukraaye huay*
> **Saathion haath barhaao ke hum haiñ aaj bhi ek,**
> **Kaun kar sakta hai taqseem adab ki jaageer**
> *Shehr bat sakte haiñ ho sakti haiñ galiyaañ mehdood,*
> *Kaun kar sakta hai ehsaas ki shiddat ko aseer*

> The dawn of the new liberation has broken,
> But there is still the same darkness in the paths of the past and
>   the present,
> We are neither idolaters, nor believers, nor celestial beings,
> Knocked about by famine and poverty,
> **Comrades! Stretch out your hands for we are one even today,**
> **Who can divide the heritage of literature?**
> Cities can be divided and streets closed off,
> But who can chain the intensity of feeling?

The highlighted lines in the poem above were an explicit critique of the idea that there could be—indeed was—such a thing as a "Pakistani literature" which could or should be separated from an Urdu literary heritage shared with India. The anti-Progressives obviously chose to interpret such sentiments as evidence that the Progressives were unable and unwilling to accept the reality of Pakistan as an independent nation-state. This affirmed the statist propaganda, which quickly became a widely shared fear in this period of chaos and insecurity, that there were "elements" within Pakistan who were hard at work trying to "undo" Partition.[49]

The other issue which became the subject of intense controversy was that of the *violence* of Partition. The imperative which faced secular progressive intellectuals on both sides of the border at this time was how to make sense of the deeply communalized violence which came to characterize Partition. The *sine qua non* of nationalist Indian politics of the last half-century had been the idea that far from being two divided and naturally incompatible communities, Hindus and Muslims in fact had a long history of peaceful coexistence and shared deep emotional ties. Moreover, the tragic events of Partition were interspersed with stories of everyday heroism in which members of one community provided refuge and safe passage to members of others, often at great risk to themselves.

Stemming the tide of retaliatory communal violence and helping heal the wounds and scars which it left was seen by the Progressives as their immediate social responsibility. In the Partition stories they wrote, therefore, they took care not to place the responsibility for the violence on any one community, and tried to present a balanced picture of the many incidents of cross-communal sympathy and solidarity. The idea was to avoid naturalizing the violence as the inevitable result of long-standing communal enmities, and to restore faith in the essential humanity of ordinary people, regardless of their religious identity. Moreover, the Progressives thought that the complexities of a literary community now split by a border put an additional onus on Urdu writers to be "responsible" and sensitive when writing about Partition.

But it was precisely this attempt to remain "balanced" that rankled with the self-styled patriotic writers and critics in Pakistan, and was seen as a travesty that had to be juxtaposed against "the truth" that Muslims were the disproportionate victims of Partition's violence. As is often the case with nationalist discourses, this narrative of victimization became an integral part of the discourse of Pakistani nationalism. Within this discourse, Partition became a moment of originary violence which retroactively justified the demand for Pakistan by proving that, had Indian Muslims not fought for a separate nation-state, they would have faced an uncertain and violent fate at the hands of the Hindu community in an undivided India.

One of the stories touted by liberal critics of the Progressives as the foremost example of what the new Pakistani literature ought to look like was Qudrutullah Shahab's *Ya Khuda*. In her unusually long preface to this story, Mumtaz Shireen (1963: 202) articulated a bitingly satirical critique of what she called the Progressive "formula" for writing about Partition,[50] which consisted of the following elements:

1. that the colonial government of the British sowed the seeds of hatred and chauvinism;
2. that the Partition and the creation of Pakistan are the [actual] roots of the riots;
3. that in these riots Muslims, Sikhs and Hindus should be shown to be equally to blame, and held equally liable;
4. that the stories should try to be intensely neutral;

5. and in the end, the mantric repetition of an idealistic wish that this enmity will eventually be erased, people will realise that they are simply human beings, and that then a new human being would be born.

The Progressive approach to Partition was also roundly criticized for being, first, a product of opportunism; secondly, insincere because it tried too hard to be objective; third, unreal because it tried too hard to be even-handed, and last, worthy of dismissal because it appealed to "popular" sentiments (Askari, 1952: 747).

Given this criticism, Shahab's *Ya Khuda* was an unusual, if not paradoxical, choice as a normative example of the new national literature, since it was extremely critical of both the Pakistani administration's treatment of (Muslim) refugees in the camps and the "civilians" who were taking advantage of the refugees' vulnerability. The story revolves around a young Muslim woman who escapes a life of potential sexual enslavement by the Sikh men in her village on the Indian side of the border after they have killed her father and scared away all the other Muslim villagers, only to be sexually exploited by fellow Muslims in the very country she had thought of as her refuge. In its explicit treatment of the violence that Muslims cynically mete out to other Muslims, *Ya Khuda* completely undermined any idea of some essential Muslim victimhood or of the Muslim nation as an essentially moral space. As Progressive critic Zaheer Babar (1949: 75) pointed out in his response to Shireen's preface, if it were "anti-Pakistan" opinions that liberals such as Shireen were looking for, they need look no further than *Ya Khuda* which was a much more severe indictment of Pakistan than anything the Progressives had ever written.

Babar (1949: 78) argued that, aside from this obvious double standard, Shireen also both blamed the Progressives for not doing enough to condemn the "barbarity" and "bestiality" of "all three nations" (that is, Hindu, Muslim and Sikh) *and* criticized them for being too political when they asserted that literature could be a tool of social and political change. Such contradictions, Babar claimed, demonstrated that the liberal attack on the Progressives had no principled basis and was purely political in its motivation.

The same charges, with their inherent contradictions, were also evident in Askari's tirades against the Progressives. Like Shireen, he poked fun at what he saw as their "obsessive" focus on ensuring that the blame for the violence did not fall on any particular community:

All along, one must keep strategically showing that along with this barbarism we also find examples of kindness and human empathy, and then make a naïve face and wonder what has happened to the good sense of Hindus and Muslims. Till yesterday they were brothers, why are they thirsty for each others' blood today? There is just the lingering threat that you could be accused of being partisan, but that is not a problem. If five hundred Hindus were killed in the beginning, then make sure that you balance the account by the end of the *afsaana* ["story"] by killing five hundred Muslims. Make sure that the blame is exactly evenly shared. The trick is to prove your humanism, kindness, anti-chauvinism and pacifism without offending anyone. (Askari, 1952: 746)

Askari's rejection of attempts by the Progressives to heal the wounds of Partition, to recover hope from devastation, and to try to salvage some kind of faith in a secular culture and polity in the face of what seemed to be relentless communal violence may seem incomprehensible. However, as Sardar Jafri (1948) pointed out, they were consistent with his rejection of "Art for the sake of Life," his "Muslim nationalism" and his animus towards the Progressives more generally.

Askari took his critique of the Progressive approach to Partition further in his preface to Sa'adat Hasan Manto's collection of Partition stories called *Siyah Hashiye*,[51] lauding Manto's exploration of the psychology of violence and of its perpetrators and contrasting it with what he saw as the Progressives' irritatingly naïve attitude towards human nature. In a complete reversal of his earlier position, he now declared that "true" literature was *not* concerned with assigning blame. Instead, its responsibility lay in trying to understand and explain the *psychology* of the oppressor and the oppressed. According to Askari, the problem with the Progressives was their obsession with the external environment and the social angle when, "[as] far as literature is concerned, the external act of oppression and its external apparatus are meaningless things." True literature, according to Askari, would address the "internal life of the oppressor and the oppressed and its relationship to oppression,"[52] just as Manto did in his Partition stories (Askari, 1952: 750).

THE IRON HAND IN THE VELVET GLOVE

Given its explicit anti-establishment stand, the APPWA remained under the strict scrutiny of the state and was subjected to repression from its founding to its forced demise in 1954. Its publications were proscribed,[53] its leading lights jailed, its members—communist and non-communist alike—harassed. The final ban on the Communist Party of Pakistan and the Progressive Writers Association came in the wake of the Rawalpindi Conspiracy Case in 1954 but was preceded by several instances of the use of coercive state power, often in collusion with lumpen elements of the Islamist *Jama'at-i Islami* party.

In a volume commemorating 50 years of the Progressive Writers Movement, the office-bearers of the Karachi and Lahore branches of the association recount the difficulties which the Association and its members faced at the hands of the state (Hameed Akhter, 1987; Ateeq Ahmed, 1987). Among the large and small indignities which they had to suffer were constant surveillance by the secret police, harassment of their members at every opportunity, disruption of meetings, and the periodic arrests of their office-bearers and other active members. In 1951, the PWA was declared a political organization, and employers were warned not to hire "communists," which was understood to include all those associated with the association. Needless to say, this had an immense impact on the PWA. Many members, even ideologically committed ones, stopped attending meetings for fear of having their names reported.

In Lahore, the PWA initially held its weekly meetings at the local YMCA. One day, the YMCA administration regretfully informed them that they were under strict orders from the secret police not to allow the PWA access to their premises and had been threatened with dire consequences if they did not comply. The PWA managed to secure the Dyal Singh College Library as a meeting place but the college administration was ultimately forced into submission after an 18-month-long battle with the Punjab government and the secret police. Similar problems were faced by the branch in Karachi.

The Association's first All Pakistan Conference held in Lahore in November 1949 was also subjected to a variety of pressure tactics. First, the provincial administration tried to deny access to the announced venue, an amphitheatre in the famous Lawrence Public Gardens. When that move proved unsuccessful, the conference was gate-crashed by a group of police stooges and *goonda*[54] elements in the pay of the local police led by Shorish Kashmiri, editor of the weekly *Chatan* which had become a major center of the warfare against the Progressives. The idea was to claim that this was a spontaneous expression of rage by the people of Lahore against the resolutions passed at the conference. Fortunately for the PWA, the attendees included representatives of peasant organizations who were armed with their traditional wooden *laathis*.[55] The gate-crashers had not anticipated this and so were easily routed. Hameed Akhtar (1987) recounts that the conference ended with the guests and speakers escorted down the main thoroughfare of the Mall Road by their new "bodyguards."

Another example of such officially sponsored harassment was the orchestrated response to the decision of the Lahore and Karachi branches of the APPWA to celebrate May Day in 1949. For weeks before and after the announcement, letters and articles were published in various right-wing Urdu dailies and weeklies, particularly *Chatan* and *Maghribi Pakistan*, flaying the Progressives.[56] These letters whipped up such fervor among the extremist religious elements in Lahore that the very commemoration of May Day was declared a *bida'at*[57] with most of the imams in the two cities issuing *fatwas* declaring the Progressives infidels and therefore *wajibul-qatl*.[58] Afterwards, the news was spread that blasphemous words against the Prophet had been uttered by attendees and speakers at the event. So great was this propaganda that the Progressives were forced to issue a rebuttal for publication in all the major Urdu and English newspapers (Ahmad, 1987).

Ultimately, the most devastating blow to the APPWA was dealt by the Rawalpindi Conspiracy Case. In 1951, Liaquat Ali Khan declared that he had just learnt of a conspiracy at the highest levels of the army which also implicated prominent communist leaders such as Faiz Ahmad Faiz and Sajjad Zaheer. This gave the state the rationale it needed to finally ban the Communist Party of Pakistan (CPP), which it did in 1954, and lent credence to the allegations made by Muslim League politicians as well as pro-establishment literary figures such as Askari that communists were enemies of the state. The arrest of Faiz and Zaheer was a setback not just to the CPP (of which Zaheer was then secretary general) but also to its other front organizations, including the APPWA. After the Conspiracy case, the government refused to accept the APPWA's claim that it was a cultural association; the Ministry of Interior declared it to be a political party in 1951 and subjected it to even greater surveillance than before (Ahmed, 1965). These scare tactics worked to weaken the PWA even before it was formally banned by order of the governor general in 1954.

The hegemony of the socialist vision of the Progressive writers in the literary milieu of the late 1940s made it imperative for the Pakistani state to discredit and marginalize them and their vision of the nation-state. Respected liberal intellectuals and writers such as M.D. Taseer and M.H. Askari consciously aided and abetted this state project.[59] It is a testament to the tenacity and the influence of the Progressive intelligentsia in Pakistan that it took the government seven years to ban the PWA and the Communist Party of Pakistan. However, even that did not sterilize the public sphere of communist and socialist ideas, thereby requiring the actual takeover of the Progressive Papers Ltd.—a group of leftist newspapers and periodicals run by Mian Iftikharuddin and an outlet for the voice of the Progressives—in 1959 by the martial law regime of General Ayub Khan on the advice of another liberal intellectual, Altaf Gauhar. Along the way, many Progressives, communist and non-communist alike, were jailed and some even lost their lives, but no amount of state repression or ideological assaults from the Right could completely stem the tide of dissidence in Pakistan, nor erase the hegemony of the Progressives within literary and cultural circles, as later chapters will testify.

"The nation" as a concept and idea is usually imagined as a community which exists above class and other petty divisions and is thus invoked in order to suppress the class question; in fact, however, it need not necessarily represent such reactionary interests. That it has generally done so points to the class character of nation-states in the modern period and the vested interests of those who, within them, have the power to define, delineate and police the boundaries of the licit and normative, including those of the "national."

The Progressives and their liberal detractors were working with two entirely different and ultimately incommensurate definitions of "the nation," and hence represented political projects which were diametrically opposed to one another. The anti-Progressive discourse of the establishment and its organic intellectuals—the liberals—was nothing less than an attempt to impose a particular conservative vision of both the Pakistani nation and the ideal Pakistani state in place of the radical nationalism proposed by the Left. By discrediting the Progressives, these liberal intellectuals attempted to exclude the social, cultural, political and economic alternatives represented by this radical nationalism from the imaginary of the Pakistani people.

Ultimately, the harangues of the liberal anti-communists and their efforts to paint the Progressives as traitors proved successful in so far as they helped prepare the ground for the state's repressive machinery to step in and resolve the "communist question." The constituency which the anti-communist liberals were seeking to convince in order to enable the marginalization of a once popular and now dangerous social vision was not the conservatives and religious reactionaries, but the majority of the Urdu literary and intellectual community, whose "structure of feeling" (Williams, 1977; Ahmad, 1993) was still defined by the "progressivism" of the pre-Independence period.

The apparently paradoxical case of liberals serving authoritarian ends was hardly unique to Pakistan, being evident in the fascist tendencies and politics of many purportedly liberal writers of the early twentieth century. The cultural Cold War was in fact founded on a liberal anti-communist consensus, and led to the witch-hunts of the McCarthy era. Pakistan was already becoming a key American ally by the early 1950s and by 1953, the US had been invited to intervene in Pakistan's political scene by the ruling clique at the center. In April 1954, Pakistan signed the Mutual Defence and Assistance Pact with the US, the first of many such formal alliances. A Pakistani branch of the Congress for Cultural Freedom, the organizational forum of this liberal anti-communism backed by the CIA, was also in operation by the 1950s (Hasan, 1986).[60] A new chapter in Pakistan's history was about to commence.

4
Ayub Khan's Decade of Development and its Cultural Vicissitudes

The dissolution of the Constituent Assembly by the governor general in 1955, along with the banning of the Communist Party, marked the end of constitutional politics in this early period of Pakistani history. In the same year, Governor General Ghulam Muhammad used the powers he arrogated to himself under the Emergency Powers Ordinance IX to pull off what had seemed impossible through the normal "democratic" channels: the amalgamation of the provinces of West Pakistan into one administrative political unit. The government had publicly expressed its desire to do this as early as November 1954, arguing that the consolidation would eliminate provincialism and ensure that there would be "no Bengalis, no Punjabis, no Sindhis, no Pathans, no Baluchis, no Bahawalpuris, no Khairpuris," and that the "disappearance" of these identities and political affiliations would "strengthen the integrity of Pakistan."[1]

The period between 1955 and 1958 was marked by increasing unrest, especially in the now formally renamed province of "East Pakistan," due in large part to rising regional inequality. Meanwhile, the ban on the Communist Party and its affiliates and the incarceration of several communist leaders, especially Faiz Ahmed Faiz, under the Rawalpindi Conspiracy Case, created a political vacuum on the Left which was eventually filled by a new political player—the National Awami Party (NAP). As Pakistan's first social-democratic party, NAP became the clearinghouse for all Left forces in Pakistan, including communists, until the emergence of the Pakistan People's Party in 1967. It was formed when several dissenters, led by Maulana Bhashani (a seasoned Bengali peasant leader) quit the Awami League after its leadership refused to take an anti-imperialist stand during the Suez Crisis of 1957. Following this, Bhashani visited West Pakistan to confer with left-wing leaders there, and an all-Pakistan conference of progressive organizations was called in July 1957. NAP was formally established at this conference with the declared aims of "[creating] an anti-imperialist democratic state ... [ending] feudalism ... [speeding up] measures to industrialise the country and ... [holding] immediate elections" (Ali, 1970: 81). In East Pakistan, the party won supporters because of its principled stand on the question of provincial autonomy, which translated, among other things, into a demand to dismantle the One Unit.

Agitation against the One Unit was intensifying in both wings of the country by 1958, as the National Assembly elections drew near. Matters escalated to such a level that the deputy speaker of the East Pakistan Assembly was killed in a riot which broke out during the Assembly session. This provided the army with a perfect excuse for taking over, which it did on October 7, 1958 in a bloodless coup led by General Ayub Khan—an event subsequently referred to in official and semi-official accounts as "the revolution." Not only was the coup not a surprise—Sibte Hasan recalls that the writing had been on the wall for anyone to read for several months (Hasan 1987: 39)—it merely formalized the status quo that had prevailed almost since the formation of Pakistan (Alavi, 1973, 1989, 1990; Ali, 1970).

Ayub Khan's regime was the most draconian period of Pakistan's short history. Immediately following the coup, many of those who were seen as having left-wing (particularly communist) political leanings were swept up in a vast dragnet. This included Faiz, who was arrested in November within two days of his return from Moscow, where he had been attending the inauguration of the Afro-Asian Writers Conference. He joined comrades such as Sibte Hasan in the Lahore District jail before being placed under solitary confinement in the infamous Lahore Fort (Hasan, 1987). Unbeknownst to him, Hassan Nasir, the charismatic young communist activist, was also being held here; and it was here that Nasir succumbed to the effects of torture in early 1962, an event that sent shockwaves through the Left.[2]

The history of anti-colonial nationalism in the subcontinent had produced a strong sense of solidarity among ordinary people with other oppressed and/or colonized people across the world, and this internationalism had carried over after Partition and Independence. As we saw in Chapter 3, it had become infused, along with socialism, into the literary mainstream of the subcontinent. As the Pakistani establishment became more and more aligned with the Cold War agenda and foreign policy of the United States—whether on Palestine, Algeria, Vietnam, Iran, or Africa—this internationalism increasingly came to be seen (quite rightly) as a threat to the interests of the establishment.[3]

Ayub Khan was particularly allergic to this (post)colonial solidarity because of its organic (and historical) connection to communist internationalism.[4] The US, of course, shared the Pakistani establishment's attitude towards this internationalism and its politico-ideological underpinnings. The anti-imperialist nature of people's movements in Asia and Africa and the radical nationalism they espoused were beginning to be seen as a major threat to American hegemony. When a bloody coup in Iraq brought a radical, anti-western regime to power in 1958, American fears about Soviet influence in the Arab/Muslim world were heightened. The resulting increase in the perceived strategic significance of Pakistan brought it more decisively into the US's Cold War ambit as an ally, and a front in the war against communism (McMahon, 1994), making these anti-imperialist solidarities even more inconvenient for the Pakistani establishment.

The US was wary of the Soviet Union's special relationship with and influence among the newly independent post-colonial nation-states. The USSR claimed that its "rapid, impressive rate of growth made it an ideal model for the world's 'new states'," (Latham, 2000: 27), and the generous amounts of foreign aid and assistance that the Soviet Union began to pledge to the likes of Egypt, Indonesia, India and Latin America forced the US to demonstrate to these new states that "development along liberal, capitalist lines could alleviate poverty and raise living standards at least as fast as revolutionary and Marxist alternatives" (ibid.: 28). "Modernization Theory," and the project of international development to which it gave birth, were the US's answer to the "Soviet model."[5] An ambitious cross-disciplinary intellectual project, "modernization theory" drew upon expertise from across the social sciences in order to lay out a teleology of economic, political, social and cultural change designed to bring the newly independent postcolonial states "up to speed" (Gilman, 2003).[6]

Although quintessentially American in its prescriptions, the intellectual and political antecedents of modernization theory lay squarely within the civilizing mission of British colonialism, itself inspired by what Karl Polanyi (1944) refers to as the "Liberal Creed." Underpinning modernization discourse was the binary of a moribund and reactionary "tradition" posited against a desirable "modernity", which included, among other things, high rates of economic growth and the reform—along liberal lines—of political, social and cultural institutions.[7] Although this list technically included the establishment of liberal democracy, modernization theorists (who were essentially Cold War social scientists[8]) saw the military in Third World states as a progressive force. Third World militaries, particularly in Arab/Muslim countries, were thus pitched as the best candidates to initiate the kinds of social reforms that were required to free those societies of the shackles of "tradition" and bring them, kicking and screaming if need be, into "modernity."[9] Of course, the real issue was that the military in post-colonial societies was an important Cold War asset for the US, seen as the institution best able to contain "communist expansion and penetration" (President's Committee to Study the United States Military Assistance Program, Vol. 11, 1959: 79, cited in Noman, 1988: 35). And so the US and its Cold War social scientists welcomed the military coup of 1958 and hailed Pakistan's first military dictator as the great reformer.[10] In fact, in Tariq Ali's words, the period of the Ayub regime was a period of "ten years of darkness, oppression and increasing material poverty" for the people of Pakistan (Ali, 1970: 20).

In keeping with the first part of the modernization agenda, the period 1958–68 was designated as the "Decade of Development."[11] A team of advisors from the Harvard Advisory Group on International Development (later to become the Harvard Institute of Development) led by Gustav Papanek arrived in Pakistan to help design its economic policy. The Five-Year Plan developed under the Advisory Group was based on the doctrine of "functional inequality" (Papanek, 1967). As articulated by neo-classical economists, "functional inequality" represented the belief that initial income inequalities were a necessary prerequisite for economic development (defined narrowly as economic *growth*), the benefits of which would eventually "trickle down" to the rest of society. This policy de-emphasized social sector development, with Mahbub-ul Haq (1963: 30), the head of the Planning Commission, famously stating that "the under-developed countries must consciously accept a philosophy of growth and shelve for the distant future all ideas of equitable distribution and welfare state. It should be recognised that these are luxuries which only developed countries can afford."

Unsurprisingly, the economic program resulted in a huge increase in the level of economic insecurity for the vast majority of people, especially for the rural and urban working poor. The consolidation of wealth was so pronounced that a full two-thirds of industrial capital came to be held by the infamous "22 families," one of which was Ayub Khan's own.[12]

The emphasis on industrialization gave birth to an urban proletariat which became increasingly organized and radical during this period, resulting in a corresponding increase in labour repression. Strikes were declared illegal and the regime decided that all industrial "disputes" would be settled through an establishment-controlled Industrial Relations Board. Communist unions had already been outlawed and replaced with the pro-establishment right-wing body called the Pakistan Confederation of Labour, which was allied with the anti-communist World Confederation of Labour. In addition, newspapers were barred from reporting on strikes and other incidents of industrial unrest. This was, of course, part and parcel of a more comprehensive and ruthless program of press censorship.[13]

The regime's agenda, however, was not limited to economic development, nor did it rely solely on overt repression in order to manage society. In keeping with the dictates of modernization theory and the imperatives of the cultural Cold War, it also initiated a project of social and cultural reform. As part of this project, reports on the Constitution, education, land reform, law, manpower, police, press, science and technology, "social evils" (such as "beggary", petty crime and prostitution, superstition, and "traditionalism"), as well as on sports, culture, art and literature were commissioned at various points over the next ten years.[14] Speaking in 1960, Ayub Khan described the regime's agenda of social and cultural reform in the following terms:

> The vast reforms and innovations that are taking place, or will take place, are no experimental gropings in the dark. They are fully calculated and carefully planned strings in the network of an overall objective to try and help society to get over the weaknesses and vices of its history, to come out of the stupor of its stagnant past and start preparing itself for onward march towards its appointed destiny.[15]

The regime's social engineering efforts were institutionalized through the creation of bodies such as a Bureau (and a Board) of National Reconstruction, a Council for National Integration, and a Central Institute of Islamic Research.[16] These efforts at "national integration" and "national reconstruction" were pitched as a moral regeneration of Pakistani society in the wake of a period of moral *degeneration* brought about by the behavior of "irresponsible" politicians.[17]

Other non-state organizations such as the Pakistan Historical Society and the Pakistan Philosophical Congress, along with Cold War cultural organizations such as UNESCO, PEN and the Pakistan Committee of the Congress for Cultural Freedom played important roles within this new front in the ideological battleground.

This period also saw the establishment of a Pakistani branch of the CIA-backed Congress for Cultural Freedom (CCF) headed by A.K. Brohi, Ayub Khan's law minister. The CCF, "a cultural formation that had a decidedly political impact during the Cold War" (Scott-Smith, 2001: 1), was a key cultural Cold War institution. Set up specifically as "the cultural-intellectual equivalent of the political economy of the Marshall Plan," it was designed as a common platform for anti-communist liberal and social-democratic intellectuals across the world (ibid.: 140).[18]

Not surprisingly, US Cold War social scientists, among them Edward Shils and Daniel Lerner, were prominent on the CCF circuit as well, although the CCF was not the only platform available to these academics for the propagation of these ideas. "Area Studies" programs, established in American universities, strengthened the ties between the US academy and the state, while conferences and other events organized by several private and semi-private institutes and agencies provided forums for the Cold War warrior-academics. While "culture" (specifically, the idea of *apolitical* culture) had worked as the organizing principle of the CCF in Europe, the social scientists felt that the Afro-Asian world was different and that here, appeals to religion would likely work better. The preface to the published proceedings of a conference, "Islam in the Modern World," conducted under the aegis of the newly established Middle East Institute argued that

> ... aside from the geographically strategic position it occupies, [the "Islamic world"] comprises one of the most significant and potentially most powerful bodies of population still uncommitted in the struggle between the Western democracies on the one hand and Soviet Communism and the states under its domination on the other. The Islamic world is inclined, for a variety of reasons, to the side of the democracies; at the same time there are potent forces not only blocking its complete identification with them but beckoning it to the other camp. (1951: iii)

The Cold War discourse in the Muslim world was thus framed by the idea that Islam would be an effective bulwark against communism.[19]

Much of the propaganda channeled through branches of the CCF—seminars, talks, published material—focused on Islam's "Third Way," the potential "middle road" between capitalism and communism. Conferences and seminars on the theme of "Islam in the modern world" and its many variations thus abounded on the CCF circuit. The Pakistan division of the CCF regularly organized seminars on topics such as "Islam and modern life" and "Tradition and change," which reflected the concerns of the American establishment *vis-à-vis* the newly independent nations of Afro-Asia.

The attitude of American social scientists towards the coup and Ayub Khan's dictatorship spoke volumes about their priorities. Their investment in authoritarianism as a tool for the management of "unruly" Third World societies was in direct contradiction to their purported concern with democracy; clearly, the concern was not so much with "modernizing" a traditional society as it was with managing a recalcitrant one.[20]

THE RISE OF THE "ESTABLISHMENT WRITER"

Up to this point in Pakistan's history, the role of the state in the realm of culture had basically been punitive and negative—books had been proscribed, the press had been censored through press laws and safety laws, and dissidents had been jailed. Under Ayub Khan's regime, these existing repressive aspects were complemented by a new proactive role for the state in the cultural sphere. Ayub Khan's primary advisers, Altaf Gauhar and Manzur Qadir, were instrumental in formulating the regime's cultural agenda.[21]

The Ayub regime made a successful bid to control the cultural sphere through a combination of the takeover of existing institutions and the creation of new ones. Qudrutullah Shahab, Ayub's secretary of information, orchestrated the most draconian policy of press control and censorship that Pakistan had yet seen (Ali, 1983; Hasan, 1987).[22] In addition to the repression of independent newspapers, a National Press Trust financed by 24 industrialists was created to "monitor and smother any traces of independent thought" (Noman, 1988: 29). Academics were not allowed to publish anything critical of the regime, and risked loss of employment if they chose to exercise their intellectual independence. As Noman notes, "These measures collectively cordoned off and tamed the intelligentsia, which has had profound implications for cultural and social development in Pakistan" (ibid.).

One of the most significant steps taken by the regime after the coup was the takeover of the Progressive Papers Ltd. (PPL) in April 1959,[23] on the trumped-up charge of receiving funds from "foreign governments."[24] The PPL had always been home to leftist intellectuals,[25] but after the APPWA and CPP were banned in 1954, it became the primary platform of the Marxist Left; in fact, the PPL *was* the Left (at least in West Pakistan) in a very real sense at this time. Its takeover thus neutralized dissent to an enormous degree. In fact, by its annexation, the regime effectively killed two birds with one stone—ousting the "dirty Communists" while acquiring a chain of propaganda newspapers (Ali, 1970: 101).

The regime wished to retain the old editorial staff in order to whitewash the obviously unpleasant and unprecedented nature of their operation, but they failed to accomplish this despite trying to prevent resignations by declaring that the newspaper came under the purview of the "Essential Services" Ordinance. However, Mazhar Ali Khan, the editor of the *Pakistan Times* stepped down in protest, with Ahmad Nadeem Qasmi, the editor of *Imroze*, following soon after. There was no question of wanting to retain Sibte Hasan, the fearless and firebrand editor of the PPL's weekly *Lail-o-Nihar,* and he was politely asked to leave. Faiz Ahmad Faiz, editor-in-chief of the PPL, was already in prison. The top editorial committee was subsequently replaced with handpicked men possessed of a "healthy" national spirit while a senior bureaucrat was appointed the administrator (Hasan, 1987).

The takeover was publicly acknowledged on April 19, 1959 through the publication of an editorial penned by Qudrutullah Shahab, which was carried by both the *Pakistan Times* and *Imroze*. In this infamous editorial—"A New Leaf" in English for the *Times* and "*Naya Varq*" in Urdu for *Imroze*—Shahab claimed that the takeover had been necessitated by the fact that "Distant orbits and alien horizons, far from the territorial and ideological boundaries of Pakistan, exercised a progressively increasing charm on the tone and policies of this newspaper which gradually began to look like a stranger in the house ... ." The implication was that the old editorial team had been comprised of fifth columnists, and that their purge had inaugurated a new era for the PPL.

While the acquisition of the PPL was an act of naked and unprecedented coercion, an important part of the regime's project of cultural hegemony was the co-optation of intellectuals and writers. In addition to being involved in the takeover of Progressive Papers Ltd., Qudrutullah Shahab was also the architect of the "Writers

Guild." Billed as a "trade union for writers" that would address issues of their financial security (most writers belonged to the petit bourgeoisie), protect their commercial rights as a community or "guild" against the designs of publishers in an increasingly commercialized literary market, and serve as a "non-partisan" literary platform,[26] the guild was actually a thinly disguised attempt by the state to co-opt writers. Many writers were more than happy to be granted such prestige by the state, and this ingenious institution gave birth to a creature which came to be known in Pakistan as the "Establishment Writer." Habib Jalib—the fiercely principled and dissident leftist poet whose poetry came to define the resistance to Ayub's regime—referred to the Establishment Writer as a "terrifyingly selfish and pro-dictatorship" creature, whose single-minded careerism made him or her an eager participant in the state's propaganda war, willing to cater to the needs of governments which "need such writers and poets to run their agencies of mass communication" (Jalib, 1991: 93).

Some saw the guild as a welcome alternative to the *Halqa-i Arbab-i Zauq* (henceforth the *Halqa*), the erstwhile literary organization to which the Progressives had migrated wholesale after the ban on the PWA. The influx of the Progressives had become a cause of consternation for old guard of the *Halqa*, which was worried that the new members would corrupt its "literary" (that is, apolitical) atmosphere (Hussain, 1997: 169).[27]

Jamiluddin Aali, a civil servant and literary figure, was picked to head the Writers Guild, which held its inaugural session in Karachi on January 31, 1959. It was widely known that the guild was an establishment initiative, and several writers felt strongly enough about this connection to refuse to attend the first meeting. On the other hand, invitations to this event quickly became seen as marks of prestige within literary circles in West Pakistan.[28] Ayub Khan was the guest of honor, and in his speech he assured writers that they were to have complete freedom of expression under one condition—"patriotism" (Aali, 2001: 107). It is telling that in a piece written in 2001—42 years after the fact—Aali cannot help but preface his remarks on the event by referring to how the glare of the afternoon sun illuminated the face of General Ayub, who was attending "despite running a 102 degree temperature." He marvels at the fact that the person who was chosen to write and read out the manifesto was a young writer who was "only a lowly major in the army" and, without a hint of irony, explains that the manifesto was in English "for the benefit of the foreign guests and press" and also because there had not been enough time to translate it into the different languages of Pakistan (ibid.: 93–4). Qudrutullah Shahab was elected the guild's first secretary general, and Aali proudly tells his readers that Shahab "had placed his dangerous 'Service'—the members of which could sacrifice the biggest of writers at the altar of his starched collar—at our disposal to do with as we pleased" (ibid.: 97), a chilling reference to the power of the information minister and a glimpse into the fascist mind-set of the Establishment Writer.

The benefits of belonging to the guild were manifold. Writers who joined the guild became part of a network of patronage which dispensed such rewards as financial awards sponsored by major industrial houses,[29] junkets within and outside the country to attend various literary and cultural events, and grants-in-aid for disabled or old writers. The prestige of being included in literary and intellectual gatherings organized both by members of the guild and by state officials was seductive. Many of the other cultural agencies and organizations, official or "private," which were created during this period, were part of this same network of patronage and prestige. A large number of events were organized addressing the social responsibility of writers, urging them to devote their energies to nation-building efforts in partnership with the state. So ubiquitous were these exhortations that they prompted a response even from liberal intellectuals such as Shaista Ikramullah (1966: 24) who declared that "in this utilitarian age … when a war is being waged for the minds of man, the writer is in great danger, for he is expected to lend his pen in support of one or the other side of the contestants." Safdar Mir (1998: 261–2), the pre-eminent leftist literary and cultural critic of his time, was characteristically more direct:

> For the politicians, and the bureaucrats who have intermittently replaced them in Pakistan, the theme of the writer's responsibility to society is a godsend. In times of scarcity of topics for pontificating upon, or of unavailability of convenient scapegoats for the ills of society, it comes in handy for delivering pious homilies and sanctimonious exhortations to the literary crowd to mend its ways and recognise the necessity of supporting government policies and programmes.

COLD WAR LITERARY TRENDS

The Cold War, in all its political and cultural dimensions, was an ever-present reality for Pakistanis during this period. According to Safdar Mir (1998: 150), "One of the functions of this new form of warfare was the use of culture and literature against the revolutionary aspirations of the people of the newly-independent [Afro-Asian] nations." The literary critic Intizar Hussain remembers this period as one characterized by an embarrassment of riches with regard to writers visiting from the US under the aegis of the United States Information Service (USIS), an institution established in 1953 with the stated mission "to understand, inform and influence foreign publics in promotion of the national interest, and to broaden the dialogue between Americans and U.S. institutions, and their counterparts abroad." The USIS in Pakistan was at the center of a network of patronage, organizing exchange trips for local and US writers and intellectuals.

The end of the 1950s marked a change in the Urdu literary field. The older generation of fiction writers came to the end of their fruitful careers and new writers keen to assert themselves arrived on the scene. However, their aggressive criticism of the work of their predecessors and their "almost morbid avidity for public acclaim" (Mir, 1998: 148–9) represented more than a mere generational effect; it was apparent that an ideological shift was underway. The older generation, even if they were not all officially members of the PWA, had nevertheless shared the general Progressive ideals in so far as they were motivated by a desire to change social reality and challenge moribund social and political structures. By contrast, the new Urdu writers of the 1950s opposed these ideals, "giving their antagonism ... the dimensions of an anti-progressive crusade" (ibid.: 149). Their endeavor found ready support from the Pakistani establishment.

A particular literary ideology was disseminated in Pakistan (as elsewhere) through the Congress for Cultural Freedom and its magazines such as *Encounter*, the aim of which was to defuse the potentially dangerous idea of socially meaningful literature and of the socially committed writer (Mir, 1998). As Mir contends, literature "was no longer to be the reflection of social reality. The only valid content for it was to be the anguish of the individual soul of the individual writer" (ibid.:149), resulting in the popularity of literary forms such as "[e]xistentialism, absurdism, symbolism, abstractionism, and linguistic anarchism"—literary movements that may have served a social function or reflected a social reality in their original context, but whose effect in Pakistan was decidedly reactionary, since they were used to wean writers away from commitment to progressive causes by inculcating a sense of purposelessness and anomie.

One striking departure from the Establishment Writer was the figure of Habib Jalib. A young writer working for *Imroze*, Jalib was well-known in working-class circles because of his political activism; he worked tirelessly for NAP and had long been a member of the CPP, which was underground at this time. But it was his poetry that made Jalib the voice of the new generation of revolutionaries and a favorite among workers and students. Faiz was still in jail,[30] and the ban on the PWA, combined with the regime's literary politics, had created an atmosphere of cultural and political torpor. Within this context, Jalib's poetry was electrifying in its directness, as it took on everything from Ayub's government to the literary opportunism of the Writers Guild, cutting through the existing hypocrisy like a knife.

Jalib first came into prominence on the national level with *Dastoor* ("Constitution"), a poem written in response to the recently promulgated Constitution, which was a classic example of speaking truth to power, as well as a harsh indictment of those who were complicit in the agenda of Ayub's regime:

> *Deep jis ka mehallaat hi mein jale*
> *Chand logoñ ki khushioñ ko le kar chale*
> *Voh jo saaye mein har maslihat ke pale*
> *Aise dastoor ko, subh-i benoor ko*
> *Main nahiñ maanta, main nahiñ maanta*
>
> *Phool shaakhoñ pe khilne lage, tum kaho*
> *Jaam rindoñ ko milne lage, tum kaho*
> *Chaak seenoñ ke silne lage, tum kaho*
> *Is khule jhoot ko, zehn ki loot ko*
> *Main nahiñ maanta, main nahiñ maanta*
>
> *Tum ne loota hai sadiyoñ hamaara sakooñ*
> *Ab na hum par chalega tumhaara fasooñ*
> *Chaaragar main tumheñ kis tarha se kahooñ*
> *Tum nahiñ chaaragar, koi maane, magar*
> *Main nahiñ maanta, main nahiñ maanta*

> The lamp of which burns only in mansions
> Which takes only the happiness of a few along with it
> Which grows in the shade of every opportunism
> That constitution, that sun-less dawn
> I refuse to accept, I refuse to accept

Flowers have begun to bloom, you claim
Libertines have begun to receive their wine, you say
The ripped shirtfronts have been mended, you say
This bare-faced lie, this rape of our intellect
I do not accept, I do not accept

For centuries you have looted our peace
But your enchantment will no longer work on us
How can I possibly call you a savior
You are not a savior; others may accept you as one
But not me, not me

First recited at a *mushaira* (poetry reading) in the hill-station of Murree where the poetic elite had collected, *Dastoor* caused a major stir. The news of the event, as well as the poem itself, soon reached Manzur Qadir, Ayub's close adviser (not to mention the principal author of the Constitution being pilloried), and Jalib was soon subjected to a long string of incarcerations and harassment. Despite this, Jalib traveled throughout Punjab whenever he could, reciting this poem to much acclaim. The government's efforts to stop him, using both coercion and bribery, proved to be in vain (Jalib, 1991: 59).

Another poem which became immensely popular was *Musheer* ("Adviser") which Jalib wrote in response to the poet Hafeez Jalandhari's appointment as an adviser to Ayub. The titular *musheer* of the poem, Jalandhari had boasted to Jalib that he had advised the "Great Man" that "the Muslim only understands the stick" and therefore he, Ayub, should feel no compunction in cracking down on all those who were agitating against him—from the lawyers that kept talking about the rule of law to the students who were taking out demonstrations against the University Ordinance (Jalib, 1991: 90). The poem is written in the voice of the adviser as he addresses his leader. A short excerpt will illustrate the tongue-in-cheek character of the poem:

Maiñ ne us se yeh kaha, maiñ ne us se yeh kaha

Tu k̲h̲uda ka noor hai
Aql hai shaoor hai
Qaum tere saath hai
Tere hi vajood se
Mulk ki nijaat hai
Tu hai mehr-i subh-i nau

Tere baad raat hai
Bolte jo chand haiñ
Sab yeh shar-pasand haiñ
Un ki khainch le zubaañ
Un ka ghont de gala

Maiñ ne us se yeh kaha ...

I said to him, I said to him
You are the light of God
You are Intellect, you are Wisdom
The nation is behind you
The country's salvation
Lies in your existence alone
You are the sun of the new dawn
After you, there is only night
Those few that dare to speak out
Are all mischief-makers
Rip out their tongues
Wring their necks
I said to him ...

Such irreverent and openly agitative poetry which Jalib fearlessly recited at street-corners, on university campuses, and at formal *mushairas* earned him the respect of students and workers across West Pakistan, who fondly gave him the title of "the people's poet." The regime became so sensitive to Jalib's influence that he was forbidden from reciting some of his most egregious verse in public, a ban which he regularly flouted to the enormous satisfaction of his fans, and to the immense frustration of the administration. As a consequence, he spent a lot of time in prison as a "guest of the government." Undeterred, he would compose yet another piece articulating dissent against the regime, calling it out for its atrocities against the people, often using humor and satire to poke fun at the power structure—a technique that set his poetry apart from that of the older generation of Progressives (such as Faiz) which tended to be more serious in its tone—which probably accounted for Jalib's popularity on the street.

MANAGING ISLAM

Ayub's campaign against the Left was not the only front on which his regime was engaged. The desire to undermine the increasing political influence of the Islamic parties and the *ulema* ("the learned ones," referring to the religious scholars) was one of the significant motivations behind the 1958 coup. Following the death of Jinnah in 1948, the Muslim League had increasingly turned towards the discourse of "Islam" to quash dissent and to try and cobble together legitimacy for itself. Additionally, political intrigues, particularly in the Punjab, had resulted in opening up space for Islamist parties to assert themselves. The anti-Ahmediyya riots of 1953 had given them their first taste of street power and the secular establishment recognized the danger of the growing Islamist influence. According to Governor General Iskander Mirza, politicians could neither resist "flirting with the mullahs" nor could they deal with the consequences of doing so. The constitution of 1956 contained concessions to the religious lobby which the secular establishment found dangerous.[31] This prompted the establishment to take action—it believed that the "progress of the country depended on purging Islam from the political process," but did not think that politicians could be trusted to do this, which meant that "secularism could only be guaranteed through martial rule" (Nasr, 1994: 148).

However, it did not take long for the regime to replace its explicitly secular agenda with a strategy of religious modernism. Even if Islam "could not immediately be sidelined ... it could be reformed, modernised, depoliticised and eventually eased out of politics' (ibid.: 150). The most important task was to undermine the *ulema*'s monopoly over Islam and so the Ministries of Interior and Education, as well as Information and Broadcasting launched a propaganda campaign which questioned the *ulema*'s loyalty to Pakistan, their ability to rise to the demands of the modern world, and even their moral authority.

Meanwhile, the actual work of devising a new version of Islam was delegated to the Institute of Islamic Culture, led by Khalifa Abdul Hakim, and to the Islamic Research Institute, headed by Fazlur Rahman, a respected scholar of South Asian Islam and a confidant of Ayub. The idea was for the state itself to formulate a particular take on Islam and to reserve the right to interpret the tenets of the religion. The religious forces did not take these efforts lying down; measures such as the nationalization of religious endowments through the Waqf Ordinance of 1959, and the enactment of the Muslim Family Laws Ordinance of 1961 led to the first of several clashes between them and the regime.

Despite its intentions, the official policy of secularism ended up being cursory at best, as the temptations of using Islam for political gain proved too seductive for Ayub to ignore. Under the 1962 Constitution, for example, political parties were revived under the condition that they adhere to "Islamic ideology," with the regime being the ultimate arbiter of what counted as "Islamic." This enabled the disqualification of all political opposition, especially that emerging from the Left, while giving Islamist parties an advantage they never had before. But this was not the full extent of the damage. Not only did Ayub Khan fail to substantively change the role played by Islam in Pakistani society and politics, but under him secularism became "associated with an unpopular, unrepresentative government," as well as a symbol of the undue influence of the West within Pakistan, especially in terms of its brazen support of a military dictatorship (Noman, 1988: 34).[32] This, of course, was a piece of immense good fortune for the religious forces, especially the *Jama'at-i Islami* which had undergone a major transformation during the martial law period, arguably emerging by the time of the 1965 presidential elections as "the most organised and robust of the political parties" (Nasr, 1994: 153).

A neo-fascist party founded and headed by Maulana Maududi, the *Jama'at-i Islami* (henceforth, the *Jama'at*) represented the reactionary sections of the petit bourgeoisie and the lower-level salariat, tapping into their justifiable anger at a politically unrepresentative and socio-culturally alien(ated) ruling class. A commissioned study by the Ministry of Information declared the *Jama'at* an "essentially … seditious and invidious force" along the lines of the Muslim Brotherhood (ibid.: 153).[33] However, instead of taking harsh action against it, the state sought to co-opt the organization, especially in its fight against a newly mobilized Left. Significantly, a pro-*Jama'at* faction, which included Ayub's law minister, A.K. Brohi (of CCF fame), also began to emerge within the government.

Notwithstanding his problems with the Islamists, Ayub did not shy away from using the *Jama'at* or Islam when faced with a decidedly secular, leftist and increasingly popular opposition. Thus, as early as 1959, he exhorted the *ulema* to reject obscurantism in favor of developing an Islam that was not just compatible with the modern world, but "more relevant to the country's development agenda" and to the fight against communism (ibid.: 150). As the regime's political confrontation with the leftists heated up, it increasingly turned to the *Jama'at*; among other things, it offered tacit support to its student wing, the *Islami Jami'at-i-Talibah*, turning it into a potent anti-Left force which clashed with the leftist National

Student Federation in East Pakistan and labor union activists in West Pakistan.

Thus the regime's relationship with the Islamist parties, and especially the *Jama'at*, like its relationship with Islam, was fraught but ultimately opportunist. Where earlier it had chastised and occasionally jailed Maududi, it now increasingly turned to a policy of appeasement as the Left began to gain political ground. Clearly, the regime understood that, unlike the Left, the *Jama'at* did not represent a fundamental threat to the status quo.

THE ANTI-AYUB MOVEMENT

Unrest against the regime, which had started in earnest following Ayub's rigging of the 1965 presidential elections (held in January), was further consolidated later that year by the moral and material support offered by the US to India during the Indo-Pak war, along with its refusal to help Pakistan in the conflict. Ayub Khan enjoyed a brief moment of popularity around the war, but this quickly evaporated with the signing of the Tashkent Agreement— the ceasefire terms negotiated between India and Pakistan by the Soviets—which was widely perceived to be disproportionately in India's favor.[34]

Sensing the build-up of popular anger and the nascent movement against Ayub, Zulfiqar Ali Bhutto, Ayub's charismatic and canny foreign minister, resigned from the government in protest against the signing of the Tashkent Agreement and soon formally joined the political opposition as the head of a new political party. Bhutto had already made a name for himself over the past few years through his fiery nationalist defense of Pakistan in the international arena against what was increasingly being seen in Pakistan as US bullying, and its preferential attitude towards India.

Ayub's economic and political policies had hurt or alienated a large cross-section of the Pakistani population, from the urban petty bourgeois to Sindhi landlords; even the *Jama'at* rode this tide of economic grievances against the Ayub regime. However, the most important political development at this time was the rise and consolidation of a genuine mass-based working-class and peasant politics for the first time in Pakistan's history. The increase in size of the urban proletariat along with its immiseration was the inevitable consequence of the regime's economic policies. As this faction became increasingly assertive, the stakes of the political game were dramatically transformed.

Key international events also contributed to shifting the balance of power in favor of the Left at this time. Popular anti-imperialist sentiment—always an important feature of Pakistani political culture—had intensified over the late 1950s and early 1960s as Pakistan became more imbricated in Cold War politics as an "ally" of the United States, and especially as US involvement in the Middle East and Afro-Asia increased. This sentiment manifested itself in popular support for Iran's Mossadegh following the CIA-engineered coup in 1953 and for Egypt's Nasser during the Suez Crisis of 1956, in the anger at the murder of Patrice Lumumba in the Republic of Congo, and the opposition to the wars of Indo-China, particularly to the US invasion of Vietnam, which led to a radicalization of student politics through the 1960s (Ali, 1970, 2005 (1987)). It's important to note that this popular anti-imperialism was in direct conflict with the official Pakistani stand in each of these instances.

Thus by the late 1960s, the mood in Pakistan was distinctly revolutionary. "Socialism" had become an increasingly popular rallying cry; its popularity at this time was testified to by the fact that most political parties made some reference to it in their platforms. Red flags, socialist slogans and cries of "Asia is Red" filled the air at the increasingly frequent political rallies. At the same time as these revolutionary forces were gathering strength, the National Awami Party split along pro-Moscow and pro-Peking lines in 1968, fracturing the Left and leaving it without a political platform.[35] The decidedly left-ward direction of the political winds had become evident to Bhutto (Noman, 1988: 101), as did the implications of the NAP split. Realizing that a successful political campaign at this time would require the support of the left-wing groups, he decided to actively court them. The party that he established—the People's Party of Pakistan (PPP)—included within its leadership a number of socialist intellectuals[36] who also authored its manifesto. The PPP adopted several accoutrements of socialist politics and political culture. For example, as the head of the party, Bhutto was referred to as the party's "Chairman." The party's printed manifesto (issued in 1970 just prior to the elections) had a red cover, and began and ended with the party's populist slogan "*Islam is our faith; Democracy is our polity; Socialism is our economy; All power to the people.*" It declared that the nation had been oppressed and betrayed by neo-colonial forces, described the relationship between East and West Pakistan as one of internal colonialism, promised the end of feudalism, and affirmed that the ultimate aim of the party was the "attainment of a classless society, which is possible only through socialism in our time" (Raza, 1997: 32). Its extremely popular election slogan demanded "*roti, kapra aur makaan*" ("bread, clothes and shelter") for every Pakistani. Left-wing groups were prominent at the party's public meetings, imbuing them, and the party, with a radical look.

Despite these trappings of socialism, however, Bhutto was far from bring a leftist, radical or otherwise.[37] He had the key support of a section of the military junta, which was critical of Ayub's handling of the Tashkent Agreement, and the backing of Sindhi landlords who were upset at the way in which Ayub's industrialization program had differentially benefited non-Sindhi *muhajir* traders. The PPP's unprecedented popularity, especially given the short time of its existence, was a direct result of Bhutto's ability to play the right political cards, and to be all things to all people:

> [He] carefully and successfully stressed the priorities of the people he was addressing. In the Punjab, he underlined confrontation with India. In Sindh, he promised to curb the *waderas* [landlords] and improve the standard of living of the people. In line with Sindhi nationalist sentiments, he stressed the injustice of One Unit. He spoke about Islamic Socialism to the industrial workers, particularly in Karachi … He held out something for almost everyone, except capitalists, and endeavoured to envelop within his fold both peasants and landlords, workers and well-to-do. He profited from the disarray of the leftists after the break-up of the NAP, and stole the leadership by calling for a socialist revolution. Subsequently, when he sought to appease religious sentiment, he talked about *Musawaat-i-Muhammadi* (Equality of Islam) instead of Islamic Socialism. (Raza, 1993: 27–8)

Further, Bhutto cashed in on the nationalist and anti-imperialist mood of the times, demanding an independent foreign policy, withdrawal from US defense pacts such as SEATO (Southeast Asia Treaty Organization) and CENTO (Central Treaty Organization), and a retraction of the Tashkent Agreement.

Thus, although the PPP was not a party *of* the working masses, the political atmosphere of the time along with the support of socialist intellectuals such as Safdar Mir made it the focal point of socialist politics.[38] It became a party that seemed to represent the interests of the "common man" against the rapacious capitalists and feudal landlords.

ANTI-COMMUNIST PROPAGANDA AND THE ATTACK ON "ISLAMIC SOCIALISM"

The anti-Ayub movement of the late 1960s was defined by two opposing radicalisms: that of the Right, increasingly represented by the *Jama'at*, and that of the Left which was embodied in the working-class and student uprisings of the time that eventually coalesced around the PPP. As the economic contradictions of the period intensified and discontent against the regime grew, the *Jama'at* belatedly came to realize the threat posed by the rise in left-wing politics and it focused its attention on "ridding Pakistan of the menace of the left" (Nasr, 1994: 149). The battle of ideas between these two forces was fought over the politically charged discursive elements of nationalism, socialism and Islam; at stake was the increasingly popular notion of "Islamic socialism," and the relationship between Islam and the Pakistani nation.

The sheer volume of the discourse around Islamic socialism in the late 1960s is astonishing and speaks to the popularity of the Left at this time, as well as to the anxiety this generated on the Right. The term itself was not a new one; its origins lay in Muslim modernist discourse of the 1930s and 1940s. Within that context, Islamic socialism had referred essentially to a kind of welfare state, the justification for which was sought and found in the "egalitarian spirit of Islam." The qualifier "Islamic" indicated its relationship to the principles of Islam, and served to distinguish it from other, "god-less" models of socialism/communism which were gaining popularity across the subcontinent at that time. This term re-emerged in the late 1960s, only this time it was deployed, not by modernists for whom communism was too unpalatable, but by leftists trying to present an "indigenized" version of socialism for popular consumption, and hoping to disrupt the Islamists' monopoly over "Islam."[39]

Anti-communism had been one of the cornerstones of the Ayub regime, and it shared this animus with the religious Right. In an effort to combat the Left, the establishment turned to the *Jama'at*, an explicitly and avowedly anti-socialist organization, whose ideology it found "very expedient as an antidote to the sudden influx of Maoism" (Mir, 1990: 1). The propaganda generated by the state as well as the anti-communist liberal intelligentsia of the earlier period made the Right's case easier and stronger. To begin with, anti-Left propaganda collapsed socialism and communism, a discursive move enabled by the fact that the term for communism (*ishtiraakiyat*) was frequently used to refer to socialism, although a different and a more appropriate translation for socialism (*ijtimaaiyat*) was readily available. According to the *Jama'at*, *ishtiraakiyat* was, by definition, the very negation of Islam, a claim for which it found ample supportive material in US anti-communist Cold War propaganda.[40] Leftist intellectuals responded by highlighting the progressive and revolutionary traditions in Islam, specifically focusing on the importance Islam placed on social justice and welfare, and arguing that socialism was the only means by which a truly Islamic society could be achieved.

In an interview appearing in a Damascus monthly *Al-Muslimin*, which was reprinted in *Charagh-i Rah* in June 1968, Maududi was asked to comment on the fact that "Communism promises a hungry man bread, whereas Islam only promises him Heaven in the afterlife." Maududi's response was that communism "promises bread at the cost of human freedom" while Islam "promises not just Heaven but a good life in this world and in the next ... and considers it important to safeguard human freedom for this purpose." In fact, argued Maududi, *communism* was the real opiate of the masses "because in making the promise for a worldly heaven it builds up the issue of hunger to such an extent that the oppressed and hungry willingly agree to trade in their freedom" (Maududi, 1968: 6). The idea of the leader of a reactionary Islamist party defending human freedom would be incomprehensible if we did not take into account the class interests represented by the *Jama'at*. As Safdar Mir pointed out in his columns in the *Pakistan Times* and *Nusrat*, the discourse of the "Maududi party" (as Mir derisively called the *Jama'at*) was at the forefront of attempts to give capitalism an "Islamic" makeover with the support of the *ulema*. Habeeb Jalib echoed this understanding of the *Jama'at's* vested interests thus:

Zameeneñ hoñ va<u>d</u>eroñ ki, mashineñ hoñ lu<u>t</u>eroñ ki
<u>Kh</u>uda ne likh ke di hai yeh tumheñ tehreer Maulana

The land should belong to the feudals, the machines to the looters,
This is what God has given to you in writing, Maulana

Mir proposed that the "slogans of 'Islamic system', 'Islamic society', 'Islamic ideology'" that the *Jama'at* and its allies were raising were designed to confuse ordinary Muslims who "despite [their] illiteracy," understood that "Islam implies justice and equality," and whose Islam was "purer and more healthy than that presented by the hypocrisy of the middle class." He went on to declare:

> I believe that the main efforts of Maududi and all the other middle class Islamic *mufassareen* [commentators] are directed at ensuring that there should develop no sense of the connection between Islam and revolution in the minds of ordinary Muslims. And if a revolutionary interpretation of the *kalima* [profession of faith] exists in their minds despite their illiteracy then they should be distracted from it. (Mir 1997a: 116)

Mir also argued that the *Jama'at*'s opposition to the anti-imperialist politics of the Left was intimately linked to neo-imperialism's new strategy within the developing world. The cover of his book *Maududiyat and the Present Political Struggle* featured a drawing of Maududi as a wrestler standing with his legs apart and hands on his hips, concealing moneybags adorned with the dollar sign.[41]

The *Jama'at* mobilized its vast propaganda machinery in its ideological assault on the Left, particularly through Urdu periodicals such as the monthly *Charagh-i Rah* and the weekly *Zindagi*.[42] In June 1969, for example, *Charagh-i Rah* published a special issue on socialism which focused almost entirely on the incompatibility of communism and religion, with special reference to the status of Muslims in the Soviet Union and China, the sad fate of organized religion within socialist/communist countries, and the repression of the Muslim Brotherhood in "socialist" Egypt. The issue included excerpts from the communist press which "proved" that communist propaganda was self-consciously designed and implemented to turn people against religion.

These publications also featured regular and sustained attacks on known Pakistani leftist intellectuals and political activists. Waheed Qureshi, a prominent right-wing and pro-*Jama'at* Urdu literary critic wrote a series in *Zindagi* "exposing" the nefarious and seditious nature of the Progressive Writers Association, drawing upon the infamous Rawalpindi Conspiracy Case which had implicated the leading lights of the Communist Party. Qureshi's series, which ran under the general title of *Taraqqi-Pasand Tehreek Apne Aainay Meiñ* ("The Progressive Writers Movement as reflected in its own mirror"), consisted of large sections reproduced from the writings of individual Progressives as well as official statements and manifestoes of the PWA, embellished by anti-Progressive polemic. Despite its framing, the articles failed to convincingly show up the PWA as a seditious and anti-Pakistan force. But then Qureshi was aware that he was really only preaching to the converted; *Zindagi* catered to an already deeply anti-socialist petit bourgeoisie audience.

Attacking the PWA may well have been considered necessary at this time, given the continuing popularity of established Progressive poets such as Faiz Ahmad Faiz and the increasing popularity of younger ones such as Habib Jalib.[43] Red-baiting was a consistent theme within the pages of *Zindagi*, through sensationalist yellow journalism as well as satirical jibes aimed at prominent Pakistani socialists such as Faiz Ahmed Faiz (the *Jama'at*'s bête noir) and Maulana Bhashani, the NAP leader. In issue after issue, Faiz was pilloried as Comrade *Ghaiz*[44]—the word means "belligerence"—while Maulana Bhashani was referred to as "Mao-lana" Bhashani. A surprisingly witty pun on "Maulana," Bhashani's honorific "Mao-lana" literally translates as "bring Mao." Another recurring feature was an ongoing dialogue between two hypothetical communists, Comrades *Laal Din* and *Laal Beg*. *Laal* is the Urdu word for "red" while *Din* is a common Punjabi peasant name, which literally translates as "creed"; *Beg* is another common last name—*Laalbeg*, however, is the Urdu word for cockroach.

Unsurprisingly, the *Jama'at* intellectuals were joined in their propaganda campaign by the representatives of the ruling establishment, which was threatened by the rise of the Left. In particular, retired Supreme Court Justice S.A. Rahman and former law minister (and established Cold Warrior) A.K. Brohi were active in articulating a critique of socialism from a modernist Muslim perspective, thereby appealing to the sections of the "Westernized" English-speaking elite that might have found the *Jama'at*'s politics unpalatable.

A ubiquitous theme in right-wing anti-socialist discourse was that Islam and socialism were fundamentally incompatible, because socialism—like capitalism—was an essentially materialist philosophy which not only rejected spirituality and religion, but was antithetical to them. Even if communism *could* deliver on its promise of the "equality of stomachs," argued Rahman, it could not achieve the "equality of souls" which Islam enjoins. Socialism was thus, at best, a naïve philosophy which did not take into account the obvious fact that "man did not live by bread alone" and needed "material as well as spiritual nourishment" (Rahman, 1974: 49). The state of Muslims in the Soviet Union should serve as a dire warning to Pakistanis flirting with socialism, claimed Rahman, because it proved that socialism could never be reconciled with Islam.

According to these intellectuals, the very term "Islamic socialism" was nothing short of a "fraud" perpetrated on Islam—a superficial and dishonest attempt to "spiritualise" socialism (Brohi, 1968: 40–41) so as to make it more acceptable to Muslims. "Islamic socialism" was an abomination because it negated Islam's claim to be a complete code of life for all Muslims across time and space. For example, Brohi declared that the very idea that Islam endorsed a particular economic system was sacrilegious since "Economic systems come and go but Islam goes on forever" (ibid.: 69). Moreover, it was unnecessary to "tack ... an economic programme borrowed from socialism" onto Islam since the latter "provides a dynamic and progressive social-political system which has the elasticity to fulfil the needs of all times and all climes" (Rahman, 1970: 6–7).[45]

Anti-socialist intellectuals also argued that Islam and communism/socialism disagreed on other fundamentals, such as the very desirability of a classless society, let alone class struggle. A.K. Sumar (1970: 55), a member of the National Assembly (and former president of the Karachi Chamber of Commerce) made a speech against Islamic socialism in the Assembly in which he argued that the idea of a classless society "was inconsistent with nature" and therefore not supported by Islam; Islam was invested in removing *class consciousness*, not "natural classes" since, in the eyes of God, the only thing that set one Muslim apart from another was piety (Sumar, 1970: 55). Others argued that socialism's focus on class divisions and class struggle actually posed a danger to the Muslim *ummah*, since it focused on the divisions among Muslims.

Most of these arguments advanced by anti-socialist intellectuals against Islamic socialism, were not unique to Pakistan or to any specifically "Islamic" context, even though they were presented as if that were the case. The idea that communism was a God-less ideology which mandated the expropriation of all property was standard fare in Cold War anti-communist discourse. However, by the end of the 1960s, the fact that nationalization was a prominent part of the PPP's election manifesto gave right-wing intellectuals in West Pakistan a very specific issue around which to focus their anxiety. Sumar proposed that the injustice and exploitation that characterized capitalism was not the result of the "private ownership of the means of production," but of "materialistic pursuits in the absence of a moral code of human conduct" which "must inevitably lead to selfishness and greed" (ibid.: 48). Thus the solution did not lie in the dissolution of private property, but in the adoption of a more moral and spiritual outlook. The Prophet, it was argued, had given his followers assurances regarding the inviolability of their property; expropriation of private property by the state was thus "unjust and immoral" (ibid.: 55), even *haraam* ("forbidden") (Brohi, 1968: 73). Rahman (1970: 10) even argued that "the possession of property [was] ... a means of achieving the goal of righteous life" and that the nationalization of "all property ... as the socialists demand ... narrowed [the scope of development of the righteous life]" to an unacceptable level.

Of course, far from demanding the forcible expropriation of all property, or even forcible nationalization, the PPP's manifesto called only for the nationalization of key industries after appropriate compensation. The repeated references to takeovers by the state were overblown, to say the least.[46] Nevertheless, even nationalization with compensation was deemed unacceptable since, it was argued, the process of "fully" nationalizing any industry and paying the requisite compensation would take so long that it effectively amounted to a form of forced expropriation (Brohi, 1968: 73).

This anti-socialist propaganda did not go unchallenged by leftist intellectuals, and the most powerful defense of socialism was one which strategically deployed the prose and poetry of the national poet Muhammad Iqbal. Iqbal was the perfect choice for several reasons: his passionate critique of capitalism and obvious sympathy for socialism, his admiration of Marx and Lenin and of the Bolshevik Revolution, which he thought of as an inspiration for Muslims and other colonized peoples—especially because of its radical project of social equality which, according to him, was very close to Islamic ideals of social justice—and (perhaps most importantly) because of his unimpeachable credentials as the pre-eminent Islamic poet and thinker of the modern period.[47] Defendants of Islamic socialism, such as Safdar Mir, quoted the following (officially censored) verses as examples of Iqbal's socialist sympathies, in order to refute the right-wing idea that socialism was antithetical to Islam:

Kaarkhaane ka hai maalik murawwak na-kardakaar
Aish ka putla hai, mehnat hai ise na-saazgaar
Hukm-i haq hai 'lais al-insaan illa maa-sai'
Khaye kyooñ mazdoor ki mehnat ka phal sarmaayadaar?

The owner of the factory is completely useless
He wallows in luxury; hard work does not appeal to him

God's word is that "There is nothing for man except that which
   he has strived for"
Then why should the capitalist enjoy the fruit of the worker's
   labour?

In *Lenin K̲h̲uda ke Huzoor Meiñ* ("Lenin in the Court of God"),
Iqbal has Lenin throwing the following challenge towards God:

Tu qaadir-o-aadil hai magar tere jahaañ meiñ
Haiñ tal̲k̲h̲ bohat banda-i-mazdoor ke auqaat
Kab d̲oobega sarmaaya-parasti ka safeena?
Dunya hai teri muntazir-i roz-i mukaafaat!

You are powerful and just, but in your world
The conditions of the working people are very harsh
When will the boat of capital-worship sink
Your world eagerly awaits the day of retribution!

In response, God, persuaded by Lenin's argument, issues a command
to his angels in Iqbal's fiery and popular verses, ordering them to
shake the palaces of the rich and burn down the fields which cannot
support those who work on them:

Ut̲ho! Meri dunya ke g̲h̲ariboñ ko jaga do
Kaak̲h̲-i umara ke dar-o-deewaar hila do
Garmaao g̲h̲ulaamoñ ka lahu soz-i yaqeeñ se
Kunjshak-i faromaaya ko shaaheeñ se lar̲a do
Sultaani-i jamhoor ka aata hai zamaana
Jo naqsh-i kohan tum ko nazar aaye, mit̲a do
Jis khet se dehk̲añ ko mayassar na ho rozi
Us khet ke har k̲h̲osha-i gandum ko jala do

Arise and awaken the poor of my world
Shake the very walls of the palaces of the rich
Warm the blood of the slaves with the fire of faith
Set the sparrow to fight the eagle
The age of democracy is dawning
Destroy all the signs of the past which you come across
The field from which a peasant cannot eke out a livelihood
Should have its every stalk of wheat burnt to the ground.

It was with reference to such well-known poems and verses that leftist intellectuals such as Mir could persuasively argue that, far from being a heresy, the demand for Islamic socialism was, in fact, the culmination of Iqbal's dream.

THE NATION OF ISLAM?

The second front in the battle of ideas between the Left and the religious Right at this time was that of nationalism. As Stuart Hall (1988: 66) points out, "the nation" is almost always at issue in popular struggles in the modern period, and this conjuncture in Pakistani history was no exception. Engaged in a battle for hearts, minds and power, the *Jama'at* decided that it needed to enter mainstream politics, taking on the accoutrements of a national political party which, in the post-colonial context, meant speaking in the language of (liberal) democracy, individual rights and, most importantly, "the nation."

While the *Jama'at* attempted to associate itself with liberal democratic discourse through the slogan of "constitutional democracy," nationalism posed a much trickier challenge. Maududi had been a strong and vocal critic of Muslim nationalism before Independence, specifically of the Muslim League and its demand for Pakistan. His opposition to the Pakistan Movement, and after the establishment of the Pakistani state, to a territorial or cultural nationalism for the new nation-state was based on his critique of nationalism as a political ideology which divided the real (global) community of Muslims or the *ummah*. According to him, nationalism was a form of idolatry and therefore heretical, a point which he drove home by consistently referring to it as *qaum-parasti* ("nation-worship") rather than using its accepted Urdu translation, *qaumiyyat*.

Maududi had always reserved special scorn for liberal and secular Muslims—from the original modernist reformer Syed Ahmed Khan to the leadership of the Pakistan Movement—denouncing them for being "Westernized" and therefore "inauthentic," and declaring their purported commitment to Islam a fraud. His preferred epithet for Jinnah in the period leading up to Independence, for example, was *Kaafir-i-Azam* ("the Great Infidel"), a play on Jinnah's sobriquet *Quaid-i-Azam* ("the Great Leader"). In the 1960s, his critique of the Ayub regime and of the Pakistani ruling establishment more generally was part and parcel of this long-standing animus against modernist Muslims. When, in 1968, he denounced Ayub as being part of a deracinated and comprador class "whose names are like Muslims, who are Muslims by birth, that are of our flesh and blood, and who have the blood of our ancestors running in their veins, but who unfortunately are foreigners in their way of thinking and their style of life is alien to us," he made sure to underscore that these were members of the same class which had been "given birth to" by British colonialism—a class which had faithfully served the British until such a time as their departure from the subcontinent, and which had been left behind by the British as their "viceregents" (Maududi, 1968: 9).

While this critique of the Muslim upper classes and their alien(ated) ways might have been well-received during the Ayub regime as long as it was seen as being aimed at the contemporary ruling class, it would not have gone down very well with the public in so far as it extended to Jinnah and the rest of the leadership of the Muslim League in the 1940s. Thus, once the *Jama'at* entered mainstream politics, Maududi's controversial ideas threatened to become a serious liability. It is worth noting that it was important, even for Maududi and the *Jama'at*, to take "the nation" into account if they wished to have any future as a mainstream political party. Too many accounts of Pakistani politics assume a simplistic relationship between Islam and Pakistan, based on a claim that Pakistan was established "in the name of Islam." While this relationship is invoked in every political conjuncture in Pakistan, it has always been (and continues to be) contested, argued over, and articulated anew. Thus, in the very country purportedly established in the name of Islam, even the *Jama'at* understood that it did not stand a chance within mainstream politics if it did not pay obeisance to "the nation" and its founding fathers. Heaping *invective* on them, even if it was purportedly done *in the name of Islam*, would result in a marginalization from the national political scene.

But the public and historically proximate nature of the pronouncements made against Pakistan and Jinnah meant that it was not possible to wish them away or to easily brush them under the rug. This left the *Jama'at* and Maududi with no alternative but to resort to a number of strategic sleights of hand. One was to try to play down the role played by Maududi's main nemesis within the Pakistan Movement, Jinnah, while at the same time seeking to replace him with a different nationalist icon with which the *Jama'at* could more easily claim affinity. Maududi settled on Muhammad Iqbal, Pakistan's official national poet. Although Iqbal himself was a towering figure within the Muslim modernist movement in late colonial India, his investment in a pan-Islamic Muslim identity and politics made him easier to co-opt than the uncompromisingly secular Jinnah.

And so, in his keynote speech delivered at the Iqbal Academy on the occasion of Iqbal Day (November 9), 1969, Mr. A.K. Brohi contended that the real architect of Pakistan had been Iqbal; Jinnah's role had been merely that of an "ordinary mason" whose contribution to the struggle for national independence had been limited to raising a structure (that is, Pakistan) on the blueprint provided by Iqbal. In making this claim, Brohi no doubt gambled on the possibility that the Muslim middle class felt a deeper emotional connection to the "poet of the East" than to the dry constitutionalism of Jinnah.[48]

As part of the attempt to shake his now-inconvenient past, Maududi made another daring bid. No doubt recognizing the impossibility of convincingly reinventing himself as a nationalist, he now chose to change the very terms of the political engagement by replacing the discourse of "the nation" with something over which he could claim authority. And so the proposition was floated that Pakistan was not, in fact, a "national" state, but an "ideological" one; that is, it had not been demanded or established on behalf of a "nation" (understood as a community held together by a shared culture, language, history, and so on) but on the basis of "Islam," which was an "ideology."[49] *Jama'at* intellectuals set about using every platform available to them to try and popularize this radically revisionist idea, which was given the rather grandiose name of "Pakistan Ideology." Despite the fact that this argument was, as Mir (1990: 53) called it, little more than a "hotch potch of obscurantist thinking," it did manage to muddy the waters when it came to attempts to outline a progressive model of Pakistani nationalism, as we shall see.

Maududi's early political essays and speeches had been published just prior to Independence as a multi-volume book called *Mussalman aur Maujuda Siyaasi Kashmakash* ("Muslims and the Present Political Struggle"). As part of the attempt to underscore Maududi's stature as a public intellectual, the *Jama'at*'s publishing house had recently reissued this book, but with one crucial omission—namely, the volume which contained the invective against Jinnah and the Muslim League. At the same time, in the face of mounting criticism, Maududi simply denied that he had ever made any statement critical of the establishment of Pakistan, and argued that his interventions at the time had been limited to attempts at infusing "a religious and moral spirit within the [Pakistan] movement."[50]

What's more, he dared his critics to prove anything to the contrary. As before, Safdar Mir happily accepted this challenge, and proceeded to serialize choice excerpts from the missing volume in the pages of *Nusrat* (the PPP's new weekly), under the tongue-in-cheek heading "*Maududiyat aur Maujuda Siyaasi Kashmakash*" ("Maududi-ism and the Present Political Struggle"). These "excavated" excerpts made Maududi's views on Pakistan, Jinnah and the Muslim League available to those members of the public—especially a younger generation of Pakistanis—who might not have come across them before. Allowing Maududi's own words to damn him was a brilliant move, designed to undermine his claim to moral authority within the space of Pakistani national politics. Among other things, these excerpts made clear that the basis of the Muslim League's demand for Pakistan was not "Islam," as Maududi was now claiming, since his indictment of the League was based on his assertion that their "orientation" was "towards nation-worship, not ... Islam" (1970: 187). In another excerpted passage, Maududi castigated the league for "nowhere [stating] ... that its ultimate purpose [was] ... to establish an Islamic system of government in Pakistan," and instead "insisting that it is in fact going to be a democratic government in which non-Muslims would have an equal share" (ibid.: 188). Other reproduced passages from the "missing" volume revealed that Maududi had referred to the establishment of Pakistan as the birth of a "monster" (with the Partition riots being its birth pangs), held the Muslim League responsible for the Partition violence, and derisively referred to Pakistan variously as *Na-Pakistan* (the "land of the impure" or "land of impurity"), *Faaqistaan* ("Land of Hunger") and *langra loola Pakistan* ("limbless/handicapped Pakistan") (ibid.: 57).

Republishing these excerpts thus served two purposes for Mir: discrediting Maududi and the *Jama'at* by exposing their animus towards both the very idea of the Pakistani nation-state and its "founding fathers," and establishing that Pakistan had *not* been conceived of as a theocratic state along the lines being proposed by Maududi. Reproducing this debate here is similarly important, in so far as it reveals that far from being simple or foreclosed, as many commentators and scholars of Pakistan would have us believe, the relationship between "Islam" and "Pakistan" was in fact open-ended, contradictory and complex.

THE PROBLEMATICS OF PAKISTANI CULTURE

This clash between Maududi and Mir over the basis of Pakistani nationalism and its relationship to Islam, had a history. The ruling establishment's moves to centralize power in the immediate aftermath of Independence, its callous disregard for the rights of the federating units, and its attempts to marginalize Hindu Pakistanis had made it clear very early on to leftist intellectuals that a progressive national project was needed that could counter the reactionary nationalism of the establishment. These intellectuals understood that only a nationalist project that drew on the cultures and histories of the various regions that were now part of the state, as opposed to the de-territorialized ideology of "Muslim nationalism" which was the cornerstone of official nationalism, held out any hope for a just social and political order in Pakistan. Articulating such a progressive national project thus became one of the major preoccupations of the Left in Pakistan.

The leading voice in the national debate over Pakistani culture in the 1950s and 1960s was indisputably that of Faiz Ahmad Faiz, the pre-eminent poet, writer, editor and public intellectual of his time. Not only did Faiz write extensively on the topic, he also engaged with the issue through talks and debates that were regularly broadcast on radio and television. In the late 1960s, Faiz chaired the government's Commission on Culture, Sports and the Arts; his report was shelved at the time, no doubt due to the fact that the popular agitation against Ayub Khan was reaching its climax. The report was to become the blueprint for Pakistan's new cultural policy under Zulfiqar Ali Bhutto.

The attempt by leftist intellectuals to construct a progressive Pakistani nationalism foregrounded the territorial and cultural aspects of nationalist identity, thus begging the question: what exactly *was* Pakistani culture?[51] Faiz's attempts to answer this reflect the complexity of the problem at hand.[52] According to him, Pakistani culture included the "religion of Islam which provides the ethical and ideological basis for the people's way of life," the "indigenous cultures of various linguistic regions," "elements of Western culture absorbed since the days of British occupation" and "distinct cultures of minority groups who form a part of the Pakistani nation" (Faiz, 1968: 16). Culture, specifically the graphic and performing arts, thus became a crucial element of the progressive nationalist project, which included within its purview both high cultural traditions associated with Indo-Muslim civilization, such as miniature painting and Hindustani classical music, as well as the folk traditions of the various regions of the new nation-state.

For the religious Right, represented by the puritanical *Jama'at*, on the other hand, culture was the Trojan horse through which atheistic leftists were attempting to storm the fortress of Islam. Perhaps as a corollary to Maududi's antipathy towards nationalism, the very idea of "culture" was anathema to them: the performing arts were obscene, hedonistic and depraved, while the graphic arts (except for calligraphy and perhaps architecture) when not actually idolatrous, always carried that potential within them.

So strong were these connections in the minds of *Jama'at* intellectuals, that in the late 1950s Naseem Hijazi, a prominent member of their fraternity, wrote a serialized radio play satirizing two hapless "comrades" deputed by their leader to go to the villages to "discover" Pakistani culture.[53] In his preface to a collected edition of these plays, *Saqaafat ki Talaash* (literally, "The search for culture"), Hijazi explained that the "Progressives" (read: communists) had, circa 1956, taken on the "mantle of culture" since their literary activities had been curtailed (a reference to the banning of the PWA), and because they had found it to be the most effective weapon in their assault on Pakistan's Islamic foundations. As he recalls:

> ... this was the time when an army of so-called progressives had declared war on the fortress of the moral and spiritual values of Pakistan through the front of "culture". Those same "great artists" who earlier used to conduct a trade in obscenity in the name of "literature" [that is, the Progressive Writers], had now, disappointed by the lack of interest shown by the people, taken on their "delicate" shoulders the weight of the service of culture. (Hijazi, 1978: i–ii)

But, argued Hijazi, one should not be fooled by this shift in emphasis because

> ... these "artists" realised that there was a strong guard of moral and spiritual values on the national fortress of Pakistan without removing which they could not hope to create a conducive environment for themselves. In this mission these spirited ones threw away their pens and took up *dhols* and *tablas*[54] instead. It was not mere accident that in this mission our progressives had the cooperation of those enemies of national unity who

thought regional cultures were the easiest means with which to awaken regional hatreds ... [this was the time when] our respected Progressives thought that the beat of *tablas* and the tinkling of *ghungroos*[55] was enough to shake the foundations of this neophyte nation-state. (Ibid.: ii)

Here, Hijazi characterizes the Progressives' defense and promotion of folk and classical performance art forms—as symbolized by the *dhol* and the *tabla* respectively—and their support for regional rights, particularly for East Bengal, as nothing less than sedition. It must be kept in mind that 1956 was the year that saw the forcible consolidation of the provinces of West Pakistan into "One Unit,"

These ideas are incorporated into the radio play itself. In Act One, Scene One of *Saqaafat ki Talaash*, the second-in-command is briefing his team on the communist strategy:

Comrade Alif[56] says that we have to change our modus operandi because we have been unable to win the people over ... we should have realized that the people of Pakistan will refuse to accept any philosophy which is explicitly against the ideology of Islam. We should, instead, try to incorporate entertainment for the people into our slogans ... For instance, we could explain to the people that despite being Muslims, it is their duty as human beings to keep their cultural traditions alive ... we should make them feel that culture is something without which human beings cannot remain human. Muslims hate dance but "tradition" and "culture" are terms with which we can easily lead them astray ... . (Ibid.: 1).

It is quite clear that his target are the "Progressives" of which Faiz was the most visible and iconic figure.[57] Faiz responded strongly to this approach to culture in his essays and talks, as well as in his report of the Commission on Sports, Culture and the Arts, pointing to the politics of such ways of thinking:

Since independence, these anti-culture attitudes inherited from the past have been seized upon by certain factions in the country for topical political ends. They first sought to equate all culture with music and dancing and then to equate all music and dance with the lewd vulgarizations of these arts by inept professionals. From these premises, it was easy to proceed to the conclusion that, as has often been done, that all art is immoral, hence anti-religious, hence ideologically unacceptable. (Faiz, 1968: 9)

The idea of a cultural or territorial basis for Pakistani nationalism, which the Left saw as crucial to a just settlement of the national question in Pakistan in the form of a federated state, was unacceptable to Maududi and the *Jama'at*. Maududi was hostile to the notion of provincial rights and especially to Bengali demands, first for recognition and later for increased autonomy from the center. This put the *Jama'at* outside of the pale of much of the oppositional politics during the Ayub period, defined as it was by a struggle against One Unit and the defense of provincial rights. Forced, however, to engage with the question of Pakistani nationalism despite his animus towards the very concept, Maududi, who had started using the vague appellation "Pakistan Ideology" in all conversations about Pakistani nationalism, led the attempt by *Jama'at* intellectuals to insist that Pakistani culture was, simply put, "Islamic culture." The term "Pakistan Ideology" represented Maududi's attempt to co-opt Muslim nationalism which had been based on its secular demands on behalf of Indian Muslims, and to re-imagine it as a religious nationalism. The content of the "Islam" in this discourse, was of course, the reactionary Islam of Maududi rather than the modernist Islam of the Muslim League leadership.

Faiz encountered this definition of "Islamic culture," especially *vis-à-vis* Pakistani nationalism, frequently during his lectures and radio presentations, and set about trying to define, pin down and put in its place this "Islamic" aspect of Pakistani culture, lest it acquire the theocratic meaning that the *Jama'at* was attempting to stick on it. However, Faiz's nuanced engagements with the complexities of Pakistani culture and his sensitivity to issues of exclusion and marginality did not always appeal to those who were looking for a simple answer. This is evident from the transcripts of radio presentations and the odd university lecture where he was invariably, and often frustratingly, asked variations on the same question: "Can we not say that Pakistani culture is Islamic culture?" (Faiz, 1988: 21). In response, Faiz drew on the accepted idea that a national culture had to be unique to the nation-state and could not be solely based on something which was shared with other nation-states—the idea was to strategically articulate a notion of Pakistani culture which would challenge the position of the *Jama'at*.[58]

In an answer to a question by a student, who asked whether it would not simply be easier to think of Pakistani culture simply as "Islamic culture," Faiz argued:

There are aspects of Islamic culture [articles of faith] which are internal and there are some external forms of these which are national in their historical and geographical contexts. This doesn't mean that they are separate, but that both these aspects combine to make what is called a 'national culture'. Thus Pakistani culture is only limited to Pakistan, and Islam is not limited by nationalism … but is universal … thus that which is Pakistani culture will be Islamic, not non-Islamic. In fact, you can call it Pakistani Islamic culture. You cannot just call it Islamic culture because you don't have a monopoly on Islam. (Ibid.: 21)

The query which followed this one enquired anxiously that if "the culture of every Islamic country is engendered by its specific geographical context, and cannot be Islamic, then that means that there is no such thing as Islamic culture" (ibid.: 24). To which Faiz responded: "Since Islam is a universal faith, therefore the culture of every Muslim nation is Islamic culture … but alongside this, every Islamic country has its own national culture as well. There is no contradiction in these two things" (ibid.: 24).

Here Faiz paused to illustrate the point with the example of Iran, which held on to both the Islamic and the pre-Islamic aspects of its culture, arguing that it was the synthesis of the two which made Persian culture unique.

This exchange, and several others like it, exemplified the clash between two different if overlapping conceptions of political and cultural identity. Faiz's effort was aimed at displacing an essentially religio-centric world-view and understanding of political and social order in favor of a cultural nationalism which, while acknowledging the importance of religion in the life of the people, also reflected the diversity of the nation's cultural geography and had the capacity to include non-Muslims. The fact that this was an intensely difficult and immensely political process—despite the hegemony of the idea of "nation"—is evidenced by the resistance displayed by the students in Faiz's audience for these lectures. It is hard not to sympathize with Faiz as he faces the same questions over and again: aren't Islamic culture and Pakistani culture one and the same thing? If not, doesn't that negate the idea that Islam is a universal religion and a complete code of life? Doesn't the claim that the culture of one Muslim country is different from the culture of another Muslim country amount to *bida'at*?[59]

What is obvious from these debates on Pakistani nationalism between leftist intellectuals and those from the religious Right is that while the relationship between Islam and Pakistan was actively under contention, and had been so since the very beginning, the idea that "Islam" (however understood) was a major constituent element of Pakistani nationalism was not. This popular understanding of the articulation between "Islam" and "Pakistan" did not, by itself, foreclose the possibility of a progressive national project, as we can see from Faiz's engagement with it, but it did make the task difficult in a context in which the *Jama'at* was actively engaged in muddying the ideological waters.

Faiz's frustrated attempts at disentangling the confusion of the students show just how difficult and complex the task of the Left was at this time, not because of the "natural" or "organic" relationship between Pakistan/Pakistani nationalism and Islam, but because of the mistrust of secular politics which the *Jama'at* had actively encouraged. The fact that secularism was associated with the unpopular regime of Ayub and the "Westernized elite classes" which it was seen as representing did not help. The political battle at this time may have been won by the PPP (and thereby, nominally, the Left) but the ideological battle over the terms "Islam," "Pakistan" and "socialism" was far from over.

In 1969, reading the writing on the wall, Ayub stepped down, but only after handing over power to another general, Yahya Khan. Yahya Khan's interim government, Pakistan's second military regime, ironically oversaw the country's first full and fair elections, as well as its break-up in the wake of a violent and rapacious military operation in East Bengal.

Yahya declared the end of the universally unpopular One Unit;[60] Bengalis were to be represented in the coming elections on the basis of their share of the population rather than any formula of "parity" (Jalal, 1990). However, it was clear that the military establishment had no intention of allowing an outcome which would undermine its interests.[61] Therefore, no mention was made of the question of provincial autonomy which had become a linchpin of Bengali demands. In March 1970 (prior to the elections), Yahya passed the infamous Legal Framework Order (LFO) which laid out a conditional framework for the transfer of power following the elections, thereby ensuring that the West Pakistani establishment would continue to call the shots in the case of the Awami League victory that appeared likely (Noman, 1988). By granting Yahya (as president) veto power over any actions undertaken by the new National Assembly, the LFO was essentially an "insurance against shifts in the balance of power to any political configuration which was aimed at circumscribing the interests of the two main institutions of the Pakistani state," namely the military and the civil bureaucracy (Jalal, 1990: 309).

The Awami League secured a clear victory, winning 160 out of 162 seats in East Pakistan, and therefore emerging as the dominant force in the future National Assembly; the PPP, whose base of support was limited to Punjab and Sindh even in West Pakistan, secured 81 out of 138 seats there.[62] Although Yahya and Mujib-ur Rahman (the leader of the Awami League) had reached an accord prior to the elections to the effect that Pakistan would remain a federal state, factions in the army demanded further reassurances before the transfer of power. Yahya thus asked to see a draft constitution before transferring power to the Awami League. Mujib, who was already wary of the vested interests of these factions within the army, in turn demanded that Yahya immediately make an announcement to call the inaugural session of the new National Assembly. Bhutto contributed to the tense atmosphere by demanding that a constitutional accord be reached before proceeding any further, and threatened to "'break the legs' of party members who dared to attend the inaugural session of the National Assembly."[63] Bhutto's aggressive posturing further strengthened the position of hawks in the army, and was in fact an explicit expression of alliance with them (Noman, 1988: 46).

As a consequence of these events, the convening of the National Assembly was indefinitely postponed, just two days before the scheduled date of March 3, 1971. As protests broke out in East Pakistan, the army planned and then launched Operation Searchlight across East Pakistan on March 25, designed to crush all intellectual, political and military resistance, and let loose an orgy of violence designed to punish the entire Bengali population. There was a virtual silence in West Pakistan over this army action,[64] except for a few brave and largely isolated voices, most of them on the Left.[65] One of them, predictably, was Jalib's; the short poem below was addressed to the Pakistani Army:

> *Muhabbat goliyoñ se bo rahe ho*
> *Vatan ka chehra khoon se dho rahe ho*
> *Gumaañ tum ko ke rasta kat raha hai*
> *Yaqiñ mujh ko ke manzil kho rahe ho*

> You are sowing love through bullets
> You are staining the country's face with blood
> You think that you are making progress
> But I know that you have lost your way

5
From Bhutto's Authoritarian Populism to Zia's Military Theocracy

Every aspect of the Pakistani state, society, politics and culture worth noting today bears the scars of the 11 years of martial law under General Zia ul Haq from 1977 to 1988, Pakistan's longest and most brutal military dictatorship. The story of how a country which appeared to be on the brink of socialist revolution in 1969 was turned into the purported bastion of "Islamist terror" is one of the most compelling in modern history. In order to understand this, we must first address the six years of the "socialist" government led by Zulfiqar Ali Bhutto which in critical ways set the stage for the military coup of 1977 that brought Zia into power, decisively changing the political, social and cultural landscape of Pakistan.

On December 20, 1971, a defeated and humiliated military command, headed by General Yahya Khan, handed over the reigns of power to Zulfiqar Ali Bhutto, the chairman of the People's Party of Pakistan. In the first of a series of ironies which were to define the tenor of this period, Pakistan's first democratically elected prime minister was also its first civilian chief martial law administrator.

The Pakistan which the new prime minister took charge of was a radically changed country. Among other things, it was literally a fraction of its former self, having lost half of its land mass and over half of its population in a brutal civil war that created the new nation-state of Bangladesh. This new Pakistan began life in the shadows of a series of crises—financial, military, political, moral and ideological—all connected to the army's brutal counter-insurgency operation in the former province of East Pakistan. Like all crises, they contained within them the seeds of opportunity. The anti-Ayub movement of 1968–69 had solidified a mainstream critique of the army that the loss of East Pakistan only exacerbated. The same period had also seen an unprecedented mass mobilization of leftist forces in West Pakistan, comprised of the radical sections of society—workers, peasants, students and intellectuals—which demanded far-reaching structural changes.

117

The objective conditions were thus ripe for a revolutionary transformation. The armed forces (which had ruled Pakistan directly or indirectly since its inception) were defeated and humiliated, the propertied classes were in disarray, the working classes had developed a political consciousness through the anti-Ayub movement, and Bhutto/PPP had clearly been elected with a popular mandate to pursue fundamental social change (Ali, 1983: 108).

Tragically, for Pakistan, however, while Bhutto was canny enough to take the revolutionary tide at the flood, he was most decidedly not the man to ride its cresting wave. Not only did he fail to transform Pakistani state and society in a meaningfully progressive way, he also put into motion processes and forces which reversed many of the democratic gains of the late 1960s, setting the stage for the radically new military regime of Zia ul Haq. In the process, he also ensured his own metaphorical (that is, political) and literal demise.

The army operation in East Pakistan had pitched the country into the throes of a moral crisis, the overcoming of which required an honest assessment and critique of the operation and the atrocities visited upon the (former) Bengali citizens of the state. Bhutto could easily have catalyzed this process, and in the bargain, disciplined and radically restructured the army, by making public the findings of the Humood-ur Rahman Commission Report. Named after the justice who led the commission of enquiry instituted to look into the performance of the armed forces during the war, the report was a strong indictment of the conduct of the military. However, Bhutto immediately suppressed the report, thus ensuring that the most pressing moral issue of the day—the use of army violence against fellow-citizens, and the subsequent shameful tragedy of the secession of the majority province from the nation-state—never became the subject of public discussion or any soul-searching at the national level.[1] Those who attempted to address it either found themselves facing a wall of silence or being criticized by friends and allies (Burney, 1996). Thereafter, the secession of East Bengal/Bangladesh became coded within official and mainstream discourse as, variously, a tragic "loss," the unfortunate amputation of a diseased limb and/ or the natural result of Bengali calumny and Indian machinations.[2]

Given his inside knowledge of the Pakistani military, Bhutto should have known that, left to its own devices, the army would never be content to play second fiddle to a civilian government. Far from being reprimanded, disciplined and defanged, however, the Pakistani Army was given a new lease on life, and soon "a new opportunity to re-occupy the country's political stage" (Ali, 1983:

118),[3] through an operation in Baluchistan under the aegis of a new commander-in-chief, General Tikka Khan, the "Butcher of Dhaka."

In the 1970 elections, the PPP had won majorities in Punjab and Sindh but had lost Sarhad (North West Frontier Province—NWFP)[4] and Baluchistan to the National Awami Party (NAP) and the *Jamiat Ulema-i Islam* ("Party of the Scholars of Islam"). Bhutto set about the task of destabilizing these provincial governments, banning the NAP and throwing its leadership into jail (Waseem, 2007; Jalal, 1990), while his machinations in Baluchistan resulted in an uprising which the army was sent in to quell. Unleashing a discredited and venal army—smarting from a recent humiliating defeat in a war in which it had already tasted the blood of its own people—on another civilian population amounted to an error of judgment so colossal that it defies comprehension. For its part, the army used Baluchistan as a political laboratory; as in East Bengal, it was an opportunity to operationalize what it had learned of guerilla warfare under American tutelage (Ali, 1983; Cohen, 2004).

At the same time that the repressive apparatus of the state was strengthened and reorganized,[5] civil rights such as freedom of expression came under attack, resulting in what a senior journalist referred to as "institutionalised tyranny" (Burney, 1996: 330).[6] Bhutto also began to move away from, and in fact undercut, the very constituencies which had brought him to power, namely the peasantry and the urban working class, while courting the landed interests. This shift in priorities was reflected within the PPP through a crackdown on organized labor and the purge of the members of the PPP's left-wing, radical and reformist sections (Noman, 1988).[7] The rightward drift of the party was also apparent in the rise in profile of the religious Right wing within the PPP as represented by Maulana Kausar Niazi, a former *Jama'at* stalwart who had fallen out with Maududi (Noman, 1988).

Thinking that Bhutto's electoral victory was tantamount to a victory of the working classes, the radicals within the PPP had begun to organize worker occupations of factories and establish people's courts. However, they were in for a rude awakening. In June 1972, during the visit of a World Bank team which had linked multilateral aid to control of the domestic labor situation, armed police shot and killed 30 workers on the streets of Karachi; later that year, a joint police and paramilitary operation killed 15 more while 4,000 others were arrested or driven underground.[8]

This was just the beginning of the regime's crackdown on the militant/revolutionary sections of the organized labor movement and its representatives within the PPP; mass arrests, torture and assassinations followed. There were 15 incidents of police firing on striking workers in various cities in 1972, 26 in 1973 and 32 in 1974 (Waseem, 2007).[9] Labor leaders were assassinated with impunity, noncompliant workers, many of whom fought back heroically, were subject to severe repression by the state, and the government looked the other way when members of their ranks were murdered by management goons (Ali, 1983). All in all, as Ahmad (1983: 103) put it, "the regime of the People's Party bequeathed to the working class a list of martyrs which is ... painfully long." At the same time, the regime moved to co-opt the trade union movement, working with mill owners and right-wing parties to break Marxist unions and replace them with PPP-dominated ones (Ahmad, 1983),[10] while its attempts to buy off workers injected cynicism into the working-class movement.

Unexpected as these actions against the radicals were, what really took insiders and observers alike by surprise was the purge of the *reformist* Left from the PPP, members of which formed a significant part of Bhutto's cabinet. The Punjabi landed elite, which had hitherto kept its distance from the PPP, correctly understood the purge as an invitation to join the PPP, which they gladly accepted, given the perks that came with membership in the ruling party. Such was the "scale and rapid pace of the process" that, as Noman (1988: 104) notes, "twenty-eight out of the thirty-three leading aristocratic families of the Punjab had representatives in the PPP by 1976."[11]

The regime's lack of commitment to social democracy was also visible in two of its most touted "socialist" initiatives—land reforms and the nationalization of key industries. Nationalization amounted to mere sound and fury (Waseem, 2007); a few industrialists were paraded in handcuffs on television, while Bhutto gave fiery speeches about blood-sucking capitalists. In actual fact, all expropriations were handsomely compensated, while foreign capital was left untouched at the behest of the IMF. The first set of land reforms were similarly superficial, doing little to change production relations in the countryside or disturb the power of the large landlords (Ali, 1983) despite the fanfare with which they were announced. In fact, the upper strata of the rural propertied classes became the main beneficiaries of Bhutto's "Green Revolution" (Ali, 1983; Hussain, 1989).[12]

For the vast majority of Pakistanis,[13] this was a period of declining living standards both economically (through an increase in the cost of living and in the rates of absolute and relative poverty) and politically (in the form of state repression and the loss of civil liberties). A rising debt burden, falling domestic savings and high inflation all contributed to the state's inability to fund social welfare programs in health and education.[14] In order to bring inflation under control, various subsidies, including those on food, were reduced or eliminated, leading to urban protests which the government sought to manage by increasing the wages of lower-level government employees and of industrial labor. The middle classes thus bore the brunt of the subsidy reduction, adding to their growing resentment (Noman, 1988).

COZYING UP TO THE GULF STATES

Bhutto, seeking to establish his credentials as an independent Third World leader, pulled Pakistan out of the Commonwealth and SEATO (and thus symbolically out of the ambit of the US sphere of influence), while actively looking elsewhere for alternative bases of support (Jalal, 1990). Certain significant global realignments of this time were fortuitous for him, even as they proved to be a Faustian bargain for the country in the long term. The same oil crisis that had exacerbated Pakistan's economic woes had resulted in the rise in international status of the oil-producing countries, especially the Arab ones, increasing their heft on the world stage. Bhutto turned to these countries for economic and political support, successfully lobbying to host the second summit of the Organization of the Islamic Conference.

By the time the summit was held in 1974, Middle Eastern countries accounted for 30.8 per cent of Pakistan's exports, up from 17.2 per cent just a year earlier (Ali, 1983), and also became major importers of Pakistani labor. This new relationship with the oil-rich countries of the Gulf (especially the UAE and Saudi Arabia) not only had a visible impact on Pakistan's economy and society, but also changed Pakistani culture and politics in ways which took a little longer to manifest. Among other things, working-class radicalism dissipated, since the turnover in these lucrative Gulf jobs ensured that a large percentage of the working class was hopeful, at any given time, of securing employment abroad. There was another, less direct but no less important impact. The tens of thousands of workers that went to these countries as immigrant laborers came back more socially conservative and more religiously inclined than before, even as their increased purchasing power contributed to the rise of conspicuous consumption on an unprecedented scale (Ballard, 1989).[15]

While Pakistan provided the Gulf oil kingdoms with, among other things, training for students in the medical and engineering fields, soldiers and military expertise, the real pound of flesh it had to surrender to its benefactors was a greater say in its internal affairs. The Saudis made it clear to the countries benefiting from their largesse that secularism was to be discouraged; in addition, it soon became obvious that they intended to support Islamist groups whose ideology corresponded most closely to their own. In Pakistan, the natural choice was the *Jama'at*, since Maududi was held in high regard by the Saudi king. Tariq Ali (1983) argues that there was a direct correspondence between the level of Pakistan's trade with Saudi Arabia and the influence of the *Jama'at* within the state apparatus. The relationship between the Pakistan armed forces and their counterparts in the Gulf oil kingdoms had its own ideological fallout, and resulted in an increase in the influence of Islamism within the armed forces (Ahmad, 1983).

The deepening relationship between Saudi Arabia and Pakistan, and the direct backing of the Saudis gave the religious right in Pakistan the wherewithal to challenge the PPP's secularism and social liberalism. Having undercut his progressive constituency which alone could have buffered him against demands made by the Islamists, Bhutto rendered himself vulnerable to the assault from the religious right.

CULTURE AND IDEOLOGY UNDER BHUTTO

Bhutto's most progressive contribution was in the cultural and ideological realm. While all the earlier regimes had been socially and culturally liberal, never before had socialist ideas and symbols enjoyed official support and sanction (nor have they since). Progressive poetry was actively promoted, and socialist iconography was ubiquitous in public spaces. Although socialism as a political ideal in Pakistan did not begin with Bhutto, it was through (and under) him that it gained a popular currency, going from a subversive ideology to "a household word and a symbol for legitimate social aspiration" (Ahmad, 1983: 105).

The socialist theme was carried over into foreign policy as well. Bhutto consciously cultivated an anti-imperialist persona, distancing Pakistan from the ambit of US influence, normalizing relations and cultivating close ties with socialist states, and supporting anti-imperialist liberation struggles and movements across Afro-Asia. This was reflected in the official media, and for the first time in Pakistan's history, socialist countries and national liberation movements were officially represented as friends of the Pakistani people (Ahmad, 1983).

The impact of this state discourse of socialism on everyday culture was immense, even in the absence of any meaningful reforms. As Ahmad puts it:

> In the terrain of ideological class struggle, the permeation of social-democratic ideas deep into the countryside, whatever their practical application or lack of it, constituted a definite advance in a country which was born in religious bigotry, was dominated by semi-feudal social structures, was fed for two decades a controlled diet of Dulles-style anti-communism, was ruled by the armed forces for thirteen years, and which therefore lacked any widespread culture of secular, democratic, progressive ideas. (Ibid.: 104–5)

Even nationalization and land reform had a progressive impact despite their actual failure as mechanisms of redistribution in so far as they symbolized and valorized the *idea* of redistribution. The propertied elite understood the potential of this symbolic socialism all too well and nervously observed its positive effects on the self-esteem and self-confidence of the poor and dispossessed.[16] This was the reason for the propertied classes' anxiety under Bhutto, despite the obvious benefits they drew from the regime. Executives of the Pakistan Chamber of Commerce actually complained about the negative portrayal of industrialists and traders in radio and television plays, citing the serialization of *Khuda ki Basti* ("The Abode of God," an award-winning Urdu novel) as a case in point.[17]

A RIGHT-WING MOVEMENT AND A COUP

The opposition to Bhutto drew from different right-wing constituencies. While the socially and culturally liberal propertied classes were deeply uncomfortable with Bhutto's socialist rhetoric, the significant *muhajir* population of the urban areas of Sindh was angry at what they perceived as the Sindhi chauvinism of the provincial and federal PPP government. These grievances were fully exploited by religious parties such as the *Jama'at* and the *Jamiat Ulema-i Pakistan* (JUP), whose membership drew heavily from the *muhajir* community.[18] Along with feeding the movement against

Bhutto, these grievances were leveraged to undermine working-class unity in urban Sindh (Waseem, 2007).

The real roots of the anti-Bhutto movement lay in the reactionary sections of the urban petit bourgeoisie,[19] who were as opposed to the regime's economic program as to its liberal cultural and social policies. Given that it was also within this class that the fascist ideology of the *Jama'at* had found the most fertile ground, the emerging movement had a distinctly "Islamic" flavor. Emboldened by the support from Saudi Arabia in particular, the religious Right wing (led by the *Jama'at*) which had been slowly gathering strength through the Bhutto regime by infiltrating key institutions such as the army, education and the press,[20] and which had been given increasing space within national politics and discourse by Bhutto himself, now decided to make a bid for power.

The mobilization against the regime started to mount towards the end of 1973. The charges of immorality against Bhutto levied by the religious Right, began to grow in intensity. Having alienated and undermined the only genuinely progressive forces within Pakistani society—namely the Left, and especially the organized working-class movement—and confident that he could outmaneuver the forces of the right, Bhutto opted for appeasement rather than confrontation.[21] The man who had once flamboyantly responded to the charge that he drank alcohol by declaring that at least he didn't drink the blood of the common man, now declared Pakistan a dry state, shut down casinos and nightclubs, changed the weekly holiday from Sunday to Friday, and outlawed gambling. But instead of appeasing the Right, these concessions only served to indicate his vulnerability, and turned up the pressure on him. In the most shocking and egregious concession of all, Bhutto officially designated members of the Ahmediyya sect non-Muslim. By doing so, he not only turned on yet another group of his erstwhile supporters, but also seriously and irreversibly damaged the secular fabric of Pakistani society and state.

By 1976, the internal pressures had started to strain Bhutto's hold on power and he dissolved Parliament, announcing new elections in early 1977. In January 1977, the opposition coalesced into a nine-party coalition called the Pakistan National Alliance (PNA). Although the PNA was comprised of both secular and religious parties, their critique of Bhutto was articulated in a distinctly moral-religious register, and their chosen slogan was a demand to institute the *Nizam-i Mustafa* ("System of the Prophet"), the details of which were left deliberately vague in order to mobilize widespread support.

Despite all the harm he had caused the working-class movement, Bhutto had not lost the support of the Punjabi and Sindhi working class and peasantry.[22] By all accounts, the PPP was set to score a decisive victory in the elections, but Bhutto made the strategic error—born of hubris and insecurity—of rigging the elections. This proved to be the catalyst that consolidated the brewing tensions and grievances against him into a "meticulously planned and well-financed post-electoral campaign" (Jalal, 1990: 318) of "destabilization" two days after the announcement of election results on March 7 (Ahmad, 1983: 109). This campaign was backed by the army, the urban and rural bourgeoisie as well as Saudi Arabia, and had the ideological support of the lumpen proletariat, the urban petit bourgeoisie, and even professional groups such as lawyers (Ahmad, 1983); the *Jama'at* and the JUP provided the organizational base while *madrassas*, mosques and commercial associations along with a few (anti-progressive) trade unions formed the key organizational units for the movement (Sayeed, 1980).[23]

The intensifying nature of the agitations forced Bhutto to hold talks with the PNA, and an agreement was reached under which new elections were scheduled. However, on July 5, Bhutto and members of his cabinet were arrested by troops under orders from the military high command. The military had launched "Operation Fairplay" and Pakistan's third—and most brutal—period of martial law was about to begin.

"PAKISTAN KA MATLAB KYA? PHAANSI, KO*RE*, GENERAL ZIA!" ("WHAT DOES PAKISTAN STAND FOR? HANGINGS, LASHINGS, GENERAL ZIA!")[24]

In 1971, the generals had handed power over to Bhutto only because they had lost national prestige and so could not hope to hold on to it. For his part Bhutto, while he feared the army and tried to manage it, failed to realize that the armed forces essentially suffered him in power only because of the level of mass support he had, and would continue to do so only as long as he had it. As soon as this support began to evaporate, the army moved in for the kill.[25]

In his first address to the nation, General Zia ul Haq (the leader of the coup) declared that the army had had to step in to prevent a break-up of the country and that it had no interest in staying in power. He promised elections in 90 days; however, it was clear from the very beginning that the army had no intention of leaving the political stage. Its actions belied its claims; the denationalization of industries, the announcement of a new Five-Year Plan, the establishment of the Islamic Ideology Council, and the reorganization of the judiciary are not the kinds of steps taken by interim regimes (Noman, 1988).

The army coup of 1977 was very different from the two earlier ones in 1958 and 1969. For one, it had no legitimacy, and no real social base of support. In 1958, the fact that the army had displaced unpopular politicians had garnered it some support; this time, however, it was displacing a popularly elected government (and a highly popular prime minister) which may have been in crisis, but certainly not of the sort that justified army intervention, let alone a takeover. In fact, the popular support which Bhutto had undermined through his policies returned in spades as soon as he was put under preventive detention.

In 1958, moreover, the army was a new political player with an untested reputation for discipline and integrity. By contrast, in 1977 it was an institution tainted by the humiliating loss of Bangladesh, the movement against Ayub Khan, and Yahya Khan's despised interregnum.[26] Most importantly, this time around, the army was actually a different beast; fresh from the killing fields of Baluchistan and East Bengal, it was a far more venal and brutal an entity. It was also increasingly imbued with a religious ideology/ethos which was in sharp contrast to the urbane secularism which characterized its earlier avatar. When Bhutto had removed the top generals in 1972 as part of his internal reshuffle of the army, he had inadvertently contributed to a demographic and ideological shift which had been taking place in the army since Independence. Under the British, the upper strata of the armed forces had been made up of British officers and, later, Sandhurst-trained scions of the landed elite, while junior officers and the rank-and-file came from the relatively prosperous peasantry of Central Punjab. With new opportunities opening up for these classes in the public and private sector after independence, recruitment to the middle and lower levels of the armed forces came increasingly from the impoverished areas of northern Punjab and from the migrants from eastern Punjab, Zia being a case in point (Noman, 1988). In addition to the fact that both groups were more socially conservative than the classes from which military recruitment had earlier been drawn, members of the migrant group were also more strongly attached to the de-territorialized nationalist ideology of an "Islamic nation" than were the non-migrants (Ahmad, 1983; Ali, 1983; Cohen, 1984; Noman, 1988).

These changes within the army were also the result of the *Jama'at*'s hard work in infiltrating crucial institutions. Having received only 5 per cent of the vote in the 1970 elections, the *Jama'at* had given up on trying to gain power through the electoral process and had started focusing instead on preparing the ideological ground for a coup (Ahmad, 1983). Given the political, demographic and cultural shifts of the time, it found fertile ground for its proselytizing efforts within the armed forces.[27] This relationship between the *Jama'at* and the army was instrumental in giving the coup its Islamic face, and the *Jama'at* a presence within the state (Jalal, 1990).[28]

At the time of the coup, no one could have foreseen that this would turn out to be the longest and most brutal martial law regime in Pakistan's history, or that it would alter Pakistani state and society so fundamentally. The 11 years of the Zia regime— cut short only because of the mysterious airplane crash of August 17, 1988 which finally killed him—were a period of unimaginable horror for Pakistani society. The coup was the military establishment's way of turning back Bhutto's "socialist" initiatives, wiping out any trace of populism from the face of Pakistani society, and restoring the *status quo ante* in which the balance of power was unambiguously in favor of the propertied classes. To this end, they did not hesitate to use the most coercive of means.

The regime's combination of an exceptionally repressive (even by Pakistani standards) martial law bolstered by a program of Maududite Islamic reforms was specifically designed to brutalize Pakistani society through a reign of terror. In fact, terror was a crucial and well-considered part of the strategy of rule for the martial law regime from the very beginning. Zia openly argued that "[m]artial law *should* be based on fear," and in keeping with this doctrine, once breezily stated that all it would take to restore law and order was a "few more hangings" (Noman, 1988: 122). In his book *The Quranic Concept of War* that was commissioned by Zia (who authored its foreword, while A.K. Brohi wrote the preface), Brigadier S.K. Malik was even more explicit about the uses of terror: "Terror struck into the heart of enemies is not only a means, it is an end in itself. Once a condition of terror into the opponent's heart is obtained, hardly anything is left to be achieved … Terror is not a means of imposing decisions upon the enemy, it is *the decision* we wish to impose upon him" (Malik, 1979: 59, cited in Cohen, 2004: 118). For the Pakistani military, "the enemy" Malik refers to were, more often than not, the citizens of Pakistan itself. The introduction of medieval punishments such as public flogging, stoning to death, and the amputation of hands and feet were similarly part of a conscious design to terrorize and brutalize Pakistani society.[29] While these atrocities are typically associated with Zia's Islamization program, it is important to note that their introduction *preceded* the announcement of the *Nizam-i Mustafa*.

Military dictatorships are inherently unstable even if they begin life with the blessings of the people; the fig leaf of a civilian government is therefore one of their first concerns. In his first speech to the nation after the coup, Zia insisted that the military had no interest in staying in power longer than was necessary to restore law and order and promised to hold elections within 90 days. Aside from the question of whether or not the army ever intended to hold elections within this promised time-frame, it definitely could not *afford* to hold them as long as they could be expected to result in a victory for Bhutto or the PPP. The main reason for this, aside from protecting the interests of the establishment, was self-preservation on the part of the coup-makers, since under the 1973 Constitution, coups had been declared acts of high treason and carried an automatic death sentence.[30] Preventing the possibility of a PPP victory thus became the *raison d'être* of the first few years of the Zia regime. The quiet, pious and unassuming general who Bhutto had promoted over the heads of more senior officers because of his apparent lack of ambition and his loyalty, turned out to be the canniest of political animals.

Bhutto was released three weeks after having been put in "protective custody" along with other PPP leaders, and immediately launched into his election campaign through a nationwide tour. The coup had resulted in increasing Bhutto's political capital, and the size of the crowds at his rallies and their emotional response made the regime realize how deeply they had underestimated the danger he posed. Bhutto was soon rearrested, this time on the charge of conspiracy to murder the father of a political opponent (Waseem, 2007). In early March 1978, Zia canceled the promised elections, claiming that he had found a number of "irregularities" in the previous regime which he felt it his duty to investigate and that elections could only be held after due "accountability." The *Jama'at* was the only member of the PNA to support this line. Subsequently, "white papers" on various aspects of the performance of Bhutto's government were produced and circulated. Political parties were banned along with all political activity.

On March 18, the Lahore High Court found Bhutto guilty of conspiracy to murder and sentenced him to death; in early February of the following year, the Supreme Court upheld the conviction and the sentence by a 4-3 decision despite the fact that a death sentence was hitherto unheard of for such a charge. Significantly, the three dissenting opinions were from the non-Punjabi judges on the bench, while all four Punjabi judges voted to uphold the High Court decision (Noman, 1988). Bhutto was killed in the early hours of the morning of April 4, despite numerous international pleas of clemency, and with unexpected swiftness; his wife Nusrat and daughter Benazir had been allowed out of their detention to see him the night before. His body was secretly airlifted to his family graveyard in Garhi Khuda Buksh in interior Sindh in order to reduce the likelihood of public protests.

Later the same year, Zia appointed himself president and after rescheduling elections twice, eventually postponed them indefinitely. The reason for this change of heart was the fact that candidates affiliated with the PPP had won a resounding victory in the non-party local body elections held in September/October that year (Ali, 1983). Political parties and activities were once again banned, and extensive press censorship with harsh punishments for infractions was put in place (Talbot, 1998; Waseem, 2007).[31]

Undermining the PPP's influence thus continued to be a major preoccupation for Zia, even after he had eliminated its charismatic leader (Siddiqa, 2007). The Political Parties (Amendment) Ordinance of 1979 declared that any party which propagated views designed to defame or bring the judiciary or armed forces of Pakistan into ridicule would not be registered by the Election Commission. When the multi-party Movement to Restore Democracy (in which the PPP played a leading role) put out a call to boycott the 1985 elections, such appeals were declared criminal acts (Talbot, 1998).

In 1983, Zia once more promised that elections would be held, but on an "Islamic basis"; in other words, candidates could not run on party platforms. Further, they would take place with a system of separate electorates, a long-standing demand of the *Jama'at*. He also made it clear that he would continue on as president. Meanwhile, the ban on political activity by PPP members was extended for another ten years. The non-party nature of the elections, another move designed to undermine the PPP, reaffirmed traditional bases of patronage and support, and prioritized local over national issues, thereby reversing the democratic gains of the late 1960s. Wealth proved vitally important in mobilizing political support, and as a result, the National Assembly which was finally elected consisted of large landlords and members of a rising industrial and commercial elite (Waseem, 2007).

Martial law stayed in effect for almost ten months following the elections while Zia sought indemnification for all acts of the martial law regime and armed the office of the president with extraordinary powers (Burki, 1991).[32] The most important of these was the Eighth Amendment to the Constitution, which conferred on the president the power to dismiss the prime minister and to dissolve the National Assembly as well as the right to appoint provincial governors and the chief of the armed forces (Noman, 1988). This effectively undermined the parliamentary system and democratic politics in general, in so far as it ensured that civilian governments would always be vulnerable to manipulation by the military establishment and an unelected president.

RESTORING THE *STATUS QUO ANTE*

The purpose of the July coup was to reverse even the minimal pro-labor and pro-peasant policies of the Bhutto government and to reassure the propertied classes that they were solidly back in the saddle. It was also deemed important to rid Pakistan of the virus of populism and to cleanse Pakistani society of the socialist ideas that had begun to circulate and proliferate during the Bhutto period.

Accordingly, one of the first actions of the martial law regime was the denationalization of industry, with Zia echoing the arguments of anti-socialist intellectuals such as Brohi and Rahman that the forcible acquisition of property by the state without "adequate compensation" was un-Islamic. The flour and rice-husking mills were denationalized soon after the imposition of martial law, and 297 of the 579 nationalized cotton-ginning factories were returned to their former owners (Sayeed, 1980). Significantly, however, institutes of higher education nationalized under Bhutto were not denationalized, since a nationalized education ensured a more effective transfer of state ideology.[33]

It was also made clear to workers and peasants that the tide of history had shifted and that henceforth no agitation from their end would be tolerated; strikes and other forms of labor unrest were criminalized and made punishable by public flogging and/ or rigorous imprisonment (Jalal, 1990).[34] On January 2, 1978, 19 workers were shot dead by police in Multan, which marked the beginning of a brutal attack on the working classes. The regime also rescinded the second set of land reforms which Bhutto had passed just prior to the 1977 elections, resulting in a sharp increase in the number of tenant evictions (Sayeed, 1980).

Despite the draconian laws against labor action, strikes and labor protests did not come to an end. The All Pakistan Labour Conference voiced its strong criticism of both denationalization and tenant evictions, and demanded that they be reversed. The Pakistan Mazdoor Kissan Party organized a Unity Conference to bring together all left-wing forces; the conference similarly denounced the government's anti-labor and anti-peasant policies and voiced its strong support of strikers (Sayeed, 1980). The regime was, however, brutal in getting its anti-labor message across; leaders and workers were, like other dissidents, arrested, tortured and killed with impunity.[35]

Zia and the military establishment had learned the right lessons from the 1968–69 movement, and so ensured that universities would no longer be the hub of left-wing dissent. To this end, student unions were banned, as was all political activity on college and university campuses. The *Jami'at Tulaba-i Islam* (the *Jama'at*'s student wing) was however given the run of the campuses where it proceeded to terrorize students and faculty alike.

THE *NIZAM-I MUSTAFA*

At the same time as he was reversing the PPP's modest reforms, Zia claimed divine sanction for transforming Pakistan into an Islamic society, and declared that this required a theocratic state. Unsurprisingly, the model for this Islamic state and society turned out to be the one laid out by Maududi. To this end, Zia officially announced the launch of the *Nizam-i Mustafa* on December 2, 1978, the first day of the new year in the Islamic calendar.[36]

Through the *Nizam-i Mustafa*, Zia was able to successfully transform Pakistani state and society in fundamental ways. That this process was neither unilateral nor smooth, even for a regime as brutal as this one, was due both to the resilience of (old and new) progressive forces within Pakistani society, as well as to the country's social, cultural and even religious diversity. The use of "Islam" to legitimate authoritarianism was not new or unique in Pakistan's short history; what was different about Zia's deployment was its ideological content. Whereas Ayub's Islam was distinctly modernist (if still anti-democratic), Zia's Islam reflected the social conservatism of the urban petit bourgeoisie and the *Jama'at*, and was close to the official *wahhabi* ideology of the Saudi ruling family. Thus, while

Zia's argument for the presidential system of governance—that it was the most appropriate one for Pakistan because it most closely approximated the position of the *amir* in Islam—was similar to Ayub's, there was little else that was common to the two dictators' versions of Islam.

In keeping with Maududi's political ideas, Zia declared that secularism, socialism, democracy and political parties were "un-Islamic." The purpose of elections was to identify the people best qualified to *implement* God's law, not to actually engage in any law-making (Noman, 1988). Accordingly, in 1981, Zia established a 284-member *Majlis-i Shoora* ("Assembly of advisers") comprised of intellectuals, scholars, journalists, and so on, all nominated by him (Burki, 1991). Needless to say, the *Jama'at* had significant representation in this august body, just as it had in Zia's original cabinet.

Zia had made known his interest in Islamizing Pakistan's legal system as early as 1978. Accordingly, in 1979, he established the shariat benches of the four provincial high courts through a Presidential Order. These benches had the power and the mandate to strike down any law found "repugnant" to Islam; they were replaced the following year by the Federal Shariat Court (FSC).[37] As it transpired, the government eventually found the FSC not amenable enough to its interests. For example, the FSC declared that the land reforms of 1972 and 1977 were perfectly in keeping with the injunctions of Islam. It also struck down a petition claiming that political parties were un-Islamic, and declared that stoning to death was not an appropriate *hadd* ("limit," or in this context, maximum) punishment for adultery, in effect declaring it to be un-Islamic. The government found itself in the embarrassing position of having to appeal to the shariat apellate bench of the Supreme Court. This potentially problematic issue was resolved once and for all by the simple expedient of appointing *ulema* (religious leaders) as judges to the FSC; the inconvenient ruling was subsequently reversed (Talbot, 1998).

From 1982 onwards, *ulema* also sat on the three-man shariat apellate bench of the Supreme Court, and *qazi*[38] courts were established to decide local cases according to the shariat.[39] By the time Zia was done, Pakistan had a legal system consisting of civil courts, military courts, and federal and lower shariat courts, with jurisprudence spread between the Pakistan Penal Code, Martial Law Regulations and an emerging body of Islamic laws.[40] This insertion of *ulema* and lesser religious functionaries (such as *qazis*) into the state was not limited to the juridico-legal system; in fact, they became fairly ubiquitous at all levels of the state. They sat on the National Film Censorship Board and were appointed to all five television stations in order to ensure that the instructions of the information minister and the president regarding matters ranging from the content of the programming to the dress code of the performers were followed faithfully. They even sat on something called the *ruat-i halal* committee, whose sole mandate was to determine whether or not the new moon signaling the Muslim holy day of Eid-ul-Fitr had actually been sighted.[41]

The deployment of Maududi's hardline model of the Islamic state by Zia, with its totalitarian emphasis on unity over diversity, its glorification of a strong (male) leader as the source of political and religious authority in an Islamic state, and its displacement of all political, economic and social issues onto the terrain of the moral, directly served the interests of the military regime. Among other things, it allowed for a repressive authoritarianism that previous regimes (civilian or military) could only have dreamt of, since it purportedly had divine sanction. It neatly resolved the shame of the humiliation of an "Islamic state" in 1971 at the hands of "infidels," by setting up a distinction between the period of "irreligion" and "immorality" before the coup and the period of true Islam which the coup had allegedly ushered in. In fact, all the problems that Pakistan faced before or since could be attributed to a lack of morality, while the solution to all problems was seen to be an increased piety, which would be imposed by force if necessary.

The regime's emphasis on public piety fundamentally (and explicitly) contravened the principle of secularism by moving religious observance from the realm of the private to that of the public (that is, the state). A media campaign was launched to exhort people to be more pious themselves (Mumtaz and Shaheed, 1987), and to ensure that their neighbors were as well, thus successfully sowing the seeds of an everyday fascism which was far more insidious than anything that had come before. The office of *Nazim-i Salaat* ("Controller of Prayers") was established in 1984 to enforce prayers in government and semi-government offices during office hours, and arrangements were made for prayers in public places such as railway stations, airports and bus stops (Siddiqa, 2007).[42] An *Ehteram-i Ramzan* ("respect for the month of fasting") Ordinance was issued under which the selling and eating of food and drink as well as the smoking of cigarettes in public and in government and semi-government offices was banned during the day during Ramadan.

A serious implication of the construction of the pious Muslim male as the ideal citizen of the Islamic Republic was the denigration of women and non-Muslims within the body politic as well as society at large. Like all conservative and reactionary religious traditions, Maududite Islam was invested in the control of women; therefore it was hardly surprising that the majority of Zia's Islamization efforts were aimed at regulating the mobility and visibility of women and effectively criminalizing their sexuality. The emergent official discourse of *"chaadar aur chaardivaari"* ("the veil and the four corners of the home"; the appropriate boundaries for women) made it clear that women were to bear the brunt of Zia's "Islamization." This was entirely in keeping with the regime's relationship with the *Jama'at* and the urban petit bourgeoisie, which felt threatened by the increase in the numbers of working and professional women which had occurred over the past few decades. As a first step, directives were issued to the five television stations to ensure that all female announcers and performers appearing on television covered their heads.[43] Men were simply instructed to wear the "national" dress. This was followed by edicts to all government offices requiring women employees to wear "Islamic" dress—a full-sleeved *shalvaar kameez* with a *chaadar* as an additional covering.[44] Zia was to make it a habit to present women with *chaadars* as gifts in his official capacity.

The policing of women's dress and deportment and their appearance in the public sphere was further aided by the government's anti-obscenity campaign, which essentially equated women in the public sphere with obscenity (Khan and Saigol, 2004). From 1980 onwards, women's appearance on televised advertisements was allowed only under certain conditions—they were not to be shown in advertisements for products which had no relevance to women, when allowed to appear, they were not to be given more than 25 per cent of the commercial time, and were always to be depicted wearing modest versions[45] of the "national dress" (Mumtaz and Shaheed, 1987: 82). The emphasis on the "national dress" for women was less about enforcing the *shalvaar kameez*, which was already commonplace, and more a campaign against the *sari*, which was considered to be a lingering and undesirable Hindu cultural influence (Khan, 1985; Khan and Saigol, 2004).[46]

Under pressure from religious groups, women athletes were at various points prevented from playing domestically as well as from participating in international sporting events elsewhere. No formal directives were issued, most likely to avoid being censured and possibly banned by international sporting authorities. Pakistan was warned, for example, that it would be formally expelled from the International Olympic Association if it prevented women's participation in sports. Only under intense pressure from the newly formed Women's Action Forum did the government finally respond; its official stand was that women would not be barred from playing sports (and would even be encouraged) as long as they did so under "Islamic" conditions. These conditions involved not "exposing" themselves to *na-mahrams*,[47] which precluded all spectator sports. In 1982, Zia finally announced that while women athletes would be free to play international teams in Pakistan, they would not be allowed to attend events abroad. The issue was hotly contested in the press and on the streets, with feminist activists and women athletes picketing the airport when the all-men's team was leaving for the Asian Games held in New Delhi (Mumtaz and Shaheed, 1987).

In 1979, Zia promulgated the first set of "Islamic" laws, the Hudood Ordinances, which covered crimes that were considered the most serious: theft/robbery, rape, pre- and extra-marital sex, consumption of alcohol, and heresy. The first one to be passed was the Offences Against Property Ordinance that covered theft and robbery. This was followed by a Prohibition Order, which replaced the punishments for the drinking and sale of alcohol that had been instituted under Bhutto in 1977 (imprisonment up to six months and a Rs 5,000 fine, or both) by 80 lashes. The law did not apply to non-Muslims who could, and still can, obtain licenses to drink, procure and manufacture alcohol.

The promulgation of the Zina Ordinance,[48] a set of "Islamic" laws delineating the bounds of "legal" sexual activity, revealed how central the issue of controlling women's sexuality was to the regime. *Zina* in Arabic means "illegitimate sex" and the Ordinance covered adultery, fornication (pre- and extra-marital sex) and rape, and made each a crime against the state. The punishment for unmarried offenders (male or female) was set at a hundred lashes each, while the maximum (*hadd*) punishment for married offenders (again, whether male or female) was stoning to death. There was no provision for rape within marriage, and the wording of the law required the testimony of four adult Muslim male witnesses of "good moral character" who had witnessed the act of penetration, in order to support a charge of *zina*. While the purported idea behind the absurd evidentiary requirements was to protect innocent people from false charges, extending it to cases of rape effectively made it impossible for a rapist to be convicted, while a woman who tried to file a charge of rape could be prosecuted by the state for *zina* because she had, in effect, admitted to having sexual intercourse outside of marriage.

As if the actual ordinance wasn't problematic enough, judges took it upon themselves to "creatively" interpret it and thereby extend its reach. Thus, one judge sentenced a woman for adultery on the evidence of her 13-year old daughter, despite the stringent evidentiary rules laid out in the ordinance. In one landmark case, a woman called Fehmida had eloped with and married one Allah Buksh. Fehmida's family charged Allah Buksh with abduction, but the police took it upon themselves to register a case of adultery. Despite the fact that there were no witnesses to testify against the couple, the judge sentenced them to *hadd* punishments for *zina*; the case was later dismissed by the Supreme Court.

This became a pattern; egregious examples of abuse of this law would emerge, and would be dismissed by the Supreme Court, no doubt because of the adverse international attention they attracted. No woman or man was stoned to death for *zina*, but in 1983, Lal Mai became the first woman to be publicly flogged (Mumtaz and Shaheed, 1987). The extra-legal effect of these laws and directives aimed at women, not to mention the administration of corporal punishment to women in public, was to create a social atmosphere where they did not feel safe in the public sphere while men were given sanction to police the behavior of all women, even those they were not related to. Predictably, incidents of violence against women mounted (Rouse, 1992). The Zina Ordinance also became an effective tool through which to punish wayward wives, daughters and sisters; thousands of women were (and continue to be) incarcerated on charges of pre- and extra-marital sex, usually brought by their own family; women from the lower middle and lower classes are the law's biggest victims (Jahangir and Jilani, 1990; Khan 2006).[49]

Within the discourse of the regime, the terms *momin* ("pious Muslim") or *mard-i momin* ("pious Muslim man") became synonymous with the normative citizen, with predictable implications for women and non-Muslims.[50] Accordingly, the new legal/constitutional regime distinguished between Muslims and non-Muslims, between women and men, and between Muslim women and Muslim men, with the pious Muslim (Sunni) male emerging as the only true subject of rights and privileges, and all others being relegated to the status of second-class citizens. The Law of Evidence, for example, originally laid out that the testimony of a Muslim woman for crimes not covered by the Hudood Ordinance or other laws was half that of a Muslim man, while non-Muslims were only allowed to provide evidence for trials involving non-Muslims. Likewise, Muslims were not allowed to testify in cases involving non-Muslims.

The second-class citizenship of non-Muslims was ensured in other ways as well. They were politically disenfranchised through the system of separate electorates, a "reform" which the *Jama'at* had been clamoring for since the formation of Pakistan when the fate of the country's minorities was first being decided. Under this system, a certain number of seats were reserved for non-Muslims at the provincial and national level, and only non-Muslims could vote for them; more importantly, non-Muslims could not vote for Muslim seats. In a context such as Pakistan's where Muslims are overwhelmingly in the demographic majority, a system of separate electorates effectively amounted to a radical disenfranchisement of non-Muslims. These changes effectively cast non-Muslims, whose presence within the body politic had always been a source of cognitive dissonance, outside of the state.

The religious lobby once again pushed for further legislation against the Ahmediyya community, the result of which was the passing of Section 298-B and 298-C of the Pakistan Penal Code which made it a criminal offense for members of this community to "pose as Muslims," to use "Islamic terminology" for their own practices, or to "preach or propagate by words either spoken or written" (Talbot, 1998: 283). The changes in the Blasphemy Law opened both Ahmedis and non-Muslim Pakistanis to violence at the hands of the state and extra-state actors.[51] A relic of the colonial past, the Blasphemy Law was originally written so as to ensure respect for "religious sentiments" but not just those of the majority community. The scope and focus of this law changed completely under Zia as the amendments added to it simultaneously widened its purview and narrowed its focus. Acts of "disrespect" to the Prophet Muhammad, to his family, his companions and Islamic symbols were made cognizable offenses, with the punishment ranging from three years of imprisonment (for disrespect to the Companions) to life imprisonment (for defiling the Quran) to death (for disrespect to the Prophet).

CHALLENGES TO THE REGIME

Islamization in Pakistan was far from a smooth or consistent project, even though (or perhaps because) it was imposed from above by a brutal military dictatorship. The various forms of resistance to it mapped onto the diversity of Pakistani society. The minority Shia community, for example, responded angrily to the compulsory deduction of 2.5 per cent from the income and savings of all Muslims under the Zakat and Ushr Ordinance, forcing the government to exempt the community from the provisions of the law (Noman, 1988).[52] Similarly, the attempt to regulate heterodox practices such as pigeon-flying at Sufi shrines were met with such intense resistance that the state was forced to backtrack.[53] In addition to the many cases of informal and everyday defiance of the regime and its policies ("Islamic" or otherwise), there was also significant organized political resistance, despite the high cost of dissent. Opposition to the regime was consolidated in the Movement for Restoration of Democracy (MRD), a coalition of parties led by the PPP. In Sindh, the MRD movement triggered a militant regional struggle which raged across the length and breadth of the province.

Both military rule and Islamization resulted in an increased centralization of power, which inflamed the national question. The Zia regime managed to pacify Baluchistan and Sarhad, but this time around it was Sindh's turn to explode. Since Bhutto was a Sindhi, Sindhis took his removal from power, his incarceration and his execution to be an attack on them. This feeling was reinforced by, among other things, the fact that the coup had resulted in the *muhajir* community in Sindh regaining the ground they had lost under Bhutto. At the same time, martial law and the expansion of the military into civilian institutions translated into increased Punjabi domination.[54] The bulk of newly irrigated lands in Sindh were allocated to retired military and civil service officers, most of whom were non-Sindhi (Noman, 1988; Waseem, 2007).[55] Led by left-wing parties and organizations such as the Sindh Awami Tehreek and the Sindh Hari Committee, and fueled by radical students, peasants and workers, the pace and intensity of the revolt was such that it took the army four months of massive repression to quell it (Noman, 1988). In the first three weeks alone, almost 2,000 people were arrested, 189 killed and 126 injured (Talbot, 1998).

Perhaps the most iconic example of organized resistance to the Zia regime and specifically to its Islamization policies, was the one led by the newly formed Women's Action Forum (WAF), an umbrella organization for feminist/women's groups and individuals.[56] One of the more compelling stories of Zia's regime is that despite the regime's attitude towards women in the public sphere (or more likely, because of it), this was also the period which saw a national women's movement come into its own, changing from the social reform model of the All Pakistan Women's Association[57] to a more overtly feminist one, as represented by WAF. Flouting the regime's discourse of *chaadar* and *chaardivari*, and refusing to give in to its attempts at limiting their rights and controlling their bodies and their mobility, women took to the streets to protest the new discriminatory laws and directives. Perhaps because of the class base of WAF's leadership, the regime did not retaliate immediately. But on February 12, 1983, a large protest against the proposed Law of Evidence jointly called by the All Pakistan Women Lawyers Association and WAF was attacked by the police. Women protestors were baton-charged, arrested and jailed for violating the ban on public assembly and for disturbing the peace. The police action stunned, but also energized, the female demonstrators, many of whom had had no prior history of activism. As Mumtaz and Shaheed describe in their classic book on the history of the Pakistani women's movement that was published during the Zia period:

> The impact of the 12 February demonstration was tremendous. All of a sudden women were being taken seriously; by politicians, for having had the courage to defy existing restrictions; by the government, for having the ability to create a law and order situation; and by other women, who were forced to examine the proposed law which had moved women like them to take on the State ... For the women who had participated, very few of whom had even seen a demonstration before, the experience was singularly liberating. (Mumtaz and Shaheed, 1987: 107)

Since public assembly was severely restricted, female activists innovated, bringing together women from all walks of life through cultural activities such as song, drama and poetry-reading (Khan and Saigol, 2004). Women also resisted the state's attempts at interpellation through various forms of cultural production and performance. In fact, it would not be an exaggeration to say that this period saw the genesis and efflorescence of cultural production by, for and about Pakistani women. Some of Pakistan's best-known and most respected cultural organizations such as the theater groups Ajoka and Lok Rehas began life as a response to the Zia regime.

Poetry, in particular, came to constitute an important site of women's dissent and the contestation of the politics of Islamization. Since the state had a monopoly over the power to define what "Islam" was, this created severe problems for a politics of opposition. Poets such as Fehmida Riaz and Kishwar Naheed appropriated a long tradition of political poetry in South Asia to articulate a unique vision of self and society which functioned as a sharp critique of the Pakistani state and its version of Islam. The significance of this poetry as a mode of protest and dissent at this time is testified to by the fact that Naheed was charged with obscenity and suspended from her government job, while Riaz was forced into exile in order to escape arrest for sedition.

These women poets did not just challenge the regime and its policies; they also challenged the literary status quo. First, as women poets in an overwhelmingly male literary milieu, secondly, as feminists within an increasingly hostile and sexist social and cultural context, and third, at the level of the poetry itself, their work subverted existing and acceptable conventions of poetic form and content. It would be incorrect to assume or conclude that as feminists they wrote "only" on "women's issues," narrowly defined; in fact, they were fierce critics of the reactionary political, social and cultural changes taking place in Pakistani society. However, given that the brunt of the state's retrogressive Islamization policies and the changes they wrought in other aspects of Pakistani life was aimed at women (and minorities), most of their poetry did overwhelmingly address laws and policies which blatantly discriminated against women.

Women's poetry, even of a more broadly progressive variety—that is, directly or indirectly subversive of the patriarchal establishment— was also not all of a piece. It ranged from the work of Parveen Shakir and Ada'a Jafri who tended to use the conventional poetic form such as the *ghazal* and whose subject matter tended more towards the personal and emotional, to that of the poets most often identified with dissent under Zia, such as Kishwar Naheed and Fehmida Riaz whose poetry was more explicitly and stridently feminist and political in its tone and its subject matter. However, given the male-dominated nature of the Urdu literary milieu, the very fact of a woman writing *ghazals* to express herself was subversive, in so far as it inverted the implicit convention that woman was the object rather than the subject (let alone agent) of romance and desire. Moreover, for women to openly and critically engage with the vicissitudes of heterosexual relationships in the context of a sexist society could not but be a political act. Feminist poets were criticized by the largely male literary status quo at the time for their "loose morality" and even their "masculinity," this last charge being most often thrown at Kishwar Naheed because of her blunt personality and her even more blunt poetry.

Since women were at the vanguard of the movement against Zia's martial law government and its policies, it is fitting that they were also the most political and prominent writers/poets/artists of the time. As Kishwar Naheed pointed out in her well-known poem, "*Hum Gunahgaar Aurateñ*" ("We Sinful Women"):

Yeh hum gunahgaar aurateñ haiñ
Jo ahl-i jabba ki tamkinat se
Na raub khayeñ
Na jaan becheñ
Na sar jhukaaeñ
Na haath joreñ
Yeh hum gunahgaar aurateñ haiñ
Ke jin ke jismoñ ki fasl becheñ jo log
Voh sarfaraaz thehreñ
Nayabat-i imtiyaaz thehreñ
Voh daawar-e ahl-e saaz thehreñ

Yeh hum gunahgaar aurateñ haiñ
Ke sach ka parcham utha ke nikleñ
To jhoot se shaahraheñ ati mile haiñ
Har ek dahleez pe sazaoñ ki daastaneñ rakhi mile haiñ
Jo bol sakti theeñ voh zubaaneñ kati mile haiñ

It is we sinful women
Who are not intimidated
By the magnificence of those who wear robes
Who don't sell our souls
Don't bow our heads
Don't fold our hands in supplication
We are the sinful ones
While those who sell the harvest of our bodies
Are exalted
Considered worthy of distinction
Become gods of the material world

It is we sinful women
Who, when we emerge carrying aloft the flag of truth
Find highways strewn with lies
Find tales of punishment placed at every doorstep
Find tongues which could have spoken, severed

Besides being a harsh indictment of those who sold out to the establishment, these words also directly subverted ideas about "femininity" and stereotypes of women as weak and ineffectual. The phrase "we sinful women," repeated like a chant throughout the poem, functioned as a slap in the face of the religious orthodoxy and the state, referring as it did to the Zina Ordinance which effectively held women responsible for all sex-crimes, including those committed against them.

Fehmida Riaz's poem "*Chaadar Aur Chaardivaari*" is another wonderful example of the way feminists used poetry as a medium of dissent against the Zia regime, and a critique of the hypocrisy of the religious orthodoxy:

Huzoor, maiñ is siyaah chaadar ka kya karoongi?
Ye aap mujh ko kyooñ bakhshte haiñ, basad inaayat!

Na sog meiñ hooñ ke is ko orhooñ
Gham-o-alam khalq ko dikhaooñ
Na rog hooñ maiñ ke is ki taareekiyoñ meiñ khaft se doob jaaooñ
Na maiñ gunahgaar hooñ na mujrim
Ke is siyaahi ki mohr apni jabeeñ pe har haal meiñ lagaooñ

Agar na gustaakh mujh ko samjheñ
Agar maiñ jaañ ki amaan paaooñ
To dast-basta karooñ guzaarish
Ke banda-parvar!
Huzoor ke hujra-e mo'attar meiñ ek laasha para hua hai
Na jaane kab ka gala sara hai
Ye aap se rahm chaahta hai
Huzoor itna karam to keeje
Siyaah chaadar mujhe na deeje
Siyaah chaadar se apne hujre ki bekafan laash dhaamp deeje
Ke is se phooti hai jo 'ufoonat
Voh kooche kooche meiñ haampti hai
Voh sar patakti hai chaukhatoñ par
Barahnagi apni dhaankti hai
Suneñ zara dil-kharaash cheekheñ
Bana rahi haiñ ajab hiyole

Jo chaadaroñ meiñ bhi haiñ barahna
Ye kaun haiñ? Jaante to honge
Huzoor pehchaante to honge!
Ye laundiyaañ haiñ!

Ke yarghamaali halaal shab bhar raheñ--
Dam-i subha darbadar haiñ

Ye baandiyaañ haiñ!
Huzoor ke natfa-i mubarek ke nasb-e virsa se mo'tabar haiñ

Ye bibiyaañ haiñ!
Ke zaujagi ka khiraaj dene
Qataar andar qataar baari ki muntazar haiñ

Ye bacchiyaañ haiñ!
Ke jin ke sar pe phira jo hazrat ka dast-i shafqat
To kam-sini ke lahu se resh-i saped rangeen ho gayi hai
Huzoor ke hujla-i mo'attar meiñ zindagi khoon ro gayi hai

Para hua hai jahaañ ye laasha
Taveel sadiyoñ se qatl-i insaaniyat ka ye khooñ chukan tamaasha
Ab is tamaashe ko khatm keeje
Huzoor ab is ko dhaamp deeje!
Siyaah chaadar to ban chuki hai meri nahiñ aap ki zaroorat

Ke is zameeñ par vujood mera nahiñ faqat ek nishaan-i shahvat
Hayaat ki shaah-raah par jagmaga rahi hai meri zahaanat
Zameeñ ke rukh par jo hai paseena to jhilmilaati hai meri mehnat
Ye chaar deewaariyaañ, ye chaadar, gali sari laash ko mubarik
Khuli fizaaoñ meiñ baadbaañ khol kar barhega mera safeena
Maiñ Aadam-i nau ki humsafar hooñ
Ke jis ne jeeti meri bharosa bhari rifaaqat!

"The Shawl and the Four Walls of the Home"

Sire! What will I do with this black *chaadar*?
Why do you bless me with it?

I am neither in mourning that I should wear it—
Announce my grief to the world
Nor am I a Disease, that I should drown, humiliated, in its
   darkness
I am neither sinner nor criminal
That I should set its black seal
On my forehead under all circumstances.

If you will pardon my impertinence
If I have reassurance of my life[58]
Then only will I entreat you with folded hands
O Benevolent One!

That in Sire's fragrant chambers lies a corpse
Who knows how long it has been rotting there?
It asks for your pity
Sire, please be so kind
As to not give me this black shawl
Use it instead to cover that shroud-less corpse in your chambers
Because the stench that has burst forth from it
Goes panting through the alleys—
Bangs its head against the doorframes
Covers its nakedness
Listen to the heartrending shrieks
Which raise strange specters
That remain naked despite their *chaadars*
Who are they? You must know them
Sire, you must recognize them
They are the concubines!
The hostages who remain legitimate through the night
But come morning, are sent forth to wander, homeless

They are the handmaidens
More reliable than the half-share of inheritance promised your
    precious sperm
These are the honorable wives!
Who await their turn in long queues
To pay their conjugal dues

These are the young girls!
Whose innocent blood
Stained your white beard red
When your affectionate hand descended upon their heads

In Sire's fragrant chambers
Life has shed tears of blood
Where this corpse lies
This, for long centuries the bloody spectacle of humanity's murder
End this spectacle now
Sire, cover it up
The black *chaadar* has become your necessity, not mine

For my existence on this earth is not as a mere symbol of lust
My intelligence shines brightly on the highway of life
The sweat that shines on the brow of the earth is but my hard
    work
The corpse is welcome to this *chaadar* and these four walls

> My ship will move full-sailed in the open wind
> I am the companion of the new Adam
> Who has won my confident comradeship

In this poem, Riaz addresses the self-styled keepers of people's conscience with mock honorifics such as *huzoor*, and the series of formulaic phrases such as *jaañ ki amaan paooñ*, *dast-basta karooñ guzaarish*, *banda-parvar* are used to enhance the sarcastic tone of the poem. By spurning the *chaadar* being offered to her by these keepers of the public conscience, Riaz rejects the Islamists' interpellation of her as a sexual object required by law to be veiled and sequestered within the four walls of the home. Since she is not in mourning nor a sinner or criminal, she argues with mock innocence, she doesn't understand why she is being offered the black shawl (or, by implication, the seclusion of the *chaardivaari*). The rest of the poem lists the crimes against humanity which the person she is addressing is guilty of, including the (sexual) exploitation of women through the institutions of concubinage and marriage, forms of sexual exploitation that often begin at a very early age. The poem ends with Riaz concluding that it is he, not her, who needs the black shawl to cover his hypocrisy and shame. Although Riaz never mentions "Islam" directly, it is the absent referent in her text, because it is under the *chaadar* ("cover/cloak") of Islam that women have been subjugated for "long centuries." The "specters" of all these female victims carrying the stench of death are the skeletons in the Islamist's closet to whom Riaz "respectfully" draws his (and our) attention.

The last stanza of the poem offers a counter-interpellation of the traditional as well as Islamist ideal of "womanhood," and proposes a new female subject, an intelligent, sentient being (as opposed to object of desire and symbol of lust), a worker whose "sweat shines on the brow of the earth," and a quintessentially modern subject whose "ship will move full-sailed in the open wind." The relationship between men and women is also redefined as one of comradeship between equals; this kind of comradeship is only possible, however, with a radically reinvented and redefined man, an "Adam" who is capable of winning her confidence and is thus worthy of her.[59]

Riaz's project is a rejection of the patriarchal and paternalistic relationship between women and men posited as normative within Islamist discourse: an obedient wife who revels in her role as the "light of the home," supported by her husband who has unquestioned authority over her in all matters. The idea of a companionate relationship is thus a radical proposition despite its heteronormative assumptions, especially when accompanied by implications of a life of unfettered freedom (the trope of the sailing ship) deliberately counterposed to the *chaardivaari*. Noteworthy also are Riaz's use of *laasha* ("corpse"), *gala sara* ("rotten"), *natfa* ("sperm"), all words not normally used in poetry; these, along with the explicit references to sex and depravity provide another layer of subversiveness *vis-à-vis* form and content.

Riaz and other women poets articulated a comprehensive critique of the Zia regime and of contemporary Pakistani society which went beyond what are narrowly understood as women's issues. Kishwar Naheed's poem "*Sard Mulkoñ Ke Aaqaoñ Ke Naam*" ("To the Masters of the Cold Nations") is a critique of western stereotypes of the Third World, while "Censorship" and "Section 144" address the loss of freedom of speech and assembly under Zia, respectively. Riaz's "*Kotvaal Baitha Hai*" ("The Police Chief is Waiting") describes her interrogation by the police, and "*Khaana-Talaashi*" ("The Search") is a description of the police search of her home. Ishrat Afreen's "*Rihaai*" ("Release") makes a powerful argument for the need to fight for liberation from "the mountains of dead traditions/blind faith/oppressive hatreds" ("*Pahaar murda rivaayatoñ ke, pahaar andhi aqeedatoñ ke, pahaar zaalim adaavatoñ ke*"), as an obligation to the next generation, while Neelma Sarwar's "*Chor*" ("The Thief") deals with the cruel disparities of wealth.[60]

Riaz's long poem "*Kya Tum Poora Chaand Na Dekhoge?*" ("Will You Not See the Full Moon?") brings together many of these themes; below is an excerpt:

"*Kya tum poora chaand na dekhoge?*"

Kya maiñ ise roz-i raushan kahooñ
Ke tapte aasmaan par cheel ne chakkar kaata hai
Aur shaah-raahoñ ke jaal meiñ
Traffic ka zakhmi darinda ghurraane laga
Baazaaroñ meiñ
Baraamadi ashiya ki shahvat aankheñ malti hui bedaar ho rahi hai
Quvvat-e khareed!
Kotwaal ki moonh-chadhi faahisha
Dekho kaise dandanaati phir rahi hai
Maili, sookhi maaeñ

Koore ke dher mein haddiyaañ dhoond rahi haiñ
Bilbilaate bacchoñ ko
Khaamosh kar dene ke liye

Shahroñ ke behurmat jismoñ par
Plazoñ aur manshanoñ ke phore nikal rahe haiñ
Kaale dhan ki faisla-kun jeet ke jhande gaarte
Kal ke akhbaaroñ meiñ in ke ishtihaar dekh lena
"Tumhaari muflisi par qahqaha lagaata hua
Tum apna sar takraao – balke kaat kar phaink do
Apni maqtool aarzuoñ ke qabristaanoñ meiñ
Hum tumhaari khopriyoñ se ik minaar chunenge
Aur is ka koi chalta hua sa naam rakhenge
'Gulzaar-e Mustafa'
'Haaza min fazl-e rabbi'
Ya aisa hi koi garma garam naam
Kyoonke kaarobaar garam hai!
Kyoonkar garam hai ye kaarobaar?
...
Ye ek bhayaanak raaz hai
Jo sab jaante haiñ aur koi nahiñ bataata
...
Hum insaan ko pees kar bauna bana rahe haiñ
Ehya al-shaikh, hamaare kaarnaame ki daad deejiye
Bakhshish! Ya akhi!
Aap ke muqaddas petrodollar ki qasam!
...

"Won't you see the full moon?"

Should I call this the day of enlightenment and hope?
When the kite circles the burning sky
And in the web of highways
The traffic begins to growl like a wounded animal
In the marketplace
The Lust for imported goods awakes and rubs her eyes
Purchasing Power!
The interrogator's favorite whore
See how shamelessly she moves around
[While] Dirty, dried-up mothers
Scavenge for bones in garbage heaps
To silence their sobbing children

On the molested bodies of cities
Mansions and [shopping] plazas have begun to erupt
Like boils
Declaring the decisive victory of the black market
You can see their advertisements in tomorrow's paper
"I scoff at your poverty
You can beat your head against the wall—have it cut off [for
    all I care]
In fact, cut it off and throw it away
Into the graveyard of your murdered desires
We'll make a minaret of your skulls
And give it some trendy name
[Like] 'The Garden of the Prophet'
[or] (in Arabic) 'This is the Benevolence of God'
Or some other piping hot name
Because business is brisk"
How and why is this business flourishing?
…
It is a horrible secret
Which everyone knows but no one mentions
…
We are grinding humans to produce dwarves
O Sheikh, praise our achievements!
(in Arabic) Alms! O brother!
I swear by your hallowed petrodollar.

In this prose poem, the moon is a metaphor for the truth. The form of the piece is itself unconventional, being the first prose poem of book length in Urdu. The use of direct and colloquial diction helps give the poet's work its political edge. If the Islamization project was a "culturalist evasion" (Amin, 1989) of the real issues facing Pakistan, Riaz exposes these issues baldly: the neo-colonial nature of the state, and the extreme income disparities with conspicuous consumption at one end and starvation on the other that defined wealthy urban centers.

The poem is littered with gothic imagery and a pastiche of strange and ominous images—the kites circling a burning sky, the city as web/trap, the pathologically sexual aspect of the desire for imported commodities which awakens the "whore of purchasing power." Needless to say, this is a stark reference to the increasing commodity fetishism of the wealthy classes. The symbols of this fetishism, such as the shopping plazas and the mansions, are themselves described as boils on the molested body of the city, in the same way that conspicuous consumption is on the diseased body politic of the nation-state. The insatiable hunger for more commodities makes people insensitive to the glaring poverty around them, and the elite's lust for "petrodollars" reduces them to a state of sub-humanity.

The gothic also comes in with the superimposition of sexuality, depravity, lustfulness and disease. Satire is evident in the references to the increasing influence of Saudi Arabia—the Sheikh—while the Pakistani bourgeoisie is reduced to begging for petrodollars with which to finance the "grinding down" of human beings. This was the era in which Pakistan increasingly looked to Saudi Arabia for affirmation in the political, economic and even cultural spheres. The casual use of Arab phrases in the poem is a direct reference to the increasing use of Arabic words on Pakistan Television, the introduction of Arabic as a compulsory subject in public schools, and the Arabization of Urdu itself, which were a result of the Zia regime's effort to move ever further away from a Persianate Indo-Islamic culture towards an "Islamic" identity defined by Arabic elements. The onward march of capital and the obscene culture of consumption it engenders are depicted in a way that highlights indifference to those on the other side of the poverty line. Fehmida Riaz's theme throughout this poem is that Islamization is simply a ruse with which the rulers defuse dissent and construct consent while dividing the nation sharply between those who have economic and political power, and those who do not.

CULTURE AND IDEOLOGY UNDER ZIA

Despite the various forms of resistance to it, Zia's project left a lasting impact on Pakistani state, society and culture. Through a combination of brute repression and ideological warfare, Zia was successful in his broad goal of undermining socialism and secularism, decimating whatever part of the organized Left that had managed to survive Bhutto's earlier attacks, perverting the relationship between citizens and the state through the *Nizam-i Mustafa*, and policing the production and circulation of progressive ideas in the public sphere. Under Zia, the influence of the *Jama'at* in Pakistan's state and society was institutionalized and entrenched in ways that the *Jama'at* itself could never have managed, even if it had won political power through the electoral process. As in the political and legal realms, Maududi's influence and preoccupations were clearly reflected in Zia's cultural policies.

Official nationalism and nationalist historiography were changed to reflect the *Jama'at*'s ideas, whose revisionist history of the Pakistan movement was enshrined within official nationalism, as was the idea of "Pakistan Ideology." School, college and university curricula for social studies and history were revamped to reflect these changes, and new textbooks were issued (Aziz, 1993). The cosmopolitan and secular Jinnah posed a problem to this Maududi-inspired national project, but since it was impossible to jettison the "Father of the Nation," Jinnah underwent his own "Islamization," which involved, among other things, a sartorial makeover.[61] Jinnah's speeches and his principled secularism had always been problematic for the establishment, but never more so than under the new regime, and so were rigorously censored, with only highly selective quotes appearing in the official media.

As with so much else, the official version of Iqbal (the "National Poet-Philosopher") also closely followed the *Jama'at* script; the Iqbal that emerged in this narrative was more heavily "Islamic" than ever. The verses of Iqbal that were circulated most frequently in the official media were the ones which the first generation of Progressives had denounced as proto-fascist, since they suited the current state project of the masculinization and militarization of Islam. These verses, along with select lines from Iqbal's writings and speeches, were also used to shore up the revisionist *Jama'at* idea that the Pakistan movement had essentially been about establishing an Islamic state. Zia therefore effectively institutionalized and thereby mainstreamed those very distorted ideas of Maududi and the *Jama'at* regarding the history of Pakistan, Pakistani culture, and Iqbal that had been vigorously challenged by leftist intellectuals such as Safdar Mir in the 1960s. Thus, even as television programming was punctuated by ubiquitous "quotes" from Jinnah and Iqbal, these were judicially edited excerpts that were designed to endorse the regime's national project. For example, probably the most ubiquitous of Jinnah's "quotes" broadcast during—and long after—Zia was the exhortation that "Unity, Faith and Discipline" must be the defining principles for Pakistanis. This slogan might have been appropriate in a newly liberated post-colonial nation-state, but in the context of a fascist military regime which had cloaked itself in Islamic colors, they took on decidedly sinister overtones.

Through public cultural institutions, formal media policies and public statements by the general himself, the regime sought to construct a new Islamic "national culture" free of obscenity, of "Hindu" and/or "western" elements, and of the "decadence" which had characterized the Bhutto government. Under Zia, the puritanical and parochial attitudes of *Jama'at* intellectuals with regard to culture and the arts effectively became official national policy. The socialist/communist writers, poets and artists they despised were harassed, imprisoned, forced into exile, or blacklisted (which meant that they could not be featured in any state-sponsored event or platform);[62] even events held in private residences were not safe from the goon-squads of the *Jama'at*. Art forms and cultural practices that were considered Hindu in origins and inspiration, such as kite-flying, classical dance and Hindustani classical music, were either banned or were constantly under threat of proscription (Hasan, 2002).

Through the Islamization project, Zia injected a heavy dose of puritanism into a society which had been historically tolerant and open. Driven by a petty-bourgeois social conservatism, this was reflected in attitudes towards women and sexuality, especially in terms of the relations between men and women. The crackdown on "obscenity" which was part of the state project of moral reform also affected art in terms of subject matter and theme, especially when it came to the representation of nude bodies (male or female). One of the iconic stories of censorship and defiance from this period involved the young artist Iqbal Hussain, whose paintings depicted women (and occasionally men) from the red-light district of Lahore, where Hussain grew up. Despite the fact that Hussain's purpose was to humanize his subjects and the paintings were far from titillating, the artist was not allowed to exhibit his work at the state-run Alhamra Art Gallery in Lahore because they were deemed "obscene." In protest, Hussain displayed them on the roadside near the gallery.[63]

Along with this moral policing of the arts went severe political censorship. Aware of the country's strong progressive tradition within literature and the arts, Zia deemed any reference to politics within the artistic realm to be unacceptable, which made the feminist poetic assault on the regime even more significant. Habib Jalib maintained his reputation as a revolutionary poet; his poem "*Sarsar ko Saba*" ("Calling the Windstorm a Morning Breeze") was a powerful indictment of Zia and his ideological project, and once again got him arrested. Another important dissident voice at this time was that of a Progressive of Jalib's generation, Ahmad Faraz, who until now had not been known for political poetry. Faraz's recital of his anti-army poem "*Pesha-var Qaatilo, Tum Sipaahi Nahiñ*" ("You

Mercenaries, You are not Soldiers") at a *mushaira* got him arrested; he went into voluntary exile soon after. The revolutionary Punjabi poet Ustad Daman penned the following tongue-in-cheek lines:

> *Mere mulakh de do khuda,*
> *Laa ilah te marshal laa.*
> *Ik rehnda ay arshaañ utte,*
> *Dooja rehnda farshaañ utte.*
> *Ohda naañ ay Allah Mian,*
> *Ehda naañ ay Jurnal Zia.*

> My country has two Gods,
> One is Allah and the other Martial Law
> One lives up in the Heavens,
> The other lives down here on the ground.
> That one's name is Allah,
> This one's name is General Zia.

Television—first set up by Ayub Khan as an instrument of propaganda to facilitate his bid for the presidency—had played an important ideological role along with radio during the 1965 war, but it was under Bhutto that it truly came into its own as a major national cultural institution. The Pakistan Television (PTV) stable featured the country's most talented singers, artists and writers, and many young graduates of the prestigious National College of Arts joined PTV as producers, writers and set designers. Television programming under Bhutto reflected the government's cultural policy as well as its professed social-democratic concerns. Talk shows, documentaries and television plays focused on issues of inequality within Pakistani society, while programs on folk culture frequently brought folk artists from the various regions of Pakistan together on a national stage.

The social-democratic and secular bent of television programming under Bhutto had irked both the propertied classes and the religious lobby. Thus it was not surprising that Zia's newly appointed information secretary, General Mujeeb-ur Rahman, began his tenure by summoning all the producers at the Lahore television station to inform them that the government knew that they were all subversives with an agenda which could be seen in their "obsessive" focus on poverty and misery in Pakistan. The producers were summarily warned that they would be "strung up by wires" if they did not cooperate with the government. The programming was dramatically altered with an exponential increase in the time devoted to religious programs. The content of the other shows was brought in line with the ideological agenda of the regime (Noman, 1988).[64] A system of double censorship was put in place whereby scripts for proposed programs were vetted by the resident *aalim* (or Islamic scholar) in the television station and then sent to the Ministry of Information for approval. Producers and artistes nevertheless managed to find creative ways of pushing back against these diktats, although not always without reprisal.[65]

ISLAM AND THE MILITARY

The brutal Zia regime had little legitimacy, despite its attempt at constructing consent through Islamization. The high level of coercion was, of course, consonant with the lack of legitimacy, but such unpopular regimes are by their very nature fragile. Yet paradoxically, Zia ruled Pakistan for 11 long years. The reason for this is to be found in crucial geo-political realignments in the region that coincided with the regime's early years. In 1979, precisely as the regime appeared to be struggling—its domestic and international legitimacy was at its lowest point yet, following the assassination of Bhutto, and it faced a serious economic crisis—the combination of the Shi'ite revolution in Iran and the Soviet invasion of Afghanistan changed the game decisively. The Afghan War almost single-hand-edly saved the military regime (Siddiqa, 2007), while changing the fortunes (both literally and metaphorically) of Pakistan's generals overnight. In the process, it enabled a decisive rightward shift in the Pakistani state and society.

Pakistan had been relegated to the status of an international outcast, especially after the assassination of Bhutto. However, on December 25, 1979, the Soviet Union invaded Afghanistan and in one fell swoop, Pakistan's military establishment went from being a pariah on the world stage to being the US's most valued and strategic Cold War ally. Zia found himself in the serendipitous position of being able to leverage Pakistan's position as a front-line state in order to dictate terms to the US. President Carter's somewhat modest original offer of aid ($400 million) reflected his unease with having to negotiate with a military regime with an abysmal record of human rights violation; the offer was famously dismissed by Zia as "peanuts" (Noman, 1988: 121). But Zia's run of luck continued with the election of Ronald Reagan to the US presidency in 1980. Zia's relationship with the US was dramatically transformed, with

Pakistan being elevated to the status of major ally and partner with its international image rehabilitated, while Zia was transformed into the hero of the free world. Under Reagan, $3.2 billion worth of military aid in the form of dollars and sophisticated military hardware flowed into the country, effectively underwriting the Zia regime while fulfilling the Pakistani military's fantasy of regional dominance.[66]

The military benefited from this injection of aid in every imaginable way. The money was immediately put to use by the regime to secure its survival by the simple exigency of buying support from key players. A large chunk was siphoned off to underwrite a system of patronage catering to the regime's only real constituency—its officers. This system not only continues to exist but has grown like a malignant and parasitic tumor within the body politic. The Cold War monies also enabled the regime to "consolidate its successful manipulation of the political process" through the "extraordinary device of handing out large sums of money to members of the national assembly ready to promote its interests" (Jalal, 1990: 325), thereby undermining/perverting democratic politics and corrupting the country's political culture. The 1985 elections were designed to wean politicians away from their parties and reorient them towards the military establishment (Siddiqa, 2007). American aid was very useful in enabling this new clientalist relationship.

The increased inflow of foreign capital into Pakistan resolved the regime's economic crises as well as its political ones, producing as it did a macro-economic revival. The Aid to Pakistan Consortium, which had refused to reschedule debt-servicing was now more than happy to do so (Noman, 1988). In 1977, the government's debt-servicing had kept pace with revenue receipts; the gap now widened exponentially (Jalal, 1990).[67] This was significant in so far as it set the stage for structural adjustment programs and condition-alities. The threat posed by the communist regime in Afghanistan and then the US-backed war there had allowed the military establishment to siphon off increasing amounts of funds from the national exchequer. In 1977–78, even before the Soviet invasion of Afghanistan gave the military *carte blanche*, defense expenditure had shot up from $960 million to $1,180 million (Waseem, 2007). Noman (1988: 174) notes that "[n]o other military government allocates such a large share of central government resources [that is, 30 per cent] to defence." The phenomenal increase in defense allocations and debt-servicing between 1977 and 1985, had an extremely adverse effect on human development in Pakistan.[68]

The Iranian revolution and the Soviet invasion of Afghanistan also helped consolidate the relationship between Saudi Arabia and Pakistan. The Saur revolution and the reforms it had almost immediately instituted in the Afghan countryside—particularly redistribution of land and abolition of rural debt and usury—had caused consternation within the Pakistani establishment in terms of its potential influence across the border in Sarhad and Baluchistan. [69] The Saudis were anxious about their own Soviet-backed communist neighbor, South Yemen and the revolution in Shi'ite Iran made it even more imperative for them to invest in a Sunni Pakistan. Saudi aid, both for domestic industry and for arms procurement, was therefore readily forthcoming. In return, and in line with its already established role as a mercenary force, the Pakistani military provided the Saudis with "well-trained military and technical manpower" (Sayeed, 1980: 186). [70]

This arrangement, whereby some 20,000 Pakistani military personnel could be stationed in Saudi Arabia at any given time on a rotation basis, also fed the military patronage system which was so important for the regime's stability (Jones, 1985). From the civil services to the industrial sector, quotas and other preferential policies ensured the military's penetration of every aspect of state and society. Despite the posturing about the evils of nationalization, most industrial units were not denationalized by the regime and in fact provided it with a large pool of desirable jobs which it could offer to retiring military officers.

The military also made inroads into the state apparatus in a far more concerted way than ever before. Retired and serving military officials began to be given important posts in civil administration. Under the martial law regime, senior generals were appointed as governors of all four provinces; military officers were placed in key positions in ministries such as interior, defense, labor, communications, housing, education and railways. Quotas were put in place for ex-servicemen for jobs in ministries and departments. Military officers occupied almost 25 per cent of the top bureaucratic posts, displacing career civil servants. The heaviest penetration of the military was in the foreign service (Rashid and Gardezi, 1983); by 1982, almost half of all ambassadors were military men (Waseem, 2007). [71] At the provincial level, military officers served dual roles as martial law administrators *and* governors (Jones, 1985). Furthermore, through legal and constitutional changes, the military and civil service were made equal partners in policy-making (Siddiqa, 2007).

Under Zia, the military spread into the economic sphere in a very major way, laying the ground for its current dominance of Pakistan's economy. An important route to this economic dominance was the establishment and expansion of welfare trusts which used the political power of the military to their own benefit (Siddiqa, 2007). For example, the army's welfare trust organization, the Fauji Foundation, had interests in the fertilizer, oil, gas and sugar industries. Alliances with the business community further cemented this new and extensive economic power. The military also acquired vast land assets by force, displacing local communities without compensation or rehabilitation.[72]

Zia also institutionalized the military's involvement in politics, which had serious consequences for Pakistan. To ensure the military's control of the political field, factionalism was encouraged so as to produce a permanently unstable national politics and prevent a strong democratic national politics from emerging and challenging the military. The use of intelligence agencies to intimidate recalcitrant politicians and political workers, and to manipulate political parties was also a hallmark of this period. The US's opportunistic support of Zia's regime essentially indemnified it and its extensive use of coercion to "manage" dissent, not to mention its suspension of civil rights (Rashid and Gardezi, 1983).

The Afghan War ripped apart the already fragile social fabric of Pakistani society. Significant among the consequences of the war was the rise of the shadowy and powerful Inter-Services Intelligence (ISI), whose current notoriety and power within Pakistan is a direct result of the role it played in the conflict, funneling arms and money from the US, China and Saudi Arabia to the *mujahideen* (Burki, 1991). The ISI also "patronised and protected" the parallel shadow economy in arms and drugs produced by the war (Jalal, 1990: 326), and Pakistan became one of the main conduits for the international trade in heroin during this period.[73] The easy availability of guns and drugs in Pakistan as a consequence of this illegal war-economy led to a rise in criminality at all levels of society. Heroin addiction soared among the poor and unemployed, while gun violence permeated every aspect and level of society, transforming the very nature of social conflict in Pakistan and decisively changing the rules of the political game from this point on.[74] In addition, the presence of 3 million Afghan refugees on Pakistani soil could not but give rise to social conflict, which the regime capitalized on.[75]

Along with enabling the increased militarization of Pakistani culture and society, the Afghan War furthered the process of the

Islamization of the military and, crucially, resulted in a militarization of Islam. The use of "Islam" as the chosen ideology for the *mujahideen* in their battle with the godless communists was the apotheosis of the US's Cold War deployment of Islamic radicals as a counter to international communism.[76]

This militarized and militant version of Zia's Islam was disseminated to recruits for the *jihad* against the Soviet Union via not only the now-notorious *madrassas* set up by the army and the Inter-Services Intelligence (ISI) with the help of the CIA, but also through the mainstream educational channels. The construction and popularization of a hyper-masculinized and militarized version of Islam was part and parcel of Zia's Islamization project (Khattak, 1997); the ideal citizen under this regime was not just a pious and practicing Muslim but one ready to "defend Islam"—essentially, a religious warrior. In his very first address to the nation, Zia had announced that he considered himself a soldier of Islam. Although there was nothing new in the invocation of Islam for political purposes in Pakistan, its deployment by the military under Zia nevertheless represented a major break with the past.[77] "Islam," as deployed by this military regime, served to consolidate the centralization of power in the army, now the protector of Pakistan's territorial *and* ideological frontiers. Rubina Saigol's (1995) excellent analysis of the social science curriculum in Pakistan demonstrates that even though the military was always extolled in school textbooks, the relationship between the military, Islam and Pakistan under Zia was presented as an organic one such that the Pakistan military was not just the defender of the country, but also of the Faith. Or rather, it was the defender of the country *because* it was the defender of the Faith. This gelled seamlessly with Maududi's "Pakistan Ideology." The "hotch potch of obscurantist thinking" that had elicited scorn from Safdar Mir not ten years earlier became, under Zia, the very basis of official nationalism.

Through the serendipity of the Afghan War, the Pakistani military was able to rehabilitate and reinvent itself, penetrating every aspect of Pakistan. As a result, Pakistan emerged from 11 years of Zia's rule a brutalized society, with a state and a culture perverted by Zia's "Islamic" reforms and his draconian martial law regulations. While Zia could not break progressive forces in society completely, he did manage to shift the balance of power decisively in favor of the forces of reaction[78] by redefining Islam and fundamentally changing the relationship between Islam and the Pakistani state and society, and by successfully fracturing an emergent national democratic politics, replacing it with new political formations and figures that were tightly connected to the military establishment.

In the words of a Pakistani feminist, the combination of militarization and Islamization under Zia "destroyed the very fabric of political and civil society; made a mockery of the constitution and of the law; depoliticized and individualized the citizenry; and spread corruption and opportunism in every aspect of life in Pakistan" (Khan, 1995: 15–16). It was hard to believe that this was the same country which, at the end of the 1960s, appeared to be on the brink of a socialist revolution led by a mass movement of left-wing forces.

6
The Long Shadow of Zia: Women, Minorities and the Nation-State

The 1990s is often dismissed as a kind of "lost decade" within Pakistan's recent history, at best an anti-climactic follow-up to the tumultuous politics of the Zia period and at worst a period of disillusionment; it has even been described as "a longish civilian prologue to Musharraf's reign" (Ali, 2008: 134). But this decade was more than an interregnum between two military regimes; it had a logic and a coherence of its own, not least because it was the period of the maturation of the social, political and cultural forces which Zia had unleashed. The attack on women and minorities which had begun under Zia gained greater momentum in this period, resulting in increasing levels of sexual(ized) violence against women and the violent targeting of religious minorities.[1] Political factionalism, along with ethnic and religious divides set into motion and/or exacerbated by Zia were instrumental in making this an exceptionally turbulent decade. In fact, the religious and sectarian violence which characterized this period were of a kind, scale and intensity never before witnessed in Pakistan. At the same time, conditionalities imposed by the IMF played a significant role in the rising levels of poverty, contributing to a sharp reversal of earlier trends. The military establishment continued to manipulate the political process, using the Eighth Amendment[2] to discipline the two main political players, who were themselves, in different ways, products of the Zia era: Benazir Bhutto, daughter of Zia's nemesis Zulfiqar Ali Bhutto and Nawaz Sharif, Zia's protege.

By the end of the 1980s, Zulfiqar Ali Bhutto's daughter Benazir—young, attractive, Harvard and Oxford-educated, and increasingly fearless in the way in which she stood up to the regime—had become the symbol of resistance to the military dictatorship. It was therefore not surprising that she led the PPP to electoral victory in the elections that followed Zia's mysterious death in a plane crash in 1988. However, her victory was diluted both by the machinations of the military establishment which brokered a deal uniting anti-PPP forces under the *Islami Jamhoori Ittehad* (the Islamic Democratic

Alliance), a coalition of largely religious parties led by Nawaz Sharif, and by her own political shortcomings.[3] In what was to become a pattern for the next decade, President Ghulam Ishaq Khan used the powers granted to him by the Eighth Amendment to dismiss the PPP government. Khan was a senior bureaucrat, and had become the *de facto* head of state following Zia's death; he was retained as president following the 1988 elections on the insistence of the military establishment. Between 1988 and 1999, Pakistan experienced four changes of government and seven administrations, testifying to the immense utility of the Eighth Amendment for the military establishment. The amendment ensured the subservience of politicians to the military establishment and undermined any possibility of the development of a meaningful democratic culture in Pakistan.[4] The political musical chairs of this period finally came to an end in October 1999 with the military coup of Pervez Musharraf, and the commencement of the second longest military regime in Pakistan's history.

Zia's *Nizam-i Mustafa* had not just been about "Islamizing" Pakistan, but about asserting an aggressive and hard-line brand of Sunni Islam, inspired and underwritten by Saudi Arabia. This sponsorship of Sunni Islam, which included state patronage of radical Sunni organizations, had produced an organized response from the Shia community which drew not only inspiration from the Iranian Revolution of 1979, but also material and moral support from the new Shi'ite regime.[5] The result was a significant rise in sectarian violence from the late 1980s onwards. Although the hostility between Shia and Sunni communities had a long history in the subcontinent, this version had radically new elements, largely due to the proliferation of weapons and the recent spurt in religious violence, both a fall-out of the Afghan War.

The Sunnification/Islamization project under Zia had involved significant changes to the structure of the state, the most obvious example of which was the corruption of the juridico-legal system through "Islamic" provisions and laws. The changes outlined in the previous chapter—the establishment of parallel shariat courts, and the placement and promotion of religious conservatives (Sunni, of course) within the judiciary—all contributed towards the increasing conservatism of the judicial system. The influence of Sunni sectarianism also began to be felt within the broader legal fraternity and the police, with serious implications for Pakistani society as a whole, but especially for women and religious minorities.

The sectarian conflict in Pakistan, as well as the rising conservatism in society as a whole, was also connected to the increasing size and influence of the conservative sections of the urban petit bourgeoisie under Zia (Rouse, 2004).[6] The support for sectarian groups came largely from the urban petit bourgeoisie, particularly the bazaar merchants, who not only contributed financially to these groups, but also lent heft to their sectarianism through their ability to shut down the markets and to bring people out on the streets for anti-minority demonstrations.

The narrowing of national identity around a particular kind of Sunni Islam and the sanctioning of violence in the name of religion both by the state and, more importantly, by non-state actors such as sectarian groups and individuals, had a major impact on Pakistani society and culture. The state sanction given to privatized violence seriously compromised law and order, and strengthened non-state forces and powerful vested interests at the expense of the weak and the vulnerable. Needless to say, the implications for women and religious minorities—and not just non-*Muslim* communities such as Christians and Hindus, but also non-*Sunni* sects such as Shias and Ahmadis—were immense.[7]

Progressive politics in Pakistan underwent a serious transformation in this post-Zia period as well. The anti-Zia/pro-democracy mobilization which brought Benazir into power dissipated with the return of formal democracy. The organized Left, already weakened by the repressive policies of Bhutto and Zia, suffered a further setback with the break-up of the Soviet Union and the privatization and downsizing undertaken as part of IMF conditionalities. Meanwhile, liberal activists who had risen to prominence during the Zia period retreated from a politics of mass mobilization into one of human rights and development NGOs. This left the political field wide open for the religious right wing, which lost no time in capitalizing on it. Perhaps the most prominent example of progressive politics during this decade was the legal activism of Asma Jahangir and Hina Jilani, pursued alongside the Human Rights Commission of Pakistan (of which they were both members).[8] While their legal activism was significant given the fact that they took up the most salient issues of the day (that is, the blasphemy law and women's rights) and did so in the face of death threats and harassment by extremists, it could not be a substitute for movement building and mass mobilization. Legal activism functions within the limits set by the law, and when the law itself becomes the problem—as it did after Zia—movements are needed in order to build pressure on legislators. Liberal progressives, however, had chosen the path of accommodation and negotiation with political parties, rather than that of mass mobilization. This was to prove to be a huge mistake, given the manner in which religious extremists were increasingly beginning to control the street and therefore the mainstream discourse. Of course, the use of violence that marked the politics of the street gave the religious right wing added leverage, but it also created disaffection among the population that progressives did not have the wherewithal to tap into.

WOMEN AND/AS PROPERTY

While it is hard to single out *the* most significant legacy of the Zia years, the precipitous fall in the status of women and religious minorities must surely rank at the top. The legal and institutional changes put in place by Zia under the umbrella of Islamization, along with the sanctioning of violence in the name of religion and the rise of a militant Sunni sectarianism from the late 1980s onwards, exposed these two groups to increasing levels of violence from state and society. This vulnerability was intensified further by the promulgation of the *Qisas* and *Diyat* Ordinance ("eye for an eye" and "blood money," respectively) by Ghulam Ishaq Khan in 1990,[9] and a crucial change in Section 295-C of the Blasphemy Law initiated by a ruling of the Federal Shariat Court (FSC) under Nawaz Sharif's administration that made the death penalty the only possible punishment for blasphemy.

Zia's *Nizam-i Mustafa* had been a heavily gendered enterprise, as we have seen, with legal changes such as the Law of Evidence and the Zina Ordinance reducing women's legal (and thereby social) worth while intensifying their sexual regulation. One of the indirect effects of the Zina Ordinance had been to eroticize women's bodies such that their mere presence in the public sphere became sexually charged. The fact that the Zina Ordinance effectively rendered it impossible for a woman to prove a charge of rape, while enabling her to be charged with *zina* ("illicit sex") should she try to report one, created a situation in which men had inordinate power over women. These laws strengthened both public and private patriarchies.[10] Thus, Zia's policies were instrumental in masculinizing the public sphere such that women's presence in it became *ipso facto* transgressive, and open to reprisal even by complete strangers, while the religious imperative now attached to their surveillance and control legitimized the use of violence as a tool of control against them. At the same time, courts lowered the bar for what counted as transgressive behavior on the part of women; in fact, in case after case, the courts upheld the (male) perpetrator's *subjective* sense that a transgression had occurred at all, and condoned his use of violence as a response (Zia, 2002).[11]

Needless to say, Zia's laws directly and indirectly led to an increase in the control that families and communities exercised over "their" women. A stark example of this was the way in which the number of women in Pakistani jails skyrocketed after the passage of the Zina Ordinance, the vast majority of them turned in by their families for daring to exercise their agency (Khan, 2006).[12] The promulgation of the Qisas and Diyat Ordinance opened the floodgates of community and familial violence against women even further by making murder a compoundable offense and a crime against persons instead of the state; the issue could now be settled by the murderer either being forgiven by the woman's next of kin, or by the payment of blood money to the family of the victim. The murder of women at the hands of their family thus became an incredibly simple matter, carrying no penalties for the murderer except perhaps the payment of blood money, as long as the next of kin could be counted on to forgive him (Jilani and Ahmed, 2004: 163).[13] This was almost assured given that the woman's murderer was usually her husband, or brother, or son, and could be pardoned by any of the others.

Zia's gendered policies reinforced feudal forms of patriarchy, especially the idea that women were, literally and figuratively, the property of their family, tribe, caste, or community. This idea conflicted with Islamic law which gave women *sui juris* status, which translated, among other things, into the right to own and inherit property. This made the sexual regulation of women even more important, and lay behind "customary" practices such as *haq bakshwana* ("relinquishing one's right") in which a woman is symbolically "married" to a Quran, or even a tree, in order to prevent her share of the family property transferring to her husband's family. Such ideas about women as the property of "their" kin-group and the repository of its honor underwrote other forms of violence against them as well, including (but not limited to) "honor killings." Women could also be subjected to sexual(ized) violence by "outsiders" as a way to humiliate their families, communities, or tribes, or as a form of revenge/reprisal.

These customary forms of violence did not begin with Zia, of course, but under his gender regime, they gained new traction. Thus it was not surprising that the first case of the explicit public use of sexualized violence against women in Pakistan—the "Nawabpur case"—should have occurred during the Zia regime. The incident took place in the eponymous town of Nawabpur in the Punjab, and involved the parading naked of several women of a particular family by their arch-rivals as revenge for an illicit relationship between members of the two feuding families (Zia, 1995). Such forms of violence became mainstream through the 1990s, but with one crucial exception: in the Nawabpur case, the perpetrators were arrested and punished, but this was not to be the case for the vast majority of the cases that followed.

The use of sexual violence against women as a tool of political intimidation also became "popular" in the 1990s. In 1991, for example, Veena Hayat, a close friend of then-Opposition leader Benazir Bhutto and daughter of veteran politician Sardar Shaukat Hyat Khan was gang-raped by goons allegedly hired by the son-in-law of President Ghulam Ishaq Khan.[14] Given the stigma attached to female victims of sexual violence (which the perpetrators must have counted on), it was significant that Hayat went public with the rape and about who she thought was responsible for it. The subsequent reluctance on the part of the police to charge anyone with the crime led her father to declare that he would take the case to his *jirga*[15] (a tribal assembly of elders) in order to get his daughter the justice which was being denied her by the state. This case made national headlines because of the social status of the victim, the shocking nature of the crime (a politically motivated rape of a woman from a prominent political family), the victim's refusal to remain silent, and also because of the legitimization of a tribal institution on the national stage.

Since Zia's corruption of the existing juridico-legal system with his "Islamic" provisions had essentially opened the door to all manner of customary laws, practices and institutions, which further undermined the idea of law as an instrument of justice, it was hardly surprising that the 1990s had the dubious honor of being the decade in which Pakistan's name became connected with "honor killings." Although not sanctioned by Islam, the increase in the frequency of such murders at this time was, paradoxically, deeply connected to Zia's Islamization project, given the religious legitimacy accorded the sexual regulation of women by any means necessary.[16] The impunity with which men were able to exercise this power in the public and private realms, even to the extent of murdering "their" women, cheapened women's lives immeasurably. In addition, the increasing power of landed elites resulted in a mainstreaming of customary institutions in the 1990s. The combined effect of the

"Islamic laws," the various customary laws, and the strengthening of feudal and tribal power at the local and national level literally proved lethal for women as well as other vulnerable groups.

The case through which the issue of "honor killings" exploded onto the national stage was that of Samia Sarwar. On April 6, 1999, Sarwar, a 29-year-old mother of two was brazenly murdered in her lawyer's office by her family for daring to get a divorce. She had been married for almost ten years to her maternal cousin, a doctor, who was a drug addict and physically abusive; she finally left him after he pushed her down the stairs while she was pregnant, and moved back into her parents' home. Sarwar had been living there for several years before taking advantage of her parents' absence from Peshawar in March 1999 to travel to Lahore in order to consult prominent attorneys Asma Jahangir and Hina Jilani. She was interested in remarrying, and wanted their help in securing a divorce from her husband. While in Lahore, she stayed at *Dastak*, the women's shelter run by Jahangir and Jilani's legal aid firm, AGHS. She refused all attempts made by her parents to reach her, convinced that her life was in danger. However, in a move that sealed her fate, she finally relented at the insistence of another prominent lawyer and agreed to see her mother on the condition that the meeting take place in her lawyer's office and that her mother come alone.

What followed shook the country for months afterwards. Sarwar's mother arrived at the AGHS offices at the appointed time, but not alone. She appeared to be limping and was accompanied by a man who she claimed was there to assist her in walking. As soon as they entered the office of Sarwar's lawyer, Hina Jilani, the "assistant" took out a gun and shot Sarwar in the head, killing her instantly; he also shot at but narrowly missed Jilani. The mother and the assassin then took a paralegal hostage on their way out. A security guard shot and killed the murderer, but Sarwar's mother managed to drag the hostage outside and into the get-away car in which her brother-in-law was waiting. The paralegal—Shahtaj Qazalbash—was dropped off unhurt at the side of a road a few hours later; in the meantime, Sarwar's parents and uncle flew back to Peshawar.

Jahangir and Jilani immediately filed an FIR[17] against Sarwar's parents for her murder. However, not only were they not arrested, they were allowed to file an FIR themselves against Jahangir and Jilani, holding them responsible for the abduction and murder of their daughter. This FIR was finally rejected under pressure from the lawyers, but to date no one has been arrested for Sarwar's murder (Jilani and Ahmed, 2004: 156).

What really set this case apart was the fact that Sarwar's parents were prominent members of Peshawar society—her mother was a doctor and her father the president of the Peshawar Chamber of Commerce—which ran counter to the accepted idea that "honor killings" were confined to the rural backwaters of Pakistan. The case polarized Pakistani society and there were loud denunciations of the heinous act, with many expressing disbelief that a mother (and a professional, educated one at that) would so actively conspire in the murder of her own daughter. However, there was an equally loud defense—even valorization—of her parents' actions by prominent media personalities, politicians and other public figures, and they became virtual heroes among certain sections of Pakistani society for defending their honor and punishing their transgressive daughter. Many a liberal parent was privately heard to comment that Sarwar had been wrong to take the actions that she had, even as they condemned the murder.

When a resolution was proposed in the Pakistan Senate condemning such "honor crimes," several senators used the opportunity to denounce Jahangir and Jilani and accuse them of corrupting young, impressionable women as part of a "foreign agenda." The most spirited and surprising defense of "honor killings" came from one of the senators from Sarhad who belonged to the secular Awami National Party. Announcing himself as a friend of the family, he defended Sarwar's parents' actions on the grounds that they had upheld the *Pukhtoonwali* code of honor which she had violated.[18] In the oddest move of all, he made this impassioned argument while proudly upholding his party's secular credentials, declaring, "We have fought for human rights and civil liberties all our lives but wonder what sort of human rights are being claimed by these girls in jeans" (Verbatim record of the Proceedings of the Senate, May 10, 1999). Leaving aside the issue of who the "girls in jeans" of the senator's rhetoric might be,[19] it was clear that as far as he was concerned, the rights that Sarwar was asking for did not fall under any legitimate definition of "human rights," or "civil liberties," which he had defended in the past. What *was* connoted by the reference to "girls in jeans" was the westernized, hence agentic, and therefore disobedient woman. According to the senator's logic, the imperatives of the *Pukhtoonwali* code trumped the rights granted to her by Islamic law and the Pakistan Penal Code, namely the right to divorce her husband[20] as well as to remarry. By choosing to exercise those rights Sarwar (knowingly) violated the *Pukhtoonwali* code, and was therefore, in essence, responsible for her own death.

Even more shocking was the reaction of veteran ANP member and senior senator Ajmal Khattak. Given his distinguished political history and his respected position within intellectual and political circles as a staunch progressive, Khattak was expected to categorically condemn "honor killings." Instead, he outdid his fellow senators in his defense of the *Pukhtoonwali* code, even going so far as to trying to justify it by using vocabulary from Islamic texts (Jafri, 2008).[21]

What the Sarwar case highlighted was that, when it came to women, overlapping legal codes and the increasing legitimacy given to customary law in Pakistan at this time enabled a "patriarchal opportunism" (Toor, 2011), whereby patriarchal elites could "cherry-pick" the most constrictive norms and codes from among the different legal systems. As Simi Kamal and Asma Khan (1997: ii) note, the effect of the "interplay of tribal codes, Islamic law, Indo-British judicial traditions and customary traditions" is that "any advantage or opportunity offered to women by one law is cancelled out by one or more of the others." What is worth noting in this patriarchal opportunism as it plays out in Pakistan is that when invoking Islam is not useful—especially in cases where the provisions of Islamic law would *undercut* the patriarchal imperative[22]—it is conveniently ignored as a source of legitimacy while paeans to "culture" and "tradition" take its place.[23]

The case of Saima Waheed, which preceded Samia Sarwar's murder by a few years, dramatically demonstrated the ways in which a right given to adult Muslim women under Islamic law became the subject of heated national debate because it went against the patriarchal imperative. In fact, a close reading of the judgments in this case reveals the ways in which "Islam" itself was being subjected to an increasingly conservative (re)interpretation at this time.[24]

In February 1996, 22-year-old Saima Waheed married against the wishes of her parents, leading to a contentious legal battle which gripped the country and generated what can only be described as a "moral panic" (Cohen, 1972: 9)[25] at the national level.[26] Legally speaking, the issue was fairly straightforward. An earlier, precedent-setting case had already established, without ambiguity, that an adult Muslim woman in Pakistan had the religious and legal right to contract marriage on her own behalf, without the intercession of a *wali* or legal guardian. Moreover, such "runaway marriages" are hardly news even—or perhaps especially—in socially conservative societies such as India and Pakistan. However, the real issue was that Waheed was the college-educated daughter of an economically and politically influential family, the Ropris. Arshad Ahmad, the man she chose to marry, was a teacher at a government college in a small town.

Waheed had informed her parents of her desire to marry Ahmad, and his parents, following prescribed social norms, had followed up by formally approaching her family with a marriage proposal. However, when it became clear that her family was not only rejecting the proposal but intended to marry her elsewhere, Waheed took decisive action. She and Ahmad married in the office of a friend of his (a lawyer) with all the required legal and religious protocols. Waheed returned home immediately afterwards, and some days later broke the news to her family, expecting that they would capitulate in the face of a *fait accompli* and agree to a formal public ceremony. Instead, she was beaten, drugged and deprived of food for several days. She finally managed to escape and elicit the services of Asma Jahangir.

Waheed's family, the Ropris, were part of the new moneyed elite which had risen to power under Zia ul Haq in the late 1970s, and were "an influential family with strong connections in the 'right' places," namely "the administration, judiciary, army and the establishment" (Beena Sarwar, cited in Hussain, 1997: 216).[27] Moreover, Waheed's father and uncle were prominent leaders of a highly conservative Sunni sect. The decision by a daughter of the house to publicly violate the norms of this new, upwardly mobile orthodoxy was therefore no laughing matter. The fact that Waheed elicited the support of Asma Jahangir and chose to live in the women's shelter run by her law firm was to add insult to injury. The Ropris responded by subjecting Ahmad's family to physical harassment, and by filing an FIR with the police charging Jahangir with abduction and challenging the legality of Waheed's marriage on the grounds that it had been contracted without her *wali*'s consent (Mullaly, 2007).

If her family's reaction to her wedding had not forced Waheed to engage legal counsel, and the lawyer in question had been anyone but Asma Jahangir, her case would probably not have entered the public sphere. It is significant that the actions of Waheed's family were not just aimed at what they obviously saw as an "encroachment" (on their property) by a member of a lower class; they were aimed at the immoral ("westernized") feminist, as represented by Asma Jahangir. After all, it must be recalled that the case was one of alleged abduction brought by Waheed's father against *Jahangir* and not Ahmad or his family. This fear of emasculation by the "uppity" and depraved woman reflected the intersection of class and patriarchal anxiety; for the upwardly mobile yet socially conservative class to which the Ropris belonged, Jahangir represented the "westernized" and "morally bankrupt" bourgeois class.

Waheed's case provides a fascinating glimpse into the habitus of her particular class, and its complex and contradictory relationship to an increasingly global capitalist modernity. Despite the conservative nature of her family, Waheed was hardly a stereotypically oppressed or even a "traditional" young woman by Pakistani standards. She was active in intercollegiate (and therefore non-segregated) events where she first met Ahmad. Her father was not only aware of her attendance at such events—despite the gender segregation that was the norm within the family—by all accounts, he took immense pride in her achievements. Waheed owned a car and a mobile phone, both symbols of mobility and autonomy as well as wealth and social status. Daughters of the Ropri family went swimming and riding, both activities associated with the westernized upper classes. Their dress code was also unconventional; they wore jeans and T-shirts at home and, even when outside, continued to wear them underneath the *hijab*.

The fact that her father explicitly exposed his daughters to the lifestyle associated with "westernized modernity" and the "depraved" upper classes *as a means to secure social status* shows the complex and contradictory relationship between desire, class and patriarchal interests especially as mediated through/by the processes of economic and cultural globalization. But these accoutrements were given to Waheed to enhance her *father's* social status, in particular by making her a more desirable commodity in the marriage market, which her father could expect to deploy to his strategic advantage, given that marriages in Pakistan (as elsewhere) are still very much about cementing relations between *men*. Waheed, on the other hand, understood her education as a means of asserting her independence. But the minute she challenged her father's authority, all these markers of privilege were summarily taken away, as was her mobility (Hussain, 1997: 221).

The judgments of the panel composed of Justices Ramday, Chaudhry and Qayyum form a rich text which deserves a close discursive analysis. This text is structured around the master binary of East/West, with "the East" (specifically the Muslim social order) understood as the sanctum of family values, and "the West" as the locus of immorality and the disintegration of the family, when in fact the contradiction which emerges in the judgments is actually that between legal Islamic provisions and cultural values which have little to do with Islam. Within this text, Waheed's exercise of a right granted to her both by secular and religious law emerged as quintessentially *transgressive*, and hence shameful both at the familial and national level. This act of moral depravity on her part was connected to the "loss of cultural purity caused by the combined influences of neo-imperial designs and the treachery of their local collaborators" (ibid.: 202), the "local collaborators" being feminist activists in general, and her lawyer, Asma Jahangir, in particular.[28] That this was no ordinary case involving the legality of a certain (female) individual's actions, but had implications for the very moral foundations of the nation, was underscored by the way in which Justice Chaudhry began his judgment: "We are national judges and as such custodians of the morals of the citizens" (*Pakistan Law Digest (PLD)*, 1997: 341).

Far from being an independent or balanced narrative, Justice Chaudhry's judgment literally rehearsed the sequence of events from the perspective of the petitioner, Waheed's father. Thus, among other things, he stated that Waheed was "allegedly" abducted by Asma Jahangir and detained at the women's shelter run by her law firm (ibid.: 313). The substitution of "abduction" for a voluntary act deprived Waheed of agency while simultaneously and paradoxically criminalizing her actions (despite the ambiguity hinted at by the word "allegedly") while ironically shifting the blame on to the legal counsel she had engaged to defend her case. This was not incidental, for following on the prominent role played by the women's movement in resisting Zia's Islamization project, Islamist discourse had begun to construct "the feminist" as the quintessential Other of a moral (that is, Islamic) order. Given the slide between Islam and nation, "the feminist" was also a seditious figure who actively worked to sully Pakistan's image abroad while destroying the social fabric of Pakistani society by leading impressionable young women astray.[29]

The Saima Waheed case reflected a contradiction between legal Islamic provisions and non-Islamic cultural norms/values specific to a particular society. Under both Islamic law and the Pakistan Penal Code, Waheed had been perfectly within her rights when she married Ahmad. The judgments of Justices Qayyum and Ramday conceded as much, even as they expressed their intense disapproval of "runaway marriages" and the lax moral standards of Pakistani society which appeared to enable them. Justice Qayyum found that the "sole question which arises for determination is as to whether a Muslim adult girl can marry without consent of her Wali," and on this question his answer "has to be in the affirmative" (ibid.: 352). The intense discomfort felt by Qayyum at having to reach this conclusion is testified to by his revelation that he did so only after having failed "*despite his best efforts* ... to discover any principle on the basis of which it can be held that Nikah of sui juris Muslim girl without consent of her Wali should be invalid" (ibid.: 352; emphasis added).

What the text of these judgments showed was the contradiction between the clear injunctions of the law which recognized the *sui juris* status of an adult Muslim woman, and the judges' own moral code which seemed to require that the agency granted by the law be somehow undermined. Their attempts to square this circle make for fascinating reading, providing a glimpse into how "Islam" was being actively reinterpreted in an increasingly conservative direction at this time. That the established provisions of Islamic law were essentially under contestation here for being too liberal demonstrated the extent of the rightward shift in Pakistan, one that was most certainly not about upholding some essential Islam or the sanctity of the shariah. Islam and the shariah were powerful but merely *ex post facto* ways to justify actions and ideas. That is, something tangible called "Islam" did not *determine* the actions and opinions of elites, clerics, state functionaries and even ordinary people in Pakistan as much as it was *pressed into service* to sanction deeply held beliefs and norms that had their basis in social institutions such as the *biradari* system,[30] tribal custom, or even, simply, petty-bourgeois conservatism.[31] When Islamic injunctions proved inconvenient or clashed with established prejudices, customs and norms, they were either quietly sidelined, or subjected to reinterpretation in light of the "the accepted norms of Islamic society." As Eqbal Ahmed (2004: 237) noted, "the pattern of violence against women suggests not so much personal deviation but social and political pathology so deeply ingrained that we confer upon it the legitimacy of religion and laws."

In an effort to override the clear injunctions of Islamic law with regard to adult Muslim women's *sui juris* status, for example, the judges in the Saima Waheed case sought to present marriage as a special and sanctified act set apart from all others, and to argue that while Muslim women may have *sui juris* status in other aspects of life, this status did not—indeed, could not—apply to marriage.

Turning the accepted understanding of the status of marriage in Islam on its head, Justice Chaudhry declared that marriage in Islam was a *social* and not a *civil* contract; the idea that it was a civil contract was a misapprehension with roots in the period of British colonialism. As a *social* contract, Chaudhry argued, a marriage was not valid in Islam unless it was publicly announced; thereby, a "runaway marriage," which was by its very nature secret, could not but be invalid under Islamic law. Not content with this radical revisionism, Chaudhry echoed the words of the prosecuting council in declaring that, in fact, marriage in Islam was no less than a form of *ibadat*, or worship.

Drawing on texts as varied as a handbook of sociology, Will Durant's *Age of Faith*, an encyclopedia of religion and ethics, and an issue of *Reader's Digest*, Justice Chaudhry also put forward the argument that the family was the fundamental unit of society across the world. This was even more so in Islam which "being religion of nature and covering all human activity from cradle to grave" took a special interest in its "integrity, upkeep and preservation"; marriage therefore was not simply the union of two individuals, but that of two *families* (PLD, 1997: 326). Clearly, decisions about such an important aspect of social life could hardly be left to the two individuals concerned, and certainly not to the woman: "The parents are responsible for marriage of the children generally and girls particularly. The learned counsel for the petitioner correctly referred to Encyclopaedia of Religion and Ethics by James Hastings to argue that this is not only in Islam but recognized by all religions" (ibid.: 326).

Given the fundamental importance of the family for society as a whole, and the dangers of letting men and women (but particularly women) make independent decisions about something as crucial as their own marriage, Justice Chaudhry felt it necessary to remind parents of their duty

> ...to marry the children *particularly girls* at the earliest point of time. They should not afford opportunity to outsiders in the house or outside to come across the young girls [who] may be visitors, servants, drivers of public conveyance. *It is absolutely essential to preserve the purity of the homes and this is why much emphasis has been laid by the Islam that females should not mix up with males.* (ibid.: 343; emphasis added)

Chaudhry also declared filial disobedience "a major sin," arguing that "obedience should and can be enforced by courts" (ibid.: 345–51). This conclusion creates a theoretical situation in which individuals can *never* attain majority—at least, not until the death of their parents. Justice Chaudhry did not appear to limit the enforcement of filial obedience to any particular kind of action, or to a specific gender, but it is difficult to imagine a consensus around the idea that adult Muslim men must be beholden to their parents' wishes in all spheres of their lives. Given his ruminations on the family and marriage, it is clear that in effect the idea is to prevent *women* from exercising agency, particularly in matters relating to choice of marriage partner.

In both Justice Chaudhry's and Justice Ramday's judgment, the West featured as a self-consolidating Other, its current moral bankruptcy testified to by the break-down of the family and the decline in the importance of marriage, both of which were caused by "the agitation of women" for equal rights (in particular, the demand for the equal sharing of assets on the dissolution of the marriage bond which had resulted in "men and women ... living without marriage bond in order to save property" (ibid.: 327). It is interesting to note that in Chaudhry's view, the demand for equal rights for women was the sole cause of the decline of Western society. Of course, this is not far removed from the arguments put forth by conservatives within the US itself, a fact reflected in Justice Chaudhry's reference to an article in a recent issue of *Reader's Digest*: "Doing drugs, abusing alcohol, stealing, getting a young woman pregnant out of wedlock—today, none of these behaviours is the deep embarrassment it should be," the writer had apparently commented. As a result, "children will grow up without the security and guidance of a caring father and mother committed to each other. Once the social ties and mutual obligation of the family disintegrate, communities fall apart" (ibid.: 327). Chaudhry referenced Hillary Clinton's "it takes a village" speech to show that even the immoral West realized the importance of the family and the community, and approvingly noted the reportedly positive response to the speech because it indicated that "the 'evil empire' of United States of America is within reach of its lost paradise. *Although it has become sole power but is feeling hollow and deficient because of collapse of family nucleus*" (ibid.: 327; emphasis added).

According to Justice Chaudhry, the lesson to be learnt from the moral decline of the West was that the fault lay in the very sort of social change, that is, secularism, "which is being thrusted [*sic*] upon Pakistan society in somewhat similar fashion, which is seen to prefaces [*sic*] the subsequent explosion of family unit in other societies in [the] west" (ibid.: 327). For, according to Chaudhry, it was secularism which had underpinned the very idea of a women's movement as well as influencing its demands; this women's movement created agentic women, which led to the rise of immorality (specifically, pre-marital sex and adultery), which then destroyed the family unit and ultimately, led to the destruction of western society as a whole. And so Justice Chaudhry uncon-ditionally dismissed Dr. Tanzil-ur-Rehman's *Code of Islamic Law*—an authoritative source of Muslim law written by a Muslim modernist—which the defense had earlier referred to:

> Suffice it to record here that learned author debated the point without keeping in mind startling results. It was lost sight of the fact that it would lead to a society free from all social and moral values ... The Muslims did not strive in the past, they are making efforts today and they would never endeavour for such a society in future. The views of the learned author also lost sight of the sufferings of [the] west by following the theory of equality and sui juris. (ibid.: 340)

Chaudhry's argument here is that the very idea of "equality and *sui juris*" status for women had led to the moral and social decline of the West and so was something which Muslims must forever remain vigilant against. Chaudhry's cavalier dismissal of this established text on Islamic law and his linking of its (modernist) precepts to moral decline, along the lines experienced by the West, is noteworthy because it reflects the marginalization of modernist Islam within the Pakistani mainstream, and the rightward shift in the ideas about what could legitimately be considered "Islamic."

The third and deciding judgment—that of Justice Ramday—was the most interesting and also potentially the most dangerous in its implications for women. Despite ultimately conceding the validity of Waheed's marriage to Ahmad, he placed such marriages on the outer margins of the licit. Much like the second judgment (that of Justice Qayyum), it set up a moral discourse, universalizing the issue in a way that both revealed and played up the intense patriarchal anxieties that the case had generated. For example, referring to other cases presided on by Justices Chaudhry and Qayyum, Justice Ramday noted that

... in all those cases, each young, unmarried girl had managed to establish contact with a man; this contact then developed into a secret liaison and this secret affair then allegedly culminated into a secret marriage; each girl disappeared from her parental home; apprehending worst of consequences, the family in each case commenced a frantic search for their daughter/sister to ultimately find out, after weeks in some cases and after months in others, that their dear-one has contracted an *alleged* marriage. (ibid.: 353; emphasis added)

The narrative builds a climactic tension through a story of intrigue and the ultimate betrayal of the patriarchal family by the transgressive, emasculating woman. The rhetorical strategy deployed (through the repetition of the words "all" and "each") projects *all* parents as being at risk of becoming victims of their daughters' (actual or potential) "dishonorable" actions.

Within the text of Ramday's judgment, Islam's superiority in having recognized women as independent legal entities long before the West, is asserted at the same time and often within the same breath as the condemnation of Waheed for having taken advantage of precisely this recognition. Ramday conceded that "the girl" (like "the boy") could decide on what kind of person she wished to marry and had the right to voice her opinion and withhold her consent should she decide to, *after* her male and female relations have identified an appropriate match (ibid.: 381). Ramday recognized the possibility of conflict between the desire/will of the potential bride (or groom) and those of her/his parents. In such a situation, he upheld the importance of freely given consent as an "indispensable condition," arguing that the "*wali* has no right to grant such a consent on behalf of the woman without her approval," and that he found the idea that "the parents or the family could have a right to force someone to marry a particular individual" insupportable. At the same time, while not going as far as Justice Chaudhry in his ideas about judicially enforceable familial rights, Ramday nevertheless felt that "the parents and family have a definite importance and place in the social set-up ordained by ALLAH" and therefore "a right to be consulted and their wishes ... entitled to respect" (ibid.: 381; emphasis in original). Thus, while (reluctantly) acknowledging Waheed's legal rights as an adult, Ramday was nevertheless disturbed at the thought that she would assert those rights in the face of her parents' disapproval: "Does it behove a person when he is grown-up," he declared, "to say that since he or she had become

SUI JURIS, therefore she or he did not need to listen to his or her parents any more or even to consult them in any matter concerning him, or her?" (ibid.: 374; emphasis in original).

Ramday was also clearly disturbed by the free access that men and women seemed to have to each other in Pakistani society, which allowed them to identify a potential spouse without the appropriate intercession of their families, warning that

> ... the concept of a young girl or a boy for that matter, venturing out in search of a spouse is alien to the teachings of ISLAM and even otherwise this scheme of HUSBAND-SHOPPING which obviously involves testing and trial of the desired material is fraught and pregnant with dangers and cannot be viewed with favour. (ibid.: 381; emphasis in original)

The phrase "husband-shopping" alone reveals the anxiety generated by the inversion of normative relations of power within the marriage market, such that the *men* become the commodities that *women* shop for. The problem posed by the Saima Waheed case for the judges lay in the fact that, as they understood it, the purpose behind Islam's conferral of *sui juris* status on adult Muslim women was not to enable them to flout their parents' wishes in the matter of marriage and/or to freely mix with men. For example, Ramday declared that Islam "abhor[red] ... establishment of liaison between men and women" and "[forbade] pre-marital relationships, secret friendships and secret marriages." His proposed solution to the unacceptable state of affairs was legislation to make "courtships, secret friendships and secret marriages ... a penal offence" (ibid.: 381).

Even the shortest judgment (that of Justice Qayyum) which declared that Waheed's marriage *was* legally valid, conceded its validity only after expressing a shared disapproval of such practices in principle. Thus he found for the defendant despite "sharing the anxiety of my learned brother that Islamic norms of our society and the sanity [*sic*] which Islam attaches to a family must be protected and safeguarded" and agreeing that it was "[t]rue enough that runaway marriages are abhorrent and against the norms of our society and must, therefore, be deplored" (ibid.: 352).

The argument that the institutionalization of women's rights leads inexorably to the complete moral decay of a society makes an appearance in Ramday's discourse as well. For example, the result of the breakdown of the "DIVINE division of labor" between men and women (as represented by the "understandable urge" that some women had "to be left outdoors to become professionals") had led in the "more permissive societies" to "legalisation of carnal intercourse against the order of nature; the so-called marriages between brothers and sisters, unmarried 'wives'; unmarried 'husbands'; unwed mothers and parentless children" (ibid.: 363). Instead, Ramday emphasized the importance of maintaining "a proper balance between the extent of the individual's freedom and the limits to which the individual's rights extended" (ibid.: 365), pointing out the "unfortunate and the unpleasant consequences faced today by the more permissive societies" who had neglected to maintain that balance. The idea of the absolute freedom of individuals amounted, according to Ramday, to "a freedom from all civilised norms of society and a freedom to take human beings back into the animal world" (ibid.: 365). The absent referent in this discourse is, of course, the "West."

Waheed's decision to marry without the consent of her parents—and Asma Jahangir's defense of her action on the basis of Waheed's *sui juris* status—was equated in the judgments of Chaudhry *and* Ramday with the blind worship of a morally bankrupt West (itself regretting its loss of a moral compass) which could only lead to the destruction of Pakistani society. Ramday ultimately ruled in favor of the marriage, not on the basis of the principle that it was Waheed's inalienable right under Islam and the law, but because "invalidating a marriage entails rather serious and even penal consequences" (ibid.: 380). Yet Waheed and Ahmad were forced into hiding out of fear of reprisal from her family, as well as threats from religious groups that disagreed with the decision.

The judgments in the "Saima Waheed love-marriage case" highlight the kind and level of anxiety—to the point of national crisis—produced by female agency as related to women's increasing access to the public sphere and "free" movement beyond the sanctity of the *chaadar* ("veil") and *chaardivaari* ("four walls" of the home). Both Justice Chaudhry and Justice Ramday referred to Islam as a "natural" religion and to the "nature" of women which required that their sexuality be controlled. In this context, acknowledging women's *sui juris* status became tantamount to granting them complete sexual licence, a possibility which could not be tolerated even at the theoretical level, due to its potentially devastating effect on the social fabric of the nation and of the larger Islamic *ummah*. This threat had to be controlled through a collusion of public and private patriarchies—hence the argument about the "DIVINE division of labour" which *required* a return of women to the protection of the *chaadar aur chaardivaari* and the plea to make filial obedience judicially enforceable. It is crucial to note the deep consensus that underlies the very different judgments over the reprehensibility of "love marriages," and the striking similarities between the contradictory judgments of Justice Chaudhry and Justice Ramday on the questions of women's rights and status, filial obedience, and the West. The obsessive (and almost comical) references to the moral decline of the West and the reasons for it show how important the West had become as a self-consolidating Other within the national discourse.

This case highlights the fact that despite ubiquitous references to "Islam," the "Shariat" and even Pakistan as the "Islamic Republic," it is in fact patriarchy—or rather patriarchies—that were at issue here. When it came to the issue of the legality of the marriage, Waheed's case could have easily been resolved by recourse to legal precedence, which is what the Lahore High Court ultimately did, albeit through a split verdict. The judgments of the three justices provide an extremely interesting lens into the complexities of patriarchy within Pakistani society. Among other things, they demonstrate that "Islam"—whether as a basis for individual/national identity, as a religious and cultural system, or as a set of injunctions encoded in theological and juridical textual sources—is an internally contested discourse rather than a coherent monolith.

The Saima Waheed case did not pit "secular liberals" against "religious conservatives," or "fundamentalists." Even members of the liberal elite who supported Waheed's actions on principle expressed a certain degree of anxiety about the precedent it set for their own daughters, underlining the fact that the control of female sexuality was not limited to a particular class or to religious conservatives.[32]

ERASING THE NON-MUSLIM "OTHER"

The circulation of "the West" as a source of immorality in the judgments of the "Saima Waheed case," while not entirely new (nor unique to Pakistan or Muslims), nevertheless points to some significant political and ideological shifts in the international realm which occurred in the 1990s. Chief among them were the end of the Cold War and the break-up of the Soviet Union, and the emergence of a new, post-Cold War geo-politics of the "New World Order" and the "Clash of Civilizations." Significantly, one of the first crises that marked this geo-political shift was the Rushdie affair which coincided with the end of the Cold War. In 1990, Bernard Lewis coined the phrase "the clash of civilizations" in an article in the *Atlantic Monthly* which purported to explain "the roots of Muslim rage." The phrase was of course immortalized by Samuel Huntington as the basis for understanding the post-Cold War world order, and its status as the legitimizing ideology of the New World Order was sealed in the 1991–92 Gulf War, the first major conflict of this new period of world history.

The end of the Cold War and the break-up of the Soviet Union also had a negative impact on an already-beleaguered Pakistani Left, while the Rushdie affair and the Gulf War, as well as the western discourse around them, served to reinforce the idea that a new age of crusades had dawned, in which a Christian West was now at war with Islam. Without the important countervailing—intellectual and political—force of the Left and the anti-imperialist framework it could have offered, Islamists were able to capitalize on the strong anti-West sentiments within Pakistani society and popularize their own culturalist framing of geo-politics. The strong resemblance between this (Islamist) discourse and Huntington's Clash of Civilizations framework has been remarked on by others, but is worth highlighting. The second Palestinian Intifada, and the heating-up of the Kashmiri struggle for self-determination—both of which occurred within the same period—were also exploited by Sunni sectarian groups, religious parties and the Pakistani establishment to build up a sense of a beleaguered global Muslim community under attack by Israel ("the Jews") and the (Christian) West. These events also bolstered an aggressive pan-Islamic nationalist identity which the Afghan War had helped consolidate.

The implications of the growing anti-West sentiment in Pakistan were severe for Pakistani Christians. Already marginalized within Pakistani society, particularly the Punjab, for their perceived "low-caste" status,[33] and from the political process via the institution of separate electorates, the discursive slide between Christianity and "the West" within mainstream discourse in Pakistan resulted in Pakistani Christians being increasingly targeted as proxies of the West. Pakistani Hindus were similarly made the target of retaliatory violence after Hindu nationalists destroyed the Babri Mosque in the Indian city of Ayodhya in 1992.[34]

With Khomeini's *fatwa* against Rushdie and its political and cultural fall-out, blasphemy became a global Muslim issue. In Pakistan, it came to bear a special salience because of Zia's amendments to Pakistan's blasphemy laws a few years previously.

Within Pakistan, Rushdie quickly became a reviled figure, and the West's defense of him, along with its denunciation of the Muslim world, only appeared to confirm the general opinion that he was an agent of the West bent on destroying the Muslim world. Sunni groups and political parties capitalized on this public feeling to mobilize protests across Pakistan.

One of the most popular Pakistani films of 1990, *International Gorillay* ("International Guerillas"), fictionalized the Rushdie affair, complete with a cathartic ending in which the villainous Rushdie is killed by flying Qurans. The film is significant in the way in which it posits Pakistan as the center of the Rushdie controversy. In the film, the fictional Rushdie is depicted as a criminal mastermind plotting to destroy the Muslim world from his lair in the Philippines where he is protected by a private Israeli army. His grand plan involves encouraging moral depravity by opening discos and casinos. Rushdie is shown to amuse himself by torturing Muslims by making them listen to excerpts from the *Satanic Verses*, and by killing the *mujahideen* who attempt to hunt him down. It is worth noting that Pakistan, as the "fortress of Islam," is shown to be central to Rushdie's plan. Rushdie's evil machinations are ultimately thwarted by three Pakistani brothers (the eponymous international guerillas) who swear revenge after their sister is killed by police when protesting against *The Satanic Verses*.

Khomeini's *fatwa* against Rushdie on the charge of blasphemy (not to mention the price put on his head) set a dangerous precedent in Pakistan for dealing with alleged "apostates," and articulated well with the newly revised (and revived) blasphemy laws in Pakistan. The original colonial-era blasphemy laws were intended to curb religious violence and to ensure protection to all religious communities from actions designed to humiliate or intimidate them. Zia ul Haq's amendments removed the crucial prerequisite of establishing malicious intent, narrowed their purview to the protection of Muslim sentiments alone (and, increasingly, to the protection of "Islam"), and left the wording of what counted as blasphemous vague and open-ended. The subjective opinion of the accuser was deemed enough to justify the charge of blasphemy, and the case could be filed by a third party who need not even have been present when the alleged crime occurred. These changes completely subverted the intent of the original blasphemy laws, turning them into dangerous weapons in the hands of a powerful and large majority community.[35] They also created a fertile environment for the playing-out of personal vendettas, professional rivalries and political ambitions.

What rendered these laws truly horrific, however, was the punishment prescribed for blasphemy under Section 295-C; as originally passed by Zia, the amendment had prescribed either life imprisonment, or death. In October 1990, under Nawaz Sharif's first government,[36] the Federal Shariat Court (established under Zia) ruled that in Islam the only acceptable penalty for blasphemy was death and that this punishment, being divinely ordained, could not be commuted.[37] The government could have appealed this decision of the FSC to the Shariat Apellate Bench of the Supreme Court within a prescribed period of time, but since it pointedly did not do so, the death penalty became the mandatory (and only) punishment available for blasphemy.[38]

Before the passage of these amendments by Zia, blasphemy was a non-issue within Pakistan; following it (and especially after the changes to Section 295-C), cases of blasphemy suddenly exploded onto the national stage, confirming concerns about their procedural flaws and their potential for abuse.[39] The addition of the death penalty as the mandatory punishment for blasphemy, the ease with which a case of blasphemy could be registered, and the lack of any accountability or punishment for false accusations, turned these laws into lethal weapons in the hands of the unscrupulous, used to further all manner of agendas.

Although these laws were used against members of all religious communities including Sunni Muslims, the most disproportionately targeted were the Ahmedis and Christians.[40] Even though the higher courts rarely held up the convictions, the mere fact of having been charged with blasphemy increasingly rendered a person vulnerable to violent reprisal from non-state actors.[41] Individuals acquitted by the courts were brazenly murdered in broad daylight, sometimes in the courtroom itself, either by private individuals "inspired" by the poisonous rhetoric of sectarian Sunni extremist groups such as the *Anjuman-i Sipah Sahaba-i Islam* (The Association of the Soldiers of the Companions of the Prophet, henceforth the SSP), or by the sectarian groups themselves.[42] Manzoor Masih, a 13-year-old illiterate Christian boy, accused of blasphemy along with two others, was killed by SSP activists as they made their way out of the sessions court after a hearing of their case; the other two—Rehmat and Salamat Masih—were seriously injured. In another case, the accused (Ayub Masih) was killed in the courtroom *during* his trial and after the court had handed down a death sentence. Thus the mere accusation of blasphemy became a virtual death-trap. Families of those accused or charged of blasphemy were forced by fear and/or threats to move to other villages, towns, or cities; those acquitted had to immediately go into hiding.

Soon, mobs and/or individuals began to exact this vigilante violence on the basis of informal charges and/or rumor alone, which would be spread by clerics via mosque loudspeakers. This strategy was evident in Shanti Nagar in 1997 following a false accusation of blasphemy, when a mob comprised of tens of thousands of Muslims descended on the village. Over seven hundred homes were destroyed, along with four churches, and more than 2,500 villagers had to flee for their lives. Members of the local district's police force were involved in inciting and organizing the violence, while others watched from the sidelines. There were reports that some even engaged in looting. The carnage ended only after the army arrived on the scene.

As Eqbal Ahmed noted at the time:

> In a morally engaged society so appalling an event would have caused self-examination and soul-searching in the media and educated sections of society. From the government and political parties we had a right to expect symbolic as well as substantive gestures to restore confidence, affirm values, and reinforce the rule of law. Yet no evidence of concern or introspection is at hand. (Ahmed, 2004: 231)

No political officer visited Shanti Nagar, and ironically, the only political leader to do so and to publicly condemn it as an atrocity was Qazi Hussain Ahmed of the *Jama'at-i Islami*.

Whenever a case of blasphemy came up for trial, sectarian Sunni groups and parties such as the SSP organized protests outside and inside the court. Lawyers who dared to defend the accused and judges who acquitted them received death threats, which carried particular weight in the aftermath of the murder of Justice Arif Iqbal Bhatti, the judge who acquitted Rehmat Masih and Salamat Masih (Manzoor Masih's co-accused). Justice Bhatti was murdered in his rooms in the Lahore High Court by a low-level government employee who, by his own account, had been carried away by the vitriolic newspaper coverage of the case. The infiltration of the SSP into the various levels of the judicial system and the courts in the Punjab added to the general atmosphere of fear generated by this violence such that lawyers became increasingly reluctant to defend those accused of blasphemy. Hina Jilani and Asma Jahangir once more proved their mettle as legal activists by taking on many of the cases in the Lahore High Court despite specific threats against their lives.[43]

A Human Rights Watch report on violence against women noted that Nawaz Sharif's efforts to continue Zia's legacy of Islamization "not only reinforced the legitimacy of Zia ul-Haq's discriminatory Islamic laws," but "bestowed greater discretion and authority on judges to give legal weight, by invoking Islamic precedents and references at random, to biased assumptions about women in a variety of civil and criminal cases" (HRW, 1999: 25). The same can be said for cases of the blasphemy law. Judges exhibited overt and explicit bias, treating the accused (especially non-Muslims) as guilty, dismissing testimony and eyewitness accounts that showed the accusation to have been spurious, and in one case declaring that a witness could not possibly be lying because his beard showed that he was obviously a good Muslim.

The Blasphemy Laws—specifically 295-C—also, predictably, became potent political weapons. A case of blasphemy was filed against Benazir Bhutto in 1993 because she had argued that the system of separate electorates and the blasphemy laws went against human rights principles. Professor Akhtar Hameed Khan, a veteran social worker and pioneer of the highly respected Orangi Pilot Project in Karachi was charged with being "anti-Islamic," no doubt because the OPP was a community development project which mobilized home-based women workers (Rouse, 1998). These cases, like all others, were eventually dismissed, but the very ease and frequency with which they occurred, and the very real possibility of violent reprisal, produced a general atmosphere of fear for those engaged in progressive projects.[44] This fear, as well as crass political opportunism has also prevented any amendment in either the Blasphemy Laws or the Zina Ordinance over the years, despite the clear miscarriages of justice associated with both.

Over the years, the use of violence has increased and changed, from acts of vigilantism against individuals to full-scale pogroms planned and executed with the collusion of religious leaders, local police and politicians. In fact, the use of violence by non-state actors such as the SSP has been increasingly condoned by the state and its functionaries at every level, from police officers to judges.[45] Even politicians refuse to condemn it, although Benazir Bhutto and even members of Nawaz Sharif's administration initially spoke out against the blasphemy laws and about the need to amend them. Whether this is out of fear, vested interest, or religious belief is immaterial—the effect is the same, namely the silencing of progressive voices and the reinforcement of reactionary forces.[46] When, during a debate in the National Assembly following the murder of Manzoor Masih, retired Supreme Court Justice Dorab Patel, himself a member of the Zoroastrian faith, declared that the blasphemy laws should be amended, he was interrupted by a member of Parliament belonging to the SSP who shouted "anyone who commits blasphemy will meet the fate of Manzoor Masih" (*AI Index*: ASA 33/08/94: 2). This episode was chilling at the time because of its unprecedented nature; today, such pronouncements have become even more frightening for having become routine.

The very existence of the blasphemy laws, the fuzziness of the definition of blasphemy, the mandatory death penalty attached to them, and their disproportionate use against members of the Muslim and non-Muslim minority communities has poisoned the body politic and shattered the state's always-tenuous accord with its minorities. With every case of blasphemy, public discourse in Pakistan, increasingly hegemonized by militant Sunni groups and their sympathizers, has moved further to the Right.[47]

Epilogue
The Neoliberal Security State

"Bhooke mar gaye maiñ aur tu, loot ke le gaya GHQ." ("You and I are dying of hunger, The GHQ has looted everything.")[1]

Between 2001 and 2003, 18 villages in the district of Okara in the Punjab were the focus of a violent crackdown by the paramilitary Pakistan Rangers. Villagers, regardless of age or gender, were subjected to a campaign of sustained harassment, arbitrary arrest, detention, torture and death. For roughly three months in 2002 and then again in 2003, the Rangers literally besieged these villages, blocking off all access roads and preventing the passage of food, medicine and people to and from them.

At issue was the refusal of over a thousand tenant farmers in this region to sign a new contract with the military which changed the terms of their sharecropping agreement, transforming their status from tenants to lessees. The refusal was born of a very real and justified fear that this new contract rendered them vulnerable: the requirement of cash payment as opposed to harvest shares meant that a bad harvest could leave them indebted or unable to pay their "rent," while the change in their status would mean that they were no longer covered by the provisions of the Punjab Tenancy Act of 1887 under which they, as long-term cultivators, could not easily be evicted and could even potentially claim ownership of the land.[2] The farmers had, in fact, been unsuccessfully petitioning the government since the 1970s for ownership under the provisions of this Act. Aside from these issues, the new contract laid out a number of other conditions which were clearly designed to facilitate the eviction of farmers. For example, the contract "severely limited the use of natural resources by the lessee," including firewood and mud for building homes, requiring lessees to obtain permission from the military authorities.

The farms in Okara are part of 68,000 acres of agricultural land owned by the provincial government in the most fertile part of the Punjab (which is itself the breadbasket of the country). At the turn of the last century, the British introduced canal irrigation to the hitherto forested area, making it prized agricultural land. Although the colonial government had promised proprietary rights to migrant farmers from eastern Punjab who had been brought in to help develop the area, it had retained control over a large portion of these "canal-colonies" which contributed towards the creation of a landed elite in the Punjab and Sindh. The military farms in question had originally been under the control (but not ownership) of the British military at the time of Partition, following which the Pakistan Army had taken them over. The actual ownership of the land rested with the Punjab government, with the army being merely a lessee, although it had been trying unsuccessfully to have the land transferred to itself.

In 2000, after the military changed the terms of the contract and tried to force the farmers to sign it, the latter organized themselves under the umbrella of *Anjuman-i Mazarin-i Punjab* (Association of Tenant Farmers of Punjab—AMP). In the early stages of the dispute, the farmers hoped to convince the military to leave their status as it was; they even agreed to the demand for cash payment. The military's intransigence, and its use of intimidating tactics against the farmers, their families and their supporters strengthened the farmers' resolve to fight the military, and turned the AMP into a militant movement of almost a million.[3] During the course of the conflict, it was discovered that the army had no legal claim to the land at all, even as a lessee, since the original lease which the British military had signed with the Punjab government had expired in 1943 and had never been renewed. Emboldened, the farmers refused to pay the military anything at all, and demanded ownership rights to the land, adopting the powerful cry *"mulki ya maut!"* ("ownership or death!"). This brought on a wave of further and more intense repression by the army, with Okara becoming the epicenter of the confrontation between the military (via its vicious paramilitary force, the Pakistan Rangers[4]) and the AMP. Amazingly, the AMP not only managed to survive, but grow in numbers and strength.

The AMP has become an enduring symbol of successful subaltern resistance to the most powerful institution in the country. Today, the farmers (unofficially) control the majority of the land in the military farms, and still steadfastly refuse to pay any rent. The army continues its harassment and the civilian government has reneged on promises made to the leadership, but the movement remains strong and undivided. In 2010, it commemorated a decade of militant struggle against the military and its feudal allies with a rally comprising 15,000 landless peasants which then made its way in a "long march" from the Okara district to the Punjab Assembly building in the provincial capital of Lahore.

The AMP's struggle not only lies at the nexus of almost all the major issues that face Pakistan today but also single-handedly undermines the dominant discourse on Pakistan in the West. At a million strong, the AMP is the largest genuinely grassroots-based social movement in Pakistan's history and yet has no connection with Islam, *jihad*, or sectarian militancy. In fact, it is a movement which exemplifies solidarity across the religious divide since it is comprised of both Christians—who represent 40 per cent of the farmers—and Muslims. The AMP also defies stereotypes of Pakistan (especially of the "backward" classes) with regard to gender; women have been at the forefront from its very beginning, leading marches and protests with their *thappas* (sticks used to beat the dirt out of clothes while washing) in the air, defying the repressive apparatus of the state despite being subjected to abduction, physical abuse and torture (Saigol, 2004).

"*JITHE VEKHO FAUJAÑ EE FAUJAÑ*" ("EVERYWHERE YOU LOOK, THE ARMY")[5]

The story of the AMP also underlines the central role of the Pakistani military in establishing a neoliberal security state. It should be abundantly clear by now that any effort to understand Pakistan's current problems—the fragility of democracy, the corruption of politics, the weakness of social and political institutions, and the issue of religious extremism and militancy—must begin and end with the Pakistani military establishment. The military dominates the state, society and the economy, creating a predatory environment which mitigates against the interest of ordinary Pakistanis as well as against peace and stability in the region.

The predatory nature of the military in Pakistan is starkly exposed in its relationship to land, which most Pakistanis were not even aware of until the confrontation between the tenants in Okara and the Rangers became national news (Siddiqa, 2007). This is astounding, when you consider that the military, as a corporate institution, is the single largest landowner in Pakistan of both urban real estate and rural agricultural land.[6] Given the economic, political and symbolic power that land-ownership confers in a primarily agricultural country like Pakistan, the military's relationship to land is the least well-understood and yet possibly most important aspect of its economic and political domination.[7] In fact, as Siddiqa (2007) has pointed out, the military's behavior towards the tenants in Okara is of a piece with its general attitude towards the poor and disenfranchised, such as landless peasants, fisherfolk communities, or even those low down in the military hierarchy such as ordinary soldiers.[8] Okara and other similar land-grabs take place against the backdrop of an acute inequity in the distribution of land in Pakistan, where rural poverty is directly linked to a lack of access to land (Zaidi, 2005).[9] Issues of skewed patterns of land ownership, therefore, pertain directly to the Pakistani military's parasitic relationship to its people. It was significant that in 2003, at the very moment that the confrontation with the AMP reached its peak, the state shut the door on any possibility of future land reforms (Ahmed, 2003).

The military's eagerness to change the terms of its contract with the tenants on the military farms reflected another aspect of the development of the neoliberal security state: the corporate control of agriculture in Pakistan. As an expert on tenancy law pointed out to Human Rights Watch, if the army was mainly interested in switching to cash payments rather than harvest share, the terms of the original contract allowed that change to be negotiated. Also, since the earnings from these military farms were "fairly paltry" (HRW, 2004: 17), the push to implement a new contract with its attendant conditionalities was clearly designed to make it easier to evict the tenants (Akhtar, 2003). In 2001, Musharraf's government passed a Corporate Farming Ordinance,[10] while the 2001–02 budget provided incentives for the further corporatization of agriculture. Such initiatives were in line with global trends and with the Pakistani establishment's pro-liberalization stance which included the privatization of state enterprises, the removal of welfare subsidies and safety nets, and the levying of taxes which disproportionately burden the poor.

It is clear, however, that more than economic interests were at stake for the military in terms of its handling of the tenant revolt in Okara. The military's extensive ownership and control of land underwrites its vast patronage network, through which it rewards its own personnel but also co-opts politicians, media personnel, and so on. Control over agricultural land is also a "resonant and enduring symbol of the powerful status of the military" (HRW, 2004: 5). Being the totalitarian institution that it is, the military was shocked at the temerity of the tenants who stood up to it, and was worried that the virus of revolt might spread if the movement were either accommodated or allowed to continue. The deployment of the Rangers and the brutal nature of the violence unleashed upon the farmers and their families and supporters was thus a carefully considered strategy. It was also very much in line with the way in which the Pakistani military and its paramilitary forces deal with dissent or resistance.[11]

The stranglehold of the military over every aspect of Pakistani state and society has also contributed in large part to the transformation of Pakistan into a heavily indebted neoliberal security state, underwritten once again by the US's latest war in Afghanistan. It is worth noting, for example, that in every budget since Independence, Pakistan's allocations and expenditure on defense have dwarfed those for development (Zaidi, 2005). Not only does this bloated defense expenditure divert money away from investment in other sectors, which might directly and indirectly improve the conditions of the poor, it also contributes in large part to the debt burden which tightens IMF and World Bank control over Pakistan's economy.

The US's new war in Afghanistan once again gave a military regime in Pakistan a new lease on life. The government of Pervez Musharraf, which had come to power in 1999 after deposing the then Prime Minister Nawaz Sharif had been fast losing legitimacy, and the Pakistani military was quick to use the "Global War on Terror" (GWoT) to consolidate its domestic power. The starkest example of this, and one which exemplifies the economic and political agenda of the neoliberal security state, is the occupation of Baluchistan. The military's fifth operation in Baluchistan was already underway when the GWoT was launched, but the latter provided a useful cover under which the military could initiate a full-scale occupation of the province. A long (and continuing) string of harassments, threats, arrests, torture and disappearances[12] designed to squash dissent and resistance was initiated, which, predictably, had the opposite effect of producing a new and even more determined Baluch insurgency. The western media's inability to parse the various forms of militancy in Pakistan proved extremely useful for the Pakistan Army, as it encouraged the discursive collapse of the resolutely secular Baluch insurgency with Islamist militancy, while diverting funds allocated for dealing with the Taliban to suppressing the nationalists (Tahir, 2010). The army also initiated a strategy of neutralizing Baluch nationalism through the infusion of Islamist ideology and the support of Islamist political groups via the intelligence agencies. This strategy has proven to be an overwhelming failure, as nationalist feelings remain high and have in fact become stronger as the military occupation of Baluchistan has grown in size and intensity ("MT,"

2010b).[13] Events such as the assassination (in August 2006) of Nawab Akbar Khan Bugti, a respected political figure and staunch Baluch nationalist, by the Pakistan military and the rape of a woman doctor by an army officer, and the subsequent refusal of the army to either hand the officer over or prosecute him further hardened the resolve of the nationalists.

This latest army operation in Baluchistan accompanied the launching of several high-profile and lucrative "development projects" in the province (many in cooperation with the Chinese government), the most significant being the Gwadar Port Project and the proposed establishment of several new cantonments in resource-rich districts. Baluchistan is of immense importance for the military—it is a resource-rich and, given its borders with Iran and Afghanistan, geo-politically strategic region. Despite its wealth of natural resources, however, Baluchistan is Pakistan's poorest province with the lowest social and human development indicators.[14] The Pakistani establishment's relationship with Baluchistan is colonial in the extreme. Baluch grievances with the center include the expropriation of the province's wealth, land-grabs and the consequent loss of livelihood (the military often displaces/evicts locals when it occupies large tracts of land), and continued high unemployment in the face of large-scale projects as jobs generated are pointedly filled by non-Baluchs. Baluchistan is also the Pakistani state's nuclear weapons testing site of choice—the Chaghai Hills that became part of mainstream nationalist lore as a symbol of the might of the Pakistani military following the explosion of nuclear devices in 1998, are located in Baluchistan. The testing was done without Baluch consent and certainly without any effort made to shield the population from the effects of radiation.

Included among the military's investments in Baluchistan are three nuclear and chemical weapons testing sites, eight naval bases (not including the strategic port of Gwadar), six missile testing ranges, seven air bases, and 59 paramilitary facilities. Seven thousand acres of land was "acquired" recently for a new airport by the Pakistan Air Force, which is also eyeing up 70,000 acres along the Coastal Highway for a new weapons-testing and firing range, and pressuring the local population to vacate the land (Lakshman, 2008).[15] The extent of the irregularities surrounding the transfer of land in Baluchistan has been such that the Supreme Court of Pakistan took cognizance of it in October 2006. The navy's control of the Makran coast has made the coastal waters—with their rich fishing grounds—inaccessible to the local fishing community, severely impacting their livelihoods. Meanwhile, the navy has struck lucrative deals with international trawlers (Talpur, 2010).

Ayesha Siddiqa (2007) has outlined the extent of the Pakistani military's economic empire, along with its implications for the well-being of the vast majority of Pakistanis and for Pakistan as a state. The Pakistani military dominates each and every aspect of the economy from agriculture to manufacturing to services and, unsurprisingly, jealously guards the information pertaining to this economic empire. This domination is based on the existence and proliferation of military-owned and operated enterprises such as agricultural farms, manufacturing companies producing everything from fertilizer to breakfast cereal, and commercial ventures such as military banks and real estate agencies. Indirect control is enabled by the ubiquitous presence of serving and retired military personnel in private and public enterprises, key government departments, and throughout the civil bureaucracy. This enables military enterprises as well as private enterprises run by (ex)military personnel to get privileged access to all possible perks including foreign investment, government subsidies and monies, and infrastructure development at public expense.

Siddiqa (2007) has convincingly shown that, in direct contradiction to the claims of the military, the military's dominance of the Pakistani economy is more like a choke-hold, strangling initiative, encouraging patronage and cronyism, and producing large-scale distortions and inefficiencies. The military's domination of the economy has severe implications for the well-being of Pakistan's citizens, especially its most vulnerable. It has a negative impact, as one can imagine, on labor rights, given the number of private and semi-private enterprises run by ex-military men and their family members. Constant increases in military expenditure, especially in the context of structural adjustment, shortchange social welfare and development.

Its domination and manipulation of the political process even when it is not technically in charge, and its hold over the country's political leadership breeds authoritarianism, while through its double-game with regard to religious extremism and militancy it actively produces instability. All these factors mitigate against (and not by accident) any hope that democracy will take root in Pakistan. Under these circumstances, and given the clear and ample empirical evidence, it is difficult to argue that the Pakistani military can in any way be considered a savior, even of a small handful of liberal elites. The military is far from an agent of progressive social change or economic development in Pakistan; the claim that the Pakistani military can not only produce political and social stability, but somehow be an agent of democracy can only be the result of willful (indeed, *willed*) ignorance.

It is important to note that the Pakistani military's stranglehold over its people has been enabled over the last half-century by the material and moral support of the US establishment, with military regimes such as Zia's and Musharraf's being given a new lease on life by the US's own military adventurism. Along the way, this support has been justified—by Cold War/establishment social scientists as well as key decision-makers in Washington, DC—on the premise that the military in Third World societies generally, or the Pakistani military in particular, is a source of stability, development and/or progress.[16] With political Islam replacing the Soviet Union as Public Enemy Number One following the end of the Cold War, the US continued to choose unrepresentative regimes, civilian or military, across the Muslim world purportedly because of their "secular" credentials, a premise that is belied by the case of the Pakistani military given its role in the creation and support of the Taliban in Afghanistan, of Kashmir-focused jihadi groups such as the infamous *Lashkar-i-Tayyaba* and of sectarian outfits such as the *Jaish-i-Muhammad* and the SSP.

THE STATE OF PROGRESSIVE POLITICS

The story of the tenant uprising against the might of the military in Okara also highlights the state of progressive politics in Pakistan today. Although NGO activists did eventually get involved once the movement had made it to the headlines—sadly, with disastrous results for the movement—their absence from what was essentially the front line of the struggle of ordinary Pakistanis was no coincidence.[17]

Major shifts occurred in the field of progressive politics in Pakistan in the 1990s, some of which were discussed briefly at the end of the last chapter. These were not unique to Pakistan, and were the result of the emerging consolidation of a global neoliberal project ushered in by the break-up of the Soviet Union. This project had, like all global projects worth their salt, economic, political, intellectual, ideological and cultural dimensions whose ultimate aim was the reorganization of the world in the interests of capital. The role of the Bretton Woods institutions and later the Washington Consensus in realizing this agenda is well known. With the fall of the Soviet Union, History itself was declared to have ended, and all alternatives to capitalism were smugly dismissed (Fukuyama, 1992). Within academia, a liberal attack on Marxism (both as an analytical frame and as an emancipatory project) was launched with much fanfare. And crucially, for our story here, the World Bank began to promote non-governmental organizations as the antidote to the unwieldy (and implicitly, totalitarian) welfare state. An abstract discourse of "universal human rights" replaced real political engagement and mobilization.

In Pakistan, as elsewhere, the organizational and ideological decimation of the Left meant that liberal politics and values came to stand in for progressivism *tout court*. The NGO-ization of this liberal politics (with its focus on the priorities of international donors, preoccupation with the funding cycle, and bureaucratization) effectively divorced it from the real issues facing the majority of Pakistanis and rendered it a politically and culturally ineffective force within the national mainstream. For all intents and purposes, then, Pakistani liberals made themselves irrelevant to national politics and were unable to provide a counter to the rightward shifts that were rapidly changing the political, social, economic and cultural landscape of the country.

The disconnect with people's issues was reflected in the fact that NGO liberals did not agitate against structural adjustment policies and programs in Pakistan, which consistently targeted the poorest and most vulnerable, nor did they see it fit to take on neoliberal globalization until international donors began to fund anti-globalization work.[18] This was in stark contrast to the critiques of globalization which were emanating from the global South and the mobilizations against it that were building across the world. NGO "activists" also did not see it fit to connect with the people's struggles which had begun to emerge, such as the AMP, until these struggles became well known nationally and internationally, and especially until donors began to take notice of them.

Not only did NGOs in Pakistan not resist neoliberal globalization, they often enabled it by taking on the state's social welfare responsibilities (Toor, 2001). The case of a well-known education NGO is illustrative. It actively bid to take over the running of government schools under the rubric of a "public-private partnership"; crucially, the state handed over the responsibility of running these public schools, but did not relinquish control over the curriculum. As one of Pakistan's most respected feminist educationists pointed out, this not only enabled the state's retreat from its social welfare responsibilities (a major focus of structural adjustment policies), but also ensured a more efficient delivery of the state's retrogressive ideological agenda as coded into the national curriculum.[19] Another, even more stark example was that of the overwhelming support given by NGOs to Musharraf's plan to devolve power to the local level in 2000–01. The "devolution plan" sounded progressive, but in fact was essentially in the same vein as Ayub's Basic Democracies and Zia's local bodies elections, designed to undermine national politics rather than devolve power to the people, and to consolidate central control over local governments rather than empower the latter (R. Khan, 2004; International Crisis Group, 2004). Not surprisingly, there was plenty of World Bank and other donor money for NGOs to participate in institutionalizing this plan. The idea of a 30 per cent representation of women at all levels made it especially appealing to NGOs and international donors alike.

NGO liberals' endorsement of this devolution plan was not an anomaly, for they were, in fact, Musharraf's biggest supporters. It may seem paradoxical for those whose bread and butter (literally) is human rights and who were, in many cases, veterans of the anti-Zia movement to be openly supportive of a military dictatorship. The explanation lies in the shifts in the political priorities of Pakistani liberals from the Zia era onwards, both in terms of their material interests and in terms of specific class-based anxieties.

Following Zia's regime, and especially after the Taliban takeover in Afghanistan in the 1990s, Pakistani liberals became increasingly obsessed with what they referred to as "Talibanization"—a catch-all term which included everything from state-led Islamization efforts to the rise in social conservatism and an increase in public displays of piety. As we have seen, the rightward shift in Pakistani politics, society and culture did, in fact, continue after the literal and metaphorical demise of Zia. However, liberals focused on only one aspect of it—the rise of a militant and narrow version of Sunni Islam—while ignoring all the others, particularly the reactionary thrust of the state's economic agenda. Unfortunately, not only did the obsession with "Talibanization" not translate into any form of organized resistance at the social, political, or cultural level,[20] but it also led Pakistani liberals in dangerous and fundamentally anti-progressive directions, a particularly egregious example of which was their open support for Musharraf's *coup d'état* in 1999.

The government of Nawaz Sharif was about to push through the controversial and draconian 15th Amendment to the Constitution, otherwise known as the "Shariat Bill," and had been taking an increasingly aggressive stance *vis-à-vis* women's rights and human rights NGOs. Binyamin, the Punjab government's minister of social welfare had openly vilified these organizations, denouncing them as fifth columnists working to undermine Pakistan and Islam, and serving the interests of Israel, India and the West, and had explicitly begun threatening those that ran them. As a result, instead of condemning the overthrow of a democratically elected government by a military dictator, most NGO activists openly celebrated it as a release and welcomed the general as a savior.

Nighat Said Khan, a prominent women's rights activist from Lahore who had been singled out for special mention by Binyamin,[21] relates her shock at the proceedings of the meeting of the Joint Action Committee for Peace and Democracy (a Lahore-based alliance of 36 organizations and political parties) convened immediately following the coup:

> I assumed that all we would be doing was deciding the wording of our immediate resolution and working out our strategy. The reaction of a majority of the organisations was stunning. They supported the Military taking over. This despite the fact that the JAC was for democracy and most of them were familiar with the history of the military as an institution and its role in politics in Pakistan. (Khan, 2004: ii–iii)

There was much excitement among the NGO elite at the fact that the NGO Bill which Nawaz Sharif's government had been trying to pass would not see the light of day. That this reaction indicated that they were "more interested in saving their NGOs than saving the nation" (ibid.: iii–iv) did not seem to register or matter, especially after Musharraf welcomed many of them into his government with open arms. In fact, so many NGO representatives joined the government in one capacity or another as Ministers, advisers, members of task forces, and consultants, that it became popularly referred to as the "NGO government" (ibid.: iv).

The welcoming of the military as a savior by women's rights and human rights stalwarts reflected a mixture of historical amnesia, political confusion and crass opportunism. Those who supported the coup justified their decision based on the general's liberal lifestyle, an argument that makes sense only if progressive politics in Pakistan can somehow be reduced to a rejection of "Islamization," and political analysis to issues of an individual's lifestyle rather than an understanding of institutions. The widespread belief that the army was a progressive force that would save the country from "Talibanization" also reflected an ignorance of the military's role in creating and sustaining the very forces of the religious Right which it was expected to protect the people from.[22]

The attitudes of "civil society activists" mirrored those of the westernized liberal elite more generally. While they had been unable to identify with Zia's petty bourgeois conservatism and smug piousness, they saw in Musharraf's westernized lifestyle and his philosophy of "enlightened moderation" a reflection of themselves. The significant growth in GNP during the first few years following the start of the GWoT—a result of renewed aid from the US and other donors, and of overseas Pakistanis repatriating their money and/or returning to Pakistan as the international climate grew more hostile towards Muslims and Pakistanis—further affirmed their faith in him as Pakistan's savior (S.R. Khan, 2004). Musharraf's abortive attempt to reform the Zina Ordinance (which sparked such a reaction from the Islamist parties that he had to backtrack even from the minor procedural change he had intended) and the passage of a Women's Protection Bill were seen as evidence of his progressive credentials, as was his plan to allocate a quota for reserved seats for women from the local to the national level.

Musharraf's liberal (that is, westernized) lifestyle—signaled by the fact that he drank alcohol and had two pet pomeranians—and his official commitment to "enlightened moderation" reassured Pakistan's "lifestyle liberals" that they were safe from the Islamists under his watch. Their support essentially translated into turning a blind eye to the terror(s) that his regime unleashed on various groups, such as the tenants on the Okara military farms, the peasants of Hashtnagar,[23] and the thousands of political activists from Sarhad and Baluchistan that were "disappeared" by intelligence agencies. Many Pakistani liberals, including some respected members of the human rights community, either explicitly or tacitly supported the US attack on Afghanistan and the Pakistani military's role in it, and continue to support the violence visited on innocent civilians under cover of the GWoT through drone attacks and army operations.

Any notion that Musharraf was a champion of women's and minority rights should have been decisively shattered by his relationship with the MMA (the *Mutahhida Majlis-i-Amal* (the MMA), or United Assembly of Action. (The MMA is the alliance of right-wing political parties which won majorities in Sarhad and Baluchistan for the first time in Pakistan's history, albeit during a much reviled election; the MMA quickly became popularly known as the Mullah-Military-Alliance.) In January 2004, Musharraf essentially bartered away the rights of women and minorities when he made a deal with the MMA; the context was his bid for a "trust vote" from Parliament which would allow him to continue as president while maintaining his status as an active member of the military corps. The MMA only agreed to this once Musharraf assured them that he would not touch Islamic laws and provisions (especially the Hudood Ordinance). As Nighat Said Khan (2004: ii) noted at the time, there was "not even a whimper from women Parliamentarians, women's organisations or individual women or the press ... the silence was deafening."

Interestingly, the same liberal intellectuals that had welcomed Musharraf and supported his regime joined the anti-Musharraf movement once it gathered momentum. The Lawyers Movement, as it came to be called because of the catalytic and leading role played by the legal fraternity, was a welcome respite from the stifling politics of the post-Zia period. The movement's focus on rule of law, while liberal, was refreshing in its support for democratic principles and its secular political idiom. The significant participation of young people from across the class divide was a hopeful sign that a new, politically engaged, progressive generation was emerging in Pakistan, and made up for the movement's urban bias. Most significant of all, there appeared to be an emerging consciousness that the problem was not one individual, but an institution, that is, the army. The use of the poetry of Jalib and Faiz by activists, connected this movement to Pakistan's earlier tradition of progressive politics.

However, this analysis was to be proved premature. It soon became clear that the liberals' obsession with "Talibanization" would continue to prove detrimental to democratic politics. The first indication of this came soon after the elections, when newly elected President Asif Zardari reneged on the PPP's promise to reinstate the chief justice of the Supreme Court as well as other judges that had been dismissed by Musharraf. This was particularly egregious given that it was Musharraf's dismissal of this chief justice which had catalyzed the Lawyers Movement to begin with, and whose reinstatement had been the movement's singular focus. When protests erupted, the government responded with sweeping raids and arrests of lawyers and their supporters; in the most astonishing move of all, Zardari blockaded all approaches to the capital city of Islamabad with trailers in order to prevent the planned culmination of a "long march" in Islamabad.

Throughout this unfolding drama, which involved the display of explicitly authoritarian and anti-democratic tendencies by the newly elected government of the PPP, several prominent liberal intellectuals refused to support the democratic demands of the Lawyers Movement and stood fast behind Zardari. Their justification for this was the same as that of the PPP—that by demanding their democratic rights, from which the PPP itself had only recently profited, the Lawyers Movement was destabilizing the government and preparing the ground for either the military or religious extremists to take over (Toor, 2009b).

Even if one were to buy this argument at face value, this essentially meant that Pakistani liberals were willing to tolerate authoritarianism of the most draconian sort as long as it was from a democratically elected civilian government that was led by a purported "secular" party. This liberal support of Zardari and the PPP did not diminish even after the shocking news that two of the ministers appointed by the leader of this "progressive" political party (with whom he also had close personal relationships) had a record of supporting customary forms of violence against women. Bijarani, a landlord from Sindh had been accused of heading a *jirga* which "awarded" five girls, ranging in age from two to five years, as compensation for the murder of a man; the case had been pending in front of the Supreme Court (which had issued orders for Bijarani's arrest) when Musharraf dismissed the judiciary. The other minister, Zehri, was a tribal leader and on record as having defended the practice of burying women alive as a "tribal tradition." He had been commenting on reports of a case in which three teenage girls had been killed in this fashion for daring to choose their own husbands. The stories had made national headlines, and many progressives (especially feminists) had strongly protested the appointments and demanded that the two ministers be dismissed (WAF, 2008), but to no avail. In the face of this, the liberal support for Zardari and the PPP is mystifying unless one realizes that Pakistani liberal politics are essentially about the liberal elite's self-preservation, and the forms of violence that feudal elites visit on the weak and vulnerable under their "jurisdiction" do not pose the kind of immediate danger to the lifestyles of liberals in Pakistan that "Talibanization" does.[24]

As for the anti-military sentiments which had appeared to be crystallizing during the anti-Musharraf movement, and which could be seen in the liberal support for the PPP, these dissipated overnight after the circulation of a video in April 2009 which claimed to show a young woman being flogged by the Taliban in Swat Valley. The timing of this video's emergence was suspiciously convenient, given that the US had just turned up the heat on the Pakistani military, demanding proof that it was actually fighting the Taliban. The video resulted in generating overwhelming support for the army's subsequent operation in Swat which displaced millions of Swatis, rehabilitating the army's image among liberals. So strong was the fear and anxiety generated by the video, that this support did not diminish even in the face of overwhelming evidence which emerged soon after the military operation showing the army's reign of terror in Swat (Toor, 2009a). Since that time, liberals have backed every military operation, as well as the expansion of the GWoT into Pakistan via drone attacks on the border areas, despite the clear evidence that drones are not the efficient "militant-killing" machines that they are promoted as being. Accompanying this unqualified liberal support for the US and Pakistani militaries and the GWoT is an overt derisiveness towards a progressive anti-war position, especially towards anti-imperialist critique. In fact, even prominent liberal intellectuals in Pakistan collapse the anti-imperialism of the Left with the anti-Americanism of the right.[25]

Another, less direct but no less important way in which the liberal obsession with the "Taliban" feeds into the military's project of a neoliberal security state is reflected in the proliferation of "security-talk," that is, the tendency to couch the very real grievances and issues of the Pakistani people in the language of security, and specifically in terms of combating "Islamist militancy." The executive director of a major policy think-tank in Islamabad made the case for addressing the food security needs of tens of thousands of Pakistanis on the grounds that to not do so would be tantamount to handing the "Taliban" and other militant Islamists new recruits (Suleri, 2009). Ahmed Rashid (2010), the quintessential liberal establishment intellectual, made the same argument when appealing for help for the victims of the recent devastating floods in Pakistan. Needless to say, this equation between deprivation and religious extremism/militancy dehumanizes the poorest and most vulnerable.

What this liberal discourse reveals is a profound dissociation from—and even a distaste for—ordinary Pakistanis and their lives, hopes, dreams and struggles, reflected in the abandonment of mass political work. Thankfully, the working people of Pakistan are not waiting for these elite progressives to initiate change, but are building movements of their own and taking on the various aspects of the monstrous system which oppresses them. The AMP's courageous stand against the leviathan of the Pakistani military is an example of one such movement; the resurgence of working-class radicalism is the other part of this story.

The rise of Left forces in the late 1960s, in particular a politically conscious working class and peasantry, had made the ruling classes understandably anxious. Therefore, as we saw earlier, there was a concerted effort by the state from the 1970s onwards to defuse and dismantle these left-wing forces, especially the militant trade union movement. This was achieved through various means: the replacement of independent trade unions with PPP ones under Bhutto, the indiscriminate use of state violence against striking workers and the leadership of left-wing trade unions, and the outright co-optation of public sector unions under Zia. As a result, there was no meaningful resistance to IMF-imposed privatization when it began in the 1980s and even when it accelerated in the 1990s, despite the fact that it resulted in massive lay-offs.[26] The fact that most of the privatized units collapsed soon afterwards only added to the misery of the working class. Private sector unions, meanwhile, were devastated by the informalization that came with the severe fragmentation of the production process which had become the norm from the 1990s onwards. Expressions of dissent or attempts at collective action on the part of workers were dealt with severely. Under Musharraf, strikes and go-slows were not just declared illegal, but prosecuted in special courts under anti-terrorism laws (passed under Nawaz Sharif's second administration in the late 1990s). Forming a trade union under the Musharraf government was tantamount to losing your job, since an application for a new union was immediately followed up by a list of workers being sent to the employer by the government for "verification" (Mahmood, 2010).

At the same time, other IMF conditionalities led to the slashing of the already modest social sector, the ending of subsidies on basic necessities, and an increase in direct taxation.[27] These measures put the burden of debt-repayment squarely on the shoulders of the working class and the poor while pulling the rug out from under their feet through privatization, downsizing and informalization. It was hardly surprising, then, that the 1990s came to be characterized by rising poverty and inequality, a trend that has continued into the new millennium. As a result, rates of suicide and self-immolation among the working classes and the poor rose exponentially by the late 1990s.

The Musharraf regime continued to push through neoliberal policies, selling off public sector enterprises at a speed which was astonishing even for Pakistan, often well below their market value.[28] However, it was soon faced with increased resistance to privatization from a working class pushed to the brink, and a newly revitalized (if still weak) left. The first such organized resistance came in 2005 from the workers of the state-owned Pakistan Telecommunications Limited (PTCL), which was slated for privatization. As a result of the hard work of a few politicized Left workers, a Unions Action Committee was formed in March 2005 which launched a nationwide protest campaign, culminating in a massive meeting at the PTCL headquarters in Islamabad on May 25, 2005. Twelve thousand workers, out of the PTCL's 62,000 came for the meeting from all over the country. The militant and uncompromising mood of the workers at the grassroots level kept the pressure on union leaders and a nationwide strike was called.

Soon after reaching an agreement with the union leadership, however, the government unleashed a wave of reprisal, arresting union leaders under the anti-terrorism statute, and declaring that the privatization of the PTCL would go on as planned. Despite this setback, the mobilization of PTCL workers and the broad Anti-Privatization Alliance which came out of it was an incredibly important turning-point in the recent history of the Pakistani working class (Akhter, 2005).

In the following years, there has been an increase in the intensity and radicalism of working-class activism in Pakistan. From the sit-in strike of the workers of the premier Pearl Continental Hotels in Karachi in May 2010[29] to the standoff between the Gadani Ship-Breaking Democratic Workers Union and the Owners Association in June that same year, a new spirit of fearless rebellion is clearly evident among the working classes of Pakistan (Usmani, 2010). Among the most salutary of developments on this front has been the establishment of the Labour Qaumi Movement (Labour National Movement) in the industrial Punjabi town of Faisalabad in 2003, by power-loom workers attempting to unionize. Today, the LQM boasts a strong membership spread across several sector offices staffed by full-time workers.[30]

These are the stories which never make it to the headlines of international newspapers—or even domestic ones. Yet, these are the mobilizations and movements that hold the most promise for Pakistan because, unlike the religious extremists or the liberal elite, they represent the hopes and aspirations of the vast majority of Pakistanis. It is therefore in their struggles that the real Pakistan exists and through their struggles that it has any hope of surviving and triumphing over the storms that threaten to engulf it.

It is fitting to close with these lines from Faiz:

Yehi junooñ ka yehi tauq-o daar ka mausam
Yehi hai jabr, yehi ikhtiyaar ka mausam
Qafas hai bas meiñ tumhaare, tumhaare bas meiñ nahiñ
Chaman meiñ aatish-e gul ke nikhaar ka mausam
Bala se hum ne na dekha to aur dekhenge
Furogh-e gulshan-o saut-e hazaar ka mausam

This is the season of passion, yet also of the yoke and noose
This is the season of repression, yet also of agency and resistance
The cage may be in your control, but you have no power over
The season when the fiery rose blossoms in the garden
So what if we do not live to see it? There will be others who
    witness
The season of the flowering garden, of the nightingale's song.

Notes

INTRODUCTION

1. The protest, which took place on June 6, 2008, was organized by the Women Workers Help Line with the help of the Labour Party of Pakistan.
2. See Alavi (2002) and Jalal (1996) on the fraught and partisan nature of this "Partition Historiography" and its implications for relations between the two states. As recently as 2005, L.K. Advani, a major political figure in Indian politics and a senior member of the Hindu nationalist Bharatya Janata Party generated a major controversy in India when, during a visit to Karachi, he described Jinnah as secular. In 2009, senior BJP leader Jaswant Singh ignited another controversy through the publication of a book on Jinnah and the Partition in which he similarly asserted Jinnah's secularism and argued that the responsibility for Partition lay with Nehru.
3. There is more than a small element of *schadenfreude* in these arguments.
4. See the works of anti-establishment Pakistani scholars such as Hamza Alavi, Ayesha Jalal and K.K. Aziz
5. *Ummat* in Urdu is the same as *ummah* in Arabic—the word refers to a supranational/global community of Muslims. The most important, even iconic, debate over nationalism among Indian Muslims took place between Muhammad Iqbal and Maulana Husain Ahmad Madani, a Muslim cleric who supported the Indian National Congress. Iqbal was strongly critical of Madani's support for a composite Indian nationalism. See Kausar (2003) and Metcalf (2007).
6. It is important to note, however, that the League did use religious symbolism in its campaigns, which was to prove disastrous in the post-Independence period. A case in point was the popular Muslim League slogan *Pakistan ka matlab kya? La ilaha illa'llah* ('What is the meaning of Pakistan? There is no God but God') (Nasr, 1994: 114).
7. In fact, it was Gandhi who first gave the Muslim clerics, particularly the hardline Sunni Deobandi *ulema*, a foothold within Muslim politics through his leadership of the Khilafat Movement in the early part of the twentieth century, thereby briefly undermining the secular leadership of the Muslim League. Gandhi even helped establish the *Jamiat Ulema-i Hind* which, in Pakistan, became the *Jamiat Ulema-i Islam*, the party which represents the hardline of Sunni fundamentalism. See Alavi, 2002.
8. In Alavi's words, they "formed a relatively cohesive social stratum. In Gramsci's language, they were an 'auxiliary' class; not the biggest class in numbers but the most articulate" (Alavi, 2002: 4515).
9. This United Front strategy of the CPI was to later come under criticism and be briefly replaced by a more militant one in 1947–48 under the leadership of B.T. Ranadive.
10. However, even after independence in 1947, such social-democratic ideals became a source of anxiety for the ruling classes. Jinnah's opening address to the first

session of the Constituent Assembly of Pakistan in which he articulated his secular, liberal-democratic vision for Pakistan caused such a stir within the ruling clique that it was banned from newspapers and the radio, until pressure from the opposition and the liberal sections of the intelligentsia forced its release after a significant delay of several days. In fact, contrary to mainstream wisdom within Pakistan, what made Jinnah's speech so objectionable was not its unqualified secularism (since the ruling classes were themselves secular), but its assumptions about the limits on the state.

11. The "first to jump off the sinking Unionist ship" (Alavi, 2002: 4522) was one Mian Mumtaz Daultana who was to have a significant impact on the politics of post-Independence Pakistan. Among other things, he was responsible for orchestrating the 1953 anti-Ahmediyya riots which contributed to the fall of the government of Prime Minister Khwaja Nazimuddin, a Bengali, and was also the mover of the "One Unit" Bill in the Constituent Assembly.

12. These were the words with which Jinnah had rejected an earlier proposal for the settlement of the "communal question" which similarly argued for a division of Bengal and Punjab along communal lines (Jalal, 1994: 121).

13. He was hailed as an "ambassador of Hindu-Muslim unity" by no less than Sarojini Naidu; this phrase became the title of the political biography of Jinnah which she wrote and published in 1918. Naidu was a senior member of the INC at that time, and later became its first female president.

14. Coined by the Bengali Hindu nationalist writer Bankim Chandra Chatterjee and featured in his novel *Anandamath*, it was the slogan used by an anti-Muslim mob.

15. The absurdity of the situation was captured by Sa'adat Hasan Manto's famous short story "Toba Tek Singh."

16. For a critical understanding of the Comintern's advice to communist parties in colonized countries and its repercussions, see Prakash (1983) and Alavi's (1997) unpublished letter to a friend titled "Marxism, ex-colonial societies and strategies of the Left." On the national question within classical Marxism, see Lowy (1976) and Debray (1977).

17. Ultimately, however, this rising militancy scared the Indian bourgeoisie, which was more interested in working out a smooth transfer of power from the colonial government. Sudhi Pradhan (1985) relates that the split in the anti-imperialist United Front started inside the Congress Socialist Party, with communists being expelled from the CSP in March 1940 (Nehru did not intervene). Consequently, no national meeting of the AIPWA was held between 1939 and 1942.

18. The CPI had originally declared World War II as an imperialist war because of the signing of the non-aggression pact between Germany and the Soviet Union. However, following Hitler's attack on the Soviet Union in June 1941, the war was officially re-designated a "People's War" resulting in a change in the CPI's stance *vis-à-vis* the colonial state from one of confrontation and antagonism to one of collaboration. See Overstreet and Windmiller (1960) and Haithcox (1971).

19. This was not an uncontroversial position within the CPI and the international communist movement. In 1946, this position was replaced by that of R. Palme Dutt, a member of the Communist Party of Great Britain (CPGB). The CPGB was one of several groups/parties which fought for control over the Communist Party of India within the International communist movement; the other important player was M.N. Roy. For details, see Overstreet and Windmiller (1960) and Haithcox (1971). Palme Dutt considered the Muslim League a

reactionary party, and argued that since the demand for Pakistan was based on religion and did not fall under the Stalinist definition of nationality, it could not be considered a national movement; the "CPI obligingly changed its position and denounced Pakistan as a plot between British imperialism and Muslim bourgeois feudal vested interests" (Ali, 1983: 39).

2   CONSOLIDATING THE NATION-STATE: EAST BENGAL AND THE POLITICS OF NATIONAL CULTURE

1. *Ekushey* is Bangla for the number "21." The events of *Ekushey* and the memory of the language martyrs are an important part of the nationalist narrative of Bangladesh, which seceded from Pakistan after a bloody civil war in 1971. In 1999, February 21 was proclaimed by the General Conference of UNESCO as the International Mother Language Day.

2. Significantly, in the same speech, Khan "strongly criticised the speeches of certain Congress leaders in the Indian Union calling upon the Indian Muslims to prove their professions of loyalty to the State," declaring it "a direct negation of the moral and political conceptions for whose success the modern world is endeavouring today" (*Pakistan Times*, October 21, 1947).

3. One League member responded to the proposal of changing the League's name in highly emotionally charged terms, arguing that "to kill the Muslim League [was] to kill the nation itself"! Such a slippage between the League and the nation was characteristic of the League leadership's self-entitlement and self-righteousness, as well as their lack of political vision. Liaquat Ali Khan himself was known to have said: "I have always considered myself as the Prime Minister of the League. I have never regarded myself as the Prime Minister chosen by the Members of the Constituent Assembly" (cited in Noman 1988: 45).

4. Specifically the "Hindi-Urdu controversy." See Fatehpuri (1987), Kumar (1990), King (1994), and Rai (1984).

5. Thanks to Peter Hitchcock of CUNY for this term.

6. India's accession of Kashmir barely a few weeks after Independence only added to this sense of insecurity.

7. For a detailed exploration of these issues, see Jalal, 1990: 29–48.

8. Both "Dhaka" and "Dacca" are different ways of spelling the name of the same city, now the capital of Bangladesh—the former is the current spelling while the latter is now defunct. "Dacca" appears in this article only when I quote a primary or secondary source from the earlier period.

9. *Muhajir* literally means "refugee" or "immigrant." In Pakistan, it refers to those Muslims who migrated to Pakistan after Partition and who considered Urdu their mother tongue. Although the majority of *muhajireen* [plural of *muhajir*] at this time belonged to the poor or lower-middle classes, they were also well-represented in the upper echelons of the Muslim League.

10. The Communist Party of East Bengal (CPEB) was also far more established and organized than its counterpart in West Pakistan, which had suffered a serious loss of membership after Partition.

11. *Dhimmi* was the term given to non-Muslim communities in the pre-modern Muslim state; *dhimmis* had state protection but no political rights. Although the official discourse of the Muslim League used the language of modern citizenship, mainstream political discourse was filled with such "Islamic" political language,

and did compromise secular-democratic politics if only by muddying the waters of mainstream political discourse.

12. The issue of the place of Bangla—and, by extension, Bengalis—in the new nation-state arose almost immediately after Independence, and gained strength in the face of continued and escalating state opposition over the course of the next five years, bookended by two violent confrontations between East Bengali language activists and the state. During this period, the demands of Bangla language activists were repeatedly rejected on the grounds that Bangla, and by implication Bengali culture as a whole, was not "Muslim" enough, while Urdu was presented as the only language that could justifiably lay claim to being Pakistan's national language given the special place it occupied within Indo-Muslim history and culture. Bangla was finally declared the second national language of Pakistan in 1952, but not before its supporters had been made to pay an unconscionably high price.

13. In fact, while it is commonly believed that Urdu was the "undisputed" lingua franca of Indian Muslims (See Oldenberg, 1985), this was not the case. At the 1937 session of the Muslim League, for example, Bengali delegates expressed their strong opposition to the proposal that Urdu be accepted as the League's official language, pointing out that Bengali Muslims constituted more than a third of India's Muslim population and that adopting Urdu would seriously undermine the League's propaganda work in this important constituency (Sayeed, 1968: 210).

14. This, of course, was not simply a "feeling"—it was based in such incontrovertible facts as the net transfer of capital from East Bengal to the center, access to important public sector jobs, and the control of East Bengali politics by the Central Muslim League and its henchmen in the East Bengal government (Umar, 2004; Jahan, 1972).

15. Tagore was officially banned from the airwaves in East Bengal and it was considered seditious activity to play or sing his songs. East Bengalis, both Hindu and Muslim, considered *Robindroshongeet* (or the songs of Tagore) to be an integral part of Bengali culture.

16. *Civil and Military Gazette*, cited in the *Pakistan Times*, February 29, 1952.

17. The attitude of the West Pakistani elite towards Bengalis also became increasingly more racialized over time, which enabled the horrific actions of the West Pakistan Army during the civil war of 1971, in which, among other things, the rape of Bengali women was justified on the basis of "purifying" their "race."

18. As the epigraph to this chapter shows, this was a sentiment that was shared by Jinnah and echoed in his visit to Dhaka in March of 1948 (Jinnah, 2004).

19. The Bangla script has Sanskritic roots, as opposed to the Arabo-Persian roots of Urdu which is written in a modified Arabic/Persian script.

20. The proposal to switch to another script was ultimately rejected on the grounds that there simply wasn't enough scientific evidence to support the claim that the Bengali script was inferior to the Arabic or Roman scripts.

21. There was, of course, historical precedence for such an attempt at cultural engineering, with its accompanying politics, the most proximate one being the splitting of Hindustani (written in both *nastaliq* and *devanagri*) into Urdu (written exclusively in *nastaliq*) and Hindi (written exclusively in *devanagri*), and the explicit choice of the Roman instead of the Arabic script for modern Turkish by Mustapha Kemal after the establishment of Turkey as a modern

nation-state. *Nastaliq* is the Arabic-derived script in which Hindustani/Urdu had been written (and in which Urdu continues to be written), while *devanagri* was the Sanskrit-derived script chosen by Hindi nationalists to distinguish Hindi from Urdu. See King, 1994.

22. The efforts by the state to engage educationists to debate the national language issue appear to be attempts at building consent. However, they can also be understood as "symbolic violence," or the exercise of the "power ... to impose meanings and to impose them as legitimate by concealing the power relations which are the basis of its force" (Bourdieu and Passeron, 1977: 4). By the time of the next pro-Bengali demonstration, the state had discarded such symbolic violence in favor of outright coercion.

23. Soon after the passage of the Objectives Resolution, committees were established to draw up the Constitution according to the principles laid out in the Resolution. The most important of these was the Basic Principles Committee (BPC). The release of its interim report in 1950 caused an uproar in East Pakistan because it proposed a bicameral legislature, with an equal number of seats for both wings in the Upper House. This effectively reduced East Pakistan's representation by as much as one-fifth. The report also proposed that the head of state be a Muslim, and a board of *ulema* (religious scholars) be set up to ensure that laws "repugnant to Islam" were not passed. An anti-BPC movement was consolidated in East Pakistan almost immediately after the release of this report.

24. Jinnah had been determined that Pakistan not be defined from within or by the outside world as a theocratic state despite its basis in the idea of a Muslim "nation" and its right to self-determination. Zaidi (2003: xi) quotes Jinnah's response to the allegation that he was avoiding the *shariah* question: "Whose Shariah? Hanafis? Hanbalis? Sha'afis? Malikis? Ja'afris? I don't want to get involved. The moment I enter the field, the ulama will take over for they claim to be the experts and I certainly don't propose to hand the field over to [them] ... I am aware of their criticism but I don't propose to fall into their trap."

25. A close examination of the "Objectives Resolution" shows that its references to the role of Islam and shariah are closer to the modernist Muslim position, which argues that shariah law must be brought in line with the demands/needs of the modern world, rather than the other way around, but all this is mere semantics when juxtaposed against the immense symbolic significance the OR came to have in terms of shifting the terms of political debate in Pakistan.

26. Ahmad Shah "Patras" Bukhari was a major literary and intellectual figure in the subcontinent. He was also an educationist and diplomat, and Pakistan's first representative to the United Nations.

27. Sri Dhirendra Nath Dutta, Debate over the Restriction and Detention (Second Amendment) Bill, Constituent Assembly Debates, November 17, 1952.

28. Mr. Abdulla-al Mahmood, Discussion on Finance Bill, Constituent Assembly Debates, March 29, 1952.

29. See *Pakistan Times* issues between February 29 and March 7, 1952.

30. Formed in 1903, the *Anjuman* had been one of the most important organizations supporting the cause of Urdu through the Hindi-Urdu movement of the twentieth century, and was venerated, along with its founder, Maulvi Abdul Haq, for the important role it played in the Muslim nationalist movement. After the establishment of Pakistan, it moved its headquarters from Delhi to Lahore—symbolizing, in effect, that Pakistan was the new "home" of Urdu.

31. Note the colonial appellation here. The Pakistani state's fear of "provincialism"—read: the self-identification of ethnic minorities—was not limited to East Bengal; from the very beginning, it also steadfastly refused the demands of the leadership of the NWFP to rename it "Pukhtunistan," the land of the Pakhtun, its ethnic majority.

32. The mandate of the Constituent Assembly was to come up with a constitution for Pakistan, and it was again a testimony to the authoritarian tendencies of the Muslim League that five years after Independence there was still no constitution.

33. "Organic intellectuals" is another technical term used by Gramsci (1971) to refer to intellectuals who articulate a class or group's ideology.

34. The stand-off between communist members of the All Pakistan Progressive Writers Association and the liberal nationalists is the subject of the next chapter.

35. He means Gautam, as in the Buddha.

36. Roy was a Hindu.

37. It may have been more pertinent to have mentioned Rabindranath Tagore, given the treatment Tagore had suffered at the hands of the Muslim League government in East Bengal and the scorn heaped on Bengali culture due to its supposedly "Hindu" influences.

38 Both versions of the BPC report were criticized by East Bengali Opposition members as proposing a legislature which reduced East Bengal's majority to a minority in the House, and also reiterated that Urdu was to be the only state language, a slap in the face of the Bengali language movement. Iftikharuddin's jibe refers to the centrality given to Islam as the basis of the Pakistani nation-state within both these versions.

39. This was a far from trivial difference, highlighting the fact that intentions, interests and effects cannot be read off the *content* of particular nationalist discourses (indeed, any discourse) alone—it is just as crucial to pay attention to the context in which the discourse is being circulated, and especially to the political projects whose interests they are intended to serve or enable (Laclau and Mouffe, 1985, Grossberg, 1986).

40. Odd as this sounds, such opportunistic disavowal was and remains standard fare for the Punjabi ruling class; to date, the Punjab is the only province in Pakistan where the official medium of instruction in government primary schools is not the mother tongue, but Urdu.

3   POST-PARTITION LITERARY POLITICS: THE PROGRESSIVES VERSUS THE NATIONALISTS

1. Sajjad Zaheer would later be deputed by the Communist Party of India (CPI) following Partition to help establish an independent Communist Party of Pakistan (CPP), and would subsequently be jailed in the Rawalpindi Conspiracy Case of 1951 on the charges of trying to overthrow the state.

2. For a more detailed discussion of *Angaray*, the reaction to it and its relationship to the Progressive Writers Association, see, *inter alia*, Ali (1988), Coppola, (1981), Mahmud (1996), and Gopal (2005).

3. It is important to note the international dimension of the events unfolding in colonial India within the literary-political sphere. Political activists, artists, writers, and so on didn't just draw inspiration from "international" (read: western) events and movements, but contributed actively to them. Events like the

Paris Conference—and especially the International Bureau of the Congress for the Defence of Culture set up at the Paris meeting—enabled the establishment of international connections and the cementing of political relationships. The communist movement is another example of this "transnational" dimension of politics and culture in this period. As a result of participation in the Paris Conference, for example, Sajjad Zaheer and Mulk Raj Anand came under the influence and patronage of Louis Aragon (they were already connected to important leftist writers and intellectuals in England—for instance, Ralph Fox and E.M. Forster). Although they attended the first meeting of the Congress as spectators, Mulk Raj Anand delivered an address at the second one, and the All India Progressive Writers Association, once formed, maintained an affiliation with the International Writers' Association until the latter's demise with the commencement of war.

4. Coppola notes that appeals from the organizational committee for this congress was also sent to writers and journals in India as elsewhere in the world, and appeared in the Urdu literary journal *Savera* of Karachi (Coppola, 1974: 13).

5. Ralph Fox was an early and influential adviser to the group.

6. See Coppola (1974: 5–12) for a detailed comparison between the two versions of the Manifesto and an analysis.

7. The Communist Party of India was established at roughly the same time as the AIPWA.

8. Except perhaps the earlier Aligarh movement led by Syed Ahmed Khan.

9. From here on, I shall use PWA to refer to the parent organization, and APPWA or AIPWA to refer to the post-independence Pakistani and Indian branches of the organization respectively. I should also clarify that I use "Progressive" as a noun to refer to a member of the PWA, and "progressive" as an adjective to refer to a more general political and social attitude which, in the subcontinent, was always posited against "reaction" and thus can be used to describe anything from Marxist to "liberal."

10. It would, however, be limiting to identify all progressivism in literature, particularly after 1947, with the Association, or to label the Association a "front" organization of the Communist Party of India (and later Pakistan) as is often done. This has been a matter of some dispute both at the height of the Association's popularity, as well as for scholars and others interested in recovering its history. I don't think that there can be much dispute about the fact that it was a front organisation, but that it simultaneously enjoyed an autonomous sphere of action. Many of its members were not communists, even though "the Marxists were in control organisationally" (Pradhan, 1985: 6), and the Association's leadership was careful from the very beginning to establish that it was an autonomous association of independent writers who had broadly shared social, cultural and political agenda of "progressivism," and was run on democratic lines.

11. Progressives were also heavily represented and very well respected in the field of journalism. In fact one of the two major English language newspapers in Pakistan after Partition was the *Pakistan Times*, owned by a leftist politician and fellow-traveler Mian Iftikharuddin (whom we have already encountered earlier). Faiz Ahmed Faiz, renowned socialist poet and general secretary of the All Pakistan Trade Union Federation was its editor at the time.

12. These literary magazines were an important part of the cultural life of the urban middle-class intelligentsia in West Pakistan, and as such helped to consolidate

a sense of community and continuity at a very fragile historical moment—the immediate aftermath of Independence and Partition.

13. *Savera* was edited at this time by Khadija Mastoor; the others were regular contributors.

14. For details of the consolidation of this international liberal anti-communist intellectual front, see, *inter alia*, Saunders (1999) and Scott-Smith and Krabbendam (2003).

15. Askari was the only member of this camp who had not had a relationship with the PWA before Partition.

16. The word came to be used to refer to those who migrated from India to Pakistan. In time, it became associated with those who hailed from North India and Hyderabad more specifically.

17. Serious work needs to be done on analyzing the extent to which the loyalty that liberal, modernist Muslims felt towards the Muslim League was mediated through the personality and charisma of Jinnah, in so far as he represented the quintessential modern Muslim leader—western-educated and yet committed to the welfare of his community.

18. Taseer and Samad Shaheen were high-level civil servants in a country ruled by the bureaucracy, but Askari had no such direct connections.

19. I use this term in the Gramscian sense of intellectuals who represent a particular class's interests in the struggle for hegemony.

20. One of these junior officers was Major Ishaq Muhammad, who would later establish the Pakistan Mazdoor Kissan Party in the late 1960s. Muhammad also wrote the introduction to Faiz's collection of poetry *Zindah-Nama* ("Prison-Letters") which the poet composed during his first term of incarceration.

21. As the APPWA's then secretary Ahmad Nadeem Qasmi argued in a report on these years to the Association, and as many Pakistani communists have variously admitted, the new strategy was one of left-adventurism, and was based on a misconception that Pakistan was now a capitalist state, and that the communist movement in India and Pakistan had entered a new stage—one of militant revolution. Ranadive admitted this in his self-criticism before the CPI in 1950 when he was replaced as general secretary.

22. See, *inter alia*, Mumtaz Hussain (1949) and Khalil-ur Rahman Azmi (1996).

23. This hardening of positions and circumscribing of what was and was not truly "Progressive" was not accepted unqualifiedly by all members of the PWA, communist or otherwise. Faiz Ahmad Faiz recalls, for example, that he stopped attending meetings of the APPWA after Iqbal's work and thought was denounced in a fashion which led him to realize that the association was going through a phase of dogmatic Left extremism (Haider, c. 1984).

24. When World War II broke out, a group of countries—all of whom were under the direct or indirect control of Great Britain—were pulled together into a currency "bloc" which either used the pound sterling as their official currency, or pegged their currency to it. The idea was to protect the external value of the pound. The Sterling Bloc remained in effect for some time after decolonization, disappearing only in the 1970s.

25. Not only did the Manifesto list the different types of reactionary literature in Pakistan, it also provocatively named its practitioners causing the commotion within the literary community, and earning it the epithet "The 'Safety Act' of Literature" among the liberals.

26. The echoes of Brecht's cry "Art is not a mirror held up to reality but a hammer with which to shape it" are obviously not coincidental here, just as one can find in Taseer and Askari's glorification of a "pure literature" free of politics the echoes of their anti-communist liberal counterparts in Europe and the United States of America.

27. Printed in *Savera* 7/8, and in *Taraqqi-Pasand Adab: Dastaavezaat* [*Progressive Literature: Documents*], Karachi, 1986. Published by the Progressive Writers Golden Jubilee Conference Committee.

28. As I show in the previous chapter on the language controversy, the Bengali demands to make Bangla the second state language after Urdu was declared by the state and by many Urdu-speaking intellectuals to be an attack on Muslim nationalism, the ideological foundation of Pakistan. The history of the alignment of Urdu with Indian Muslim nationhood, and the labeling of Bengali as "not Muslim enough" and in fact "too Hindu" is also outlined in that chapter.

29. The second-in-command of the Indian National Congress, after Nehru.

30. Literally, "The Great Leader," the unofficial title by which Muhammad Ali Jinnah, the head of the Muslim League and the first governor general of Pakistan came to be known during the struggle for independence.

31. The reference is again to the agitation around the language issue in East Pakistan, which the state had dismissed as a communist conspiracy to undermine Pakistan.

32. Sibte Hasan (1986: 217) quotes a letter from Askari (who was based in Lahore) to Shirin (in Karachi) in which he enquired about the "literary atmosphere" of Karachi in these terms: "How many [writers] are Pakistanis and how many are progressives?"

33. *Savera*, number 5/6, as quoted in Fateh Muhammad Malik, *Khayaal Ka Khauf* ("The Fear of Thought"), *Ta'asubaat* (1991: 51). See also the accounts of Ateeq Ahmed (1987) and Hameed Akhter (1987).

34. The reference here is to Sajjad Zaheer who was on deputation from the CPI to set up the Communist Party of Pakistan, and was the general secretary of the CPP at this time.

35. It used to be published from Bangalore, but moved to Pakistan after Independence.

36. *Naya Daur*, numbers 14/15.

37. Literally, "the self." "*Khudi*" was a concept popularized by Muhammad Iqbal who saw the awakening and strengthening of the Muslim (man)'s *khudi* as the prerequisite to the Muslims' return to glory on the world stage. Taseer's choice of words is thus entirely conscious—linking the establishment of Pakistan to Iqbal's "dream" of Muslim glory—and the reference would have been instantly understood by his readership.

38. One *crore* = 10 million

39. *Savera*, numbers 5/6, as quoted in Fateh Muhammad Malik (1991: 51–2).

40. In South Asia studies, "communal" has a very specific and negative meaning— the word comes from the tendency of British administrators and anthropologists to categorize their Indian subjects in terms of their religious affiliation—thus "community" in the South Asian context is always already understood as a *religious* community and therefore the opposite of "secular." In the context of Partition, the relevant communities which engaged in and were also the victims of a cycle of violence were Hindus, Muslims and Sikhs.

41. It was such a singularly defining event for both countries that it has come to be known as "the Partition," and continues to generate much emotion on both sides of the border.

42. The most prominent and highly respected Progressive poet of the Indian subcontinent, Faiz was also a member of the Communist Party of Pakistan and an editor of one of the major national dailies. Unsurprisingly, he spent a large amount of time in this period as "a guest of the state," that is, in prison.

43. The poem's alternative title is *Sahar* ("Morning"). See *Naya Adab* [New Literature], c. 1948: 193.

44. Republished in *Naya Adab*, c. 1948: 191.

45. The lines rely on a play on the words <u>gh</u>am ("sadness," "grief") and *haasil* ("achievement," "sum")—thus while the past was *haasil-i* <u>gh</u>am or the result or sum of grief, the present is nothing but <u>gh</u>am-i *haasil*, the anticlimactic or even tragically ironic grief which accompanies the attainment of one's goals. The "goal" in question being, of course, Independence.

46. For this, Faiz was roundly criticized by Sardar Jafri. Recall that such "ambiguity" was considered problematic and potentially reactionary for and by Progressives at this time.

47. Saifuddin Saif, for instance.

48. See also Arif Abdul Mateen's (1948: 102) *Pakistan ke she'ri rujhanaat* ("The poetic trends of Pakistan") in *Savera*, number 3/4.

49. This idea of the reversal of the Partition was a reigning fear in the years immediately following Partition. It had as its basis the cry of *Akhand Bharat* ("United India!") raised by Hindu extremists such as the Hindu Mahasabha during this period; it was built up by the Pakistani establishment in order to maintain a permanent sense of insecurity. It was never articulated by the CPI or any communist to my knowledge, yet verses such as this were included in anti-Progressive discourse as proof that communists were working to destabilize Pakistan and "place it at the feet of Nehru and Patel" as Askari (2001: 64) declared in one of his anti-Progressive diatribes.

50. See also Shireen's (1963) *Fasaadat par hamaare afsaane* ("Our stories on Partition"). Askari (2001: 91) reiterated this charge, arguing that "this clique articulated a strong and unwavering position on the establishment of Pakistan and the riots of 1947 and also came up with a new formula for writers, which was that the expression of barbarism by human beings should be presented in extremely horrific ways so that people may be ashamed of their actions." This was simply not true; as Zaheer Babar pointed out, it was writers like Manto and Shahab who consciously represented the violence of Partition in extremely graphic terms; see Babar's (1949: 73–83) *Ya* <u>Kh</u>uda aur is ka Dibaacha ("Ya Khuda and its Preface"), in *Naqush*, number 5.

51. Manto was already one of the most famous Urdu short-story writers of his generation, and would go on to be justifiably considered the pre-eminent writer on Partition. His relationship with the PWA had always been tenuous; he had never been a formal member but had always considered himself a "fellow-traveler." Of late, however, this informal connection had been transformed into outright estrangement. One of the major causes of the rift was Sardar Jafri's critique of what he understood to be gratuitous sexual explicitness as well as a dangerous cynicism in Manto's Partition stories.

52. This binary of "external context" versus "interiority"—<u>kh</u>aarjiyat versus daa<u>kh</u>liyat—was another contested issue between Progressives and the liberal

non-Progressives. The latter accused the Progressives' social(ist) realism of focusing on the former at the expense of the latter, while the Progressives critiqued the liberals' preference for *daakhliyat* as an effort to psychologize social phenomena and therefore as *ipso facto* reactionary.

53. For example, in 1948 alone, three Progressive magazines—*Naqush*, *Savera* and *Adab-i-Latif*—were banned under the new Public Safety Act for six months each. *Naqush* was proscribed for publishing Manto's controversial short story *Khol Do* ("Open It"), while *Savera* and *Adab-i-Latif* were not even formally charged.

54. A term used to refer to thugs or goons.

55. Staffs.

56. It was an open secret within literary circles in Pakistan that a significant number of these were written by Taseer under several of his preferred pseudonyms.

57. Literally, "innovation"—unacceptable under Islamic law and tantamount to heresy.

58. This means, literally, that the person has been declared an apostate or a heretic and that it was incumbent upon all good Muslims to kill him.

59. Intizar Hussain, an anti-Progressive liberal himself, admits in his memoirs that one of the reasons Askari did not begin writing earlier than he did (that is to say, a few months after Partition) was because of the hegemony of the Progressives: "This was the era of the zenith of the Progressive Writers Movement in the entire subcontinent. Even those who weren't Progressives accepted guidance from them/were effected by them in some degree or form. If there was a dissident, he didn't have the guts to voice opposition to them" (Hussain, 1997: 44).

60. Sibte Hasan (1986: 218), a well-respected leftist journalist and major figure in the Progressive Writers Association, actually argues that the PWA was banned "under American pressure." Hasan also mentions that branches of a CIA-sponsored publishing house called Franklin Publications were opened in the three main urban and cultural centers of Karachi, Lahore and Dhaka. The publishing house also employed and contracted Pakistani writers to translate American books into Urdu, paying them handsomely for their services; these books were then distributed free of cost to local booksellers.

4 AYUB KHAN'S DECADE OF DEVELOPMENT AND ITS CULTURAL VICISSITUDES

1. "West Pakistan as one unit": Text of the prime minister's broadcast to the nation, on November 22, 1954, announcing that West Pakistan is to be constituted into a single unit: Government of Pakistan, Karachi, 1954.

2. See Ali (2005: 88).

3. For details of student radicalization around the Algerian war of independence and the state's reaction, see Ali, 2005.

4. Of course, a large part of this post-colonial solidarity felt by ordinary Pakistanis came out of a sense of a shared global *Muslim* identity, given that this period was defined by the Algerian War, the Suez canal crisis and the Mossadegh affair. However, at this time such "Muslim solidarity" was strongly inflected by anti-imperialism, as exemplified in the work of the poet Muhammad Iqbal, and was extended to non-Muslim colonial and post-colonial contexts, such as the murder of Patrice Lumumba and the Vietnam War.

5. The ideological project of modernization theory was the brainchild of a group of social scientists in the US, led by MIT economist W.W. Rostow, whose *Stages of Economic Growth: A Non-Communist Manifesto*, written explicitly as a response to the Soviet challenge was the classic text of this era. Rostow and Max Millikan (a fellow MIT economist and director of the CIA) and the Ford Foundation-funded Center for International Studies had made a case for the strategic significance of modernization as early as 1954. Rostow had written a memo in this regard to CIA director Allen Dulles, a declassified version of which was published in 1957 under the title *A Proposal: Key to an Effective Foreign Policy* and was widely circulated in Washington, DC, impressing then-Senator John Kennedy. Millikan and Rostow (who became the White House deputy national security adviser in 1961 and later the chairman of the State Department's Policy Planning Commission) were part of an extensive network of social scientists involved in planning and policy-making within the Kennedy administration. Many of these Cold War social scientists, among them Edward Shils and Daniel Lerner, were an integral part of the Cold War cultural circuit as well through the Congress for Cultural Freedom.

6. While "modernization theory" was a quintessentially American product (Latham, 2000) with roots in the European Enlightenment, it was in fact Mustapha Kemal Ataturk who first used the term "modernization" to refer to "a political and economic program" (Gilman, 2003: 30).

7. Here I am employing a structuralist understanding of the binary as a relationship which embodies power, such that one term is dominant while the other is subservient.

8. On the enterprise of Cold War social science see, *inter alia*, Gilman (2003), Latham (2000), Engerman et al. (2003), Robin (2001), Packenham (1973), Pearce and Pearce (2001), Rohde (2007, 2009), Williams (2001) and the essays in *Radical History Review* 63 (Fall 1995).

9. See, for example, Lerner and Robinson's (1960) article on the Turkish Army as a modernizing force. As an example of this orientation in studies of Pakistan, one need look no further than Herbert Feldman's (1967) contemporary and embarrassingly laudatory account of Ayub Khan's coup and the period immediately following it.

10. See Feldman (1967).

11. The term "Decade of Development" was used officially for the first time in 1968 in the context of the launch of an ill-advised propaganda exercise celebrating the regime's ten years in power, just as the agitation against it was building to a climax.

12. This "revelation," made in the late 1960s by Mahbub-ul Haq himself, contributed significantly to the already increasing agitation against Ayub Khan. By the time agitations against Ayub began, 66 per cent of industrial capital in Pakistan was in the hands of 22 families (these same families also controlled 80 per cent of the country's banking and 97 per cent of its insurance industry). Of the remaining 34 per cent, half was owned by foreign firms (Ali, 1970: 152).

13. The late Zamir Niazi (1986; 1994), a highly respected journalist and historian of media censorship in Pakistan, argues that while this censorship was state-imposed, it became internalized by journalists, editors and publishers to such an extent that they engaged in pre-emptive self-censorship in order to accommodate an authoritarian state.

14. Most of the reports of these commissions were never made public because Ayub did not agree with their recommendations.

15. From a speech given on August 13, 1960 and cited on the frontispiece of *The Emerging Society*, published by the Bureau of National Reconstruction (Government of Pakistan, 1962).

16. Revealingly, the Bureau of National Reconstruction was part of the Ministry of National Reconstruction and *Information*, and was actually set up as a "Goebbels-type" propaganda organization for the regime, but failed to act as one despite the aspirations of its architect, Brigadier F.R. Khan, who also masterminded the take-over of Progressive Papers Ltd.; see Tariq Ali (1970: 101).

17. In other words, they were attempts at what Corrigan and Sayer call "moral regulation" (1985: 5), which they define as "a project of normalizing, rendering natural, taken for granted, in a word 'obvious', what are in fact ontological and epistemological premises of a particular and historical form of social order. Moral regulation is coextensive with state formation, and state forms are always animated and legitimated by a particular moral ethos. The reality is that bourgeois society is systematically unequal, is structured along lines of class, gender, ethnicity, age, religion, occupation, locality. States act to erase the recognition and expression of these differences ... ."

18. For more information on the CCF and its role in the Cultural Cold War, see *inter alia* Coleman (1989), Saunders (1999), and Scott-Smith (2001).

19. As part of this strategy, the CIA began to actively court and patronize radical Islamist individuals and organizations around the world. For details, see Johnson (2010) and Dreyfuss (2005).

20. See Feldman (1967) for a laudatory account of Ayub's coup and the new regime.

21. Manzur Qadir was one of Pakistan's leading jurists and Ayub's foreign minister between 1958 and 1962.

22. We first came across Qudratullah Shahab in the context of the stand-off between the Progressives and their detractors in the previous chapter. He was the then-young author of the well-received novella *Ya Khuda* written in the immediate aftermath of Partition.

23. Tariq Ali calls the PPL "the most powerful left-wing force in the country" and reports that despite the fact that they had been extremely careful after the imposition of martial law not to attack the regime outright, "there was no doubt that their continued existence was a major irritant to the new regime." For example, the day after the coup, every newspaper but the PPL's *Pakistan Times* had printed editorials hailing Ayub as a savior. The *Pakistan Times*, notes Ali (1970: 100), "had an editorial on soil erosion."

24. An indication of the premium placed by the regime on control of the cultural sphere, the takeover was the brainchild of Manzur Qadir and Altaf Gauhar, and was orchestrated by Brigadier F.R. Khan (the head of the Bureau of National Reconstruction) with the support of Qudrutullah Shahab. The brigadier had been assigned to the Home Ministry which dealt with "Communist subversion and similar activities."

25. Faiz Ahmed Faiz was the editor-in-chief of PPL's three influential publications—the English-language *Pakistan Times* and the Urdu-language *Imroze*, and the Urdu weekly *Lail-o-Nihar*.

26. The claim of "non-partisanship" was a clear reference to the PWA.

27. This migration was also ironic, given that the Halqa had been established in 1939 along the principles of "Literature for the sake of literature" ("*Adab baraa-i adab*") explicitly as a counter to the AIPWA and its commitment to "Literature for Life" ("*Adab baraa-i zindagi*") (Hasan, 1987: 25).

28. Ironically enough, Mohammad Askari, the liberal anti-communist, was one of those who boycotted the proceedings, while Progressives like Safdar Mir not only did not, but argued that it was important to attend. Of course, several of the most prominent Progressive writers, such as Faiz, were still in jail.

29. The biggest and most prestigious of these was the Adamjee Adabi [Literary] Award (known popularly as the Adamjee Award, sponsored by and named after the Adamjee Group of Companies) which Jalib lampoons in one of his verses. The Adamjees were one of the infamous "22" families. This award reflected the close relationship between the state and industrial and commercial capital which developed under Ayub, and was a testimony to the importance the regime accorded to matters cultural.

30. In many ways, the major literary highlights of this period were Faiz's collections of poetry, produced under various phases of incarceration in the 1950s. *Dast-i Saba*, for example, was published in 1952, when Faiz was in jail for complicity in the Rawalpindi Conspiracy Case; *Zindaan-nama* in 1956 just after his release; while *Dast-i Tah-i Sang* contained many of his most famous poems, composed while incarcerated by Ayub Khan.

31. Pakistan was declared an Islamic Republic, and a "repugnancy" clause was incorporated into the declaration which declared that no new law could be enacted which was repugnant to Islam, and that all existing laws would be examined and amended in light of this provision.

32. Not only was the secularism of the regime superficial, but like all regimes in Pakistan before and since, it used Islam and Islamist political parties such as the *Jama'at* opportunistically. For example, Ayub sought to legitimize his increasing centralization of power as well as executive control over the legislature "by reference to historical parallels during the early days of Islam" and specifically to the figure of the caliph Omar (Noman, 1988: 34).

33. The relationship posited here between the *Jama'at* and the Muslim Brotherhood is interesting, to say the least, given Maududi's well-documented influence on Sayyid Qutb, the founder of the Muslim Brotherhood. See, *inter alia*, Mamdani (2004).

34. In one of the more embarrassing episodes within the history of the Pakistani Left, the pro-Beijing faction of the Left followed China's lead in declaring Ayub an anti-imperialist and the war with India a "people's war." See, *inter alia*, Ali, 1983.

35. The NAP split in 1968 into a West-Pakistan-based pro-Moscow faction led by Wali Khan and an East Pakistan pro-Peking group under Maulana Bhashani. In West Pakistan, Maoists broke away from NAP-Wali Khan to form the NAP-Mazdoor Kissan, which eventually became the Mazdoor Kissan Party. See Muhammad (1982).

36. Such as J.A. Rahim and Jamil Rashid.

37. Much of the engagement with Bhutto even within mainstream academic scholarship on Pakistan remains mired in psychological or simplistic class explanations for Bhutto's politics, which are not particularly useful.

38. The role played by Muhammad Safdar Mir—Progressive journalist, poet, writer and critic who was given the affectionate title of "the boxer of the PWA"—in

the politics of this period was complex, to say the least. While on the one hand the most astute and prolific of socialism's defenders, especially against the *Jama'at*, he was also a member of the pro-Peking West Pakistani Left which briefly declared Ayub an anti-imperialist.

39. In fact, by all accounts it was its very slipperiness that made it particularly appealing to Bhutto.

40. Sibte Hasan (1986) is one of many who contended that the *Jama'at* was supported by the CIA, citing (among other things) the vast propaganda machinery which the organization had at its disposal. See also Johnson (2010) for details of the links between the CIA and the Muslim Brotherhood and at least one member of the *Jama'at* as part of the US's Cold War propaganda among Muslims from the 1950s onwards.

41. This image had originally graced the cover of the issue of the *Nusrat* in which Mir's series had premiered.

42. *Zindagi* was issued under different names after it was banned by the government, and was brought out by the same group that published the *Urdu Digest*, which itself was modeled on that popular mainstay of the Cold War in America, *Readers Digest*.

43. Of course, it wasn't just poets that were attacked; all important members of the PWA were fair game. For example, between August 25, 1970 and October 27, *Zindagi* featured a six-part series attacking Syed Sibte Hasan.

44. See, for example, *Janab-i Ghaiz ki ek nayi nazm* ("Mister Ghaiz's new poem") by one *Tamashaai* ("spectator"; a pseudonym) in *Zindagi*, May 25, 1970.

45. This idea of a "dynamic," "elastic" and "progressive" Islam that had the capacity to respond positively to the challenges of modernity was, of course, the *sine qua non* of Muslim modernism. However, this capacity depended ultimately on the support and cooperation of the *ulema* for *ijtehad* (independent reasoning).

46. The more radical sections of the Left did, of course, call for all that and more, but the references to "nationalization" in right-wing discourse make it clear that those radical leftists were not the cause of the anxiety.

47. For a detailed discussion of Iqbal and socialism, see Toor (2005). A selection of Iqbal's poems were collected and translated by the British Marxist historian and essayist Victor Kiernan (1955).

48. In response, Safdar Mir (1990: 63) quoted from a published letter of Iqbal to Jinnah in which he addressed Jinnah as "the only Muslim in India today to whom the community has a right to look for safe guidance," sarcastically speculating why Iqbal did not write this letter to "'any other mason', for instance, Mr. Brohi, or Maulana Maudoodi."

49. For Maududi, the very concept of "culture" (like that of nationalism) reeked of secularism. The idea of a "national culture," then, was a compound evil.

50. In an interview given to *Imroze* on June 30, 1969.

51. As I have explained before, this problem was exacerbated by the generally held normative understanding that authentic nations and national cultures were hermetically sealed entities (See Handler, 1988).

52. Of course, as a serious body of scholarship on nationalism has shown us, this complexity wasn't—and isn't—unique to Pakistan, being a feature of all nationalist projects.

53. Naseem Hijazi is best known for his series of historical novels featuring important events and individuals from Muslim history, several of which were turned into television plays, particularly during the Zia era.

54. Traditional percussion instruments.

55. Dancers' ankle-bells. General Zia was to ban their use (Hasan, 2002).

56. '*Alif* is the first letter of the Urdu (as it is of the Arabic and Persian) alphabet, and here is a sly reference to Mian Iftikharuddin, the senior left-wing politician and owner of Progressive Papers Ltd., whose name in Urdu begins with '*alif*.

57. For this, Faiz was subjected to much red-baiting at the hands of the *Jama'at* during the mid to late 1960s.

58. These complex counter-arguments also point to the difficulty—and often impossibility—of separating the "religious" from the "secular." At the same time, Faiz's continuous attempts to do so point to the necessity from a secular/liberal/leftist perspective of drawing a distinction between these two or at least expanding what is meant by "the religious" aspects of culture.

59. Literally, "innovation," but understood in the sense of being almost heretical.

60. Significantly, the *Jama'at* was the only political party aside from the Muslim League, to support One Unit. This was odd, given that the cultural justification for One Unit was, as we have seen, completely contradictory to the idea of a unitary basis for Pakistani nationhood which the *Jama'at*—and the Establishment—generally held to be sacrosanct. However, it shows the degree to which the *Jama'at*'s political project was in sync with that of the establishment even if it appeared otherwise.

61. Ayesha Jalal (1990: 308–9) notes that the military establishment was not of a piece: "The ideological polarisation of Pakistani society which the recent mass protests had brought to the surface reflected itself in the composition of the regime. While some in the council of ministers and the upper echelons of the bureaucratic-military axis wanted to neutralise left wing groups by bringing about a genuine redress of social and economic grievances, those linked with right-wing groups like the Jamat-i-Islami and big business surreptitiously worked to sabotage the reforms."

62. Neither party won seats in both East and West Pakistan.

63. Since the PPP would be a minority in the National Assembly, the only leverage Bhutto had was at this time through an alliance with the anti-Mujib elements in the army.

64. All foreign journalists were made to leave East Pakistan prior to the launch of Operation Searchlight.

65. The Communist Party of Pakistan issued a statement opposing the army action.

5   FROM BHUTTO'S AUTHORITARIAN POPULISM TO ZIA'S MILITARY THEOCRACY

1. Bhutto's refusal to hold the army publicly accountable was not without reason. For one thing, he bore a certain amount of responsibility for the army action against East Bengal in so far as he had refused any power-sharing arrangement with Sheikh Mujeeb and the Awami League in the aftermath of the 1970 elections. For another, far from dismantling the repressive apparatuses of the state, Bhutto was invested in maintaining and expanding them, even if he *was* interested in restricting their autonomy (Jalal, 1990).

2. The army's poor performance in the battlefield was explained by placing the blame on the lack of adequate supplies, or on the personal failings of certain senior generals; these so-called "Yahya generals" were summarily purged (Ali, 1983: 101).

3. Under Bhutto, the army was brought under civilian control to a great degree, but Bhutto's practice of involving generals in political deliberations undermined this process as well as the efforts to de-politicize and re-professionalize the army. For a detailed discussion of Bhutto's relationship to the military, see Waseem (2007: 292–7) and Siddiqa (2007: 78–82).

4. The designation "North West Frontier Province" was a hangover from the colonial period. Until very recently, the Pakistani state resisted the demand of the majority Pukhtoon population of the province to name it after them, out of fear that this would strengthen Pukhtoon nationalism. It was not until 2010 the the NWFP was formally renamed "Khyber-Pukhtoonkhwa."

5. Bhutto established the paramilitary Federal Security Force (FSF), which was created to ensure his independence from the army when it came to maintaining law and order. The FSF quickly became an instrument of terror and a major source of popular anger against the PPP government (Ziring, 2001), since Bhutto regularly unleashed it against his political "enemies"—from the leadership of organized labor to current or former dissidents of the PPP (Waseem, 2007).

6. The measures taken against the press, for example, were more severe than anything that had yet been seen in Pakistan (Niazi, 1994).

7. The PPP's left wing was not a monolithic bloc, but consisted of different groups that had joined the party independently of one other, each representing a different mobilization of workers and peasants, and various levels of radicalization.

8. For a detailed analysis of the 1972 labor actions and the state's response, see Asdar Ali (2005).

9. Another indicator of the extent of the state repression of the labor movement (as well as of the suspension of civil and democratic rights that this represented) is the fact that over the four-year period of this unrest, the infamous Section 144 (the colonial-era law which criminalizes public assembly) was imposed on Karachi for all but 160 days (Waseem, 2007).

10. Ironically, this period of the first three years which saw the purge of the left wing from the party was also the period which saw the most rapid unionization in Pakistan's history—more trade unions were registered in this period than during the entire preceding two decades (Ahmad, 1983).

11. The top leadership of the PPP included 27 landlords, a representation that was far greater than that of any other demographic category, the next largest group being middle-class professionals, with seven members.

12. Hussain (1989) notes that the Green Revolution essentially made it possible to increase agricultural growth without having to bring about any real change in the power structure (that is, production relations) in the countryside.

13. The 1972 labor laws protected a small minority of industrial workers from arbitrary dismissal, gave them the right to appeal to a labor court, provided for medical and welfare funds, improved pension rights, and offered educational allowances for workers' children. Significantly, these provisions were passed before the left wing was excised from the PPP. However, oppressive labor laws from the 1930s, which granted employers arbitrary powers of dismissal, were not repealed (Waseem, 2007).

14. Defense spending, however, managed to miraculously increase despite the budgetary constraints, with allocations for the military and internal security more than doubling over four years to 55 per cent of the total; the combined expenditure on health and education was a quarter of this (Ahmad, 1983).

15. Ironically, it was Zia who reaped the benefits of this Gulf migration, since it was not until the late 1970s and early 1980s that it began to bear fruit (Noman, 1988), becoming Pakistan's single most important source of external revenue by the early 1980s, and accounting for over half of its total foreign exchange inflow (Ballard, 1989). An elite-focused policy ensured that these remittances not only failed to produce economic development (either nationally or in the migrants' home villages and towns) but that they actually translated into benefits for the elite. The "windfall inflow of remittances" allowed the Pakistani government to maintain a liberal imports policy (Ballard, 1989: 120). By deliberately overvaluing the rupee, this policy cheapened the value of remittances while keeping the cost of imports—particularly of luxury goods—low, thus effectively resulting in a net transfer of wealth from the migrant workers to the consuming elite.

16. The propertied class was affronted by the workers' willingness to make demands based on some of their modest, newly granted rights. This "insubordination" produced such anger that, following Bhutto's incarceration under martial law, landed elites taunted the tenants they were now free to evict by sardonically asking them to call on their protector (Bhutto) to save them.

17. _Khuda ki Basti_ had earned its author, Shaukat Siddiqi, the first ever Adamjee Award for Literature in 1960.

18. Maududi opposed this language policy explicitly on the grounds that it would encourage the consolidation of a Sindhi identity _across_ religious affiliation, that is, it would unify Sindhi Hindus and Sindhi Muslims; see Sayeed (1980).

19. Scholars have noted that this period saw the beginnings of a cross-regional class consciousness among members of the urban petit bourgeoisie (Sayeed, 1980), though it was under Zia that they actually managed to consolidate their power (Rouse, 2004).

20. The _Jama'at_ also infiltrated trade unions, some of which—specifically those associated with the right-wing National Federation of Trade Unions (established as a counter to the predominantly left-wing union movement in Pakistan at the time)—joined the mobilization against Bhutto (Sayeed, 1980).

21. Like Ayub before him, Bhutto thought that he could "out-maneuver" the religious lobby on their own turf by deploying Islam strategically, and like Ayub before him, he was forced to concede more and more ground to them. Bhutto's defeat at the hands of the religious forces was largely due to the fact that he did not take the opportunity of his initially strong public mandate to lay the groundwork for countering these groups' religious ideology by the structural and institutional means at his disposal.

22. Bhutto cynically set about to revive his mass base in this period, announcing new land reforms and making a highly successful tour of the countryside (Waseem, 2007). In another populist move, he delivered on the promise he had made during the 1970 election campaign to grant property rights to _kutchi-abadi_ (slum) dwellers, but only when faced with the massive PNA demonstrations (Sayeed, 1980). Even this series of transparently opportunistic actions translated into significant political gains for Bhutto, a testimony to how little the poor people of Pakistan had to hold on to. The fact that elite groups lent their support

to the PNA gave credibility to the PPP's claim of (still) being a party of the poor (Waseem, 2007).

23. In Lahore, the labyrinthine streets and alleys of the old city where small merchants and traders lived, also proved to be strategically useful for the movement, since they were difficult for the police to navigate. Mosques became centers of the agitation in large part because Section 144 of the Pakistan Penal Code which prohibits public assembly (and which was in effect at this time) did not apply to places of worship. Among the many strategic miscalculations made by Bhutto at this time was the decision to allow police and the Federal Security Force to storm mosques in order to beat up and arrest activists. This only served to validate the PNA's claim that Bhutto was an enemy of Islam.

24. "What does 'Pakistan' stand for? Hangings, lashings, General Zia!": a popular political slogan during the Zia regime, it was a clever take on the pre-Independence Muslim League call "*Pakistan ka matlab kya? la Ila ha Illallah!*" ("What does 'Pakistan' stand for? There is no God but God").

25. Bhutto responded to a wheel-jam strike called by the PNA on April 20, by imposing martial law in Karachi, Hyderabad and Islamabad. By all accounts, the generals were unhappy with this turn of events, but their proximity to Bhutto as he lost his grip on the situation played an instrumental role in the decision to overthrow him (Siddiqa, 2007).

26. Aijaz Ahmad has argued that this coup was also "structurally" different from the ones that came before it because it set out to "transform the state in such a manner that the ultra-Right shall now be propelled into a hegemonic position in all the basic structures of authority" (Ahmad, 1983: 120).

27. Zia actively aided this infiltration and thereby the army's ideological transformation. Aijaz Ahmed (1983: 123) notes that Mian Tufail, the then-chief of the *Jama'at*, was a close relation of Zia's, and that the *Jama'at*'s propaganda among troops was "officially sanctioned by commanding officers on the battalion level and above." As a result, it was the only political organization to have the opportunity to set up secret cells inside the armed forces.

28. Jalal (1990) notes that the old secular ethos of the armed forces did not disappear completely and so Zia did not have a completely free hand when it came to Islamization.

29. Thanks to the intervention of the senior judiciary, public flogging was the only one of these punishments to actually be deployed by the state (Hasan, 2002).

30. In fact, in November 1978, Bhutto's wife Nusrat filed a case in the Supreme Court challenging the validity of the coup and the martial law under which her husband and other members of the PPP had been detained, and arguing that the coup amounted to an act of treason under the 1973 Constitution (which Zia claimed had not been abrogated but only held "in abeyance"). As in 1958, a compliant Supreme Court used the convenient "Doctrine of Necessity" to legitimate the military coup, and rejected Nusrat Bhutto's case. It is worth noting that the federal minister for law under Zia, and the one representing the Federation of Pakistan in this case was none other than Mr. A.K. Brohi.

31. Editors of "defamatory" publications could now receive ten lashes and 25 years of rigorous imprisonment. Journalists were whipped for the first time in 1978 (Siddiqa, 2007).

32. Even after Martial Law was lifted in December 1985, Zia continued to occupy the position of chief of army staff.

33. Understanding the crucial importance of education as a social institution, Zia institutionalized several reforms of the education system. For details, see Saigol (1995).
34. In addition to the various forms of state action against organized labor, the *Jama'at* was engaged in trying to sabotage it by infiltrating the trade union movement; see Sayeed (1980: 180).
35. Migration to the Gulf had reached record levels and this no doubt had a negative impact on the mobilizing capacity of organized labor.
36. Ironically, he did so while criticizing the tendency of politicians to deploy Islam opportunistically. See "General Mohammad Zia ul Haq: Address to the Nation. Measure to Enforce Nizam-e-Islam," Pakistan Directorate of Films and Publications, Ministry of Information and Broadcasting, Islamabad, December 1, 1978.
37. Interestingly, the shariat courts were barred from reviewing Martial Law Orders, as well as family and fiscal laws as laid out in the Pakistan Penal Code. See Waseem (2007: 38).
38. In *qazi* courts, the judge rules in accordance with *shariah* law.
39. *Shariat* is Urdu for *shariah,* which is an Arabic word.
40. This system of concurrent penal systems produced conditions for exploitation by law enforcement agencies. See Waseem (2007: 380).
41. Interestingly, Saudi Arabia used (and still uses) astronomical data; this was one of the small but significant ways in which Zia's model of Islamization deviated from the Saudi one, and was representative of the regime's war on science and rational thought.
42 The government also instructed that all heads of government departments were to lead prayers in their offices; this caused some confusion, given that there were many government departments and offices headed by women who were not allowed to lead the prayers. This was fairly typical of the "Islamic" directives issued by the regime; they were often followed by embarrassing retractions.
43 In an act of defiance which is remembered to this day, a popular and well-respected female compere, Mehtab Channa, lost her job because of her principled refusal to cover her head.
44. "Additional" because a *dopatta* (a long scarf, usually of diaphanous material), worn casually across the neck/chest was the common, traditional and prefered covering for most women in Pakistan, rather than the *chaadar.* The head-covering known as *hijab,* now increasingly popular among some segments of the middle and upper middle classes, was not to arrive in Pakistan until the 1990s.
45. That is, full-sleeved and preferably loose, unlike the tight, sleeveless versions that had become popular in the 1960s and 1970s.
46. In 1978, a prohibition was placed on women dancing on television on the basis of the claim that this was part of Hindu culture (Noman, 1988). Interestingly, attempts to ban the Punjabi kite-flying festival of Basant by the same logic were scuttled due to the immense backlash they produced, but keep resurfacing even today.
47. *Na-mahrams* are those with whom the woman doesn't have the kind of relationship that would make modesty unnecessary; a woman's *mahrams* are her husband, father, husband's father, son, brother, brother's son, sister's son, and so on.
48. Formally called the Zina (Enforcement of Hudood) Ordinance.

49. It is important to note here that while women have become the Zina Ordinance's overwhelming (if not exclusive) victims, two of the three cases which highlighted the potential problems with the ordinance involved men who were accused of adultery and sentenced to death by stoning along with their female partners.

50. In fact, all *non-Sunnis* were excluded, because the official Islam of the regime was actually an extremely narrow and intolerant Sunni sectarianism which was also antagonistic to the popular and mystical forms of Sunni Islam.

51. For details of cases of such violence, see Waseem (2007).

52. The community's resistance and the regime's capitulation were both a result of the recent clerical revolution in Iran.

53. This pragmatism sometimes brought Zia, ironically, into conflict with the *ulema* and religious parties. When he did not respond immediately to demands from *ulema* to tighten the noose on the Ahmediyya community, a rumor was started that his reluctance was due to the fact that he was a secret Ahmedi himself. Zia was thus forced to publicly deny this charge and to denounce Ahmedis as *kafirs* (infidels), while passing the anti-Ahmediyya legislation demanded by the religious lobby.

54. Pukhtuns, interestingly, were the next best-represented ethnicity. The Soviet invasion of Afghanistan and Pakistan's participation in the subsequent CIA war there actually resulted in a quelling of the national question in Sarhad at this time. Baluchistan, too, was relatively quiet under Zia.

55. Waseem (2007) points out that Sindhis' sense of deprivation was well-founded, even *vis-à-vis* the other non-Punjabi provinces. The "Gulf bonanza" had not benefited Sindh, since most of the emigration was from rural parts of the Punjab. Sindhis were under-represented in the industrial working class which, in Sindh, was almost entirely *muhajir*. There was no Sindhi business class, and Sindhis were also under-represented in the army and bureaucracy.

56. It is important to note that WAF cannot stand in for the Pakistani women's movement in its entirety, or represent the full spectrum of women's political engagement at this time. For one thing, WAF was an urban phenomenon. The other significant women's group engaged in agitation against Zia was the *Sindhiani Tehreek*, a women's movement based in rural Sindh, which was formed in 1983 during the MRD movement in Sindh and was affiliated with the *Awami Tehreek*. WAF and *Sindhiani Tehreek* have a history of solidarity.

57. Established in 1949 by Rana Liaquat Ali Khan, wife of the then prime minister.

58. Riaz is sarcastically using conventional forms of address reserved for royalty.

59. This poem can be juxtaposed with Ishrat Aafreen's "*Adhoore Aadmi se Guftagu*" ("Dialogue with an Incomplete Man") in which Aafreen declares that she is unable to accept her male addressee as a comrade-in arms given his immaturity: "*Main tumheñ apna adraak-o-ehsaas kis tarha dooñ, Fikr ke is safar meiñ tumheñ saath kis tarha looñ*" ("How can I share my thoughts and feelings with you, How can I take you along on this journey of the intellect?"). Despite his "artistic skills ... stature ... [and] personality," her addressee is no more mature than a callow boy because he is pathologically attracted to abject helplessness, and is willing to sacrifice his dignity for any adolescent desire. "*Sirf ek larke ho tum, Jo ke roti hui larkioñ, ya uraanoñ se mehroom zakhmi-badan titlioñ, saahil se bandhi kishtioñ, fakhtaaoñ ke toote paroñ meiñ sisakti hui lazzat-azaarioñ meiñ panaaheñ talaashe, Jo khilandri si khwahish ke peeche lapakte huay, Apne adarsh bhi tor de*" ("You are just a boy / Who searches for refuge in weeping girls, flightless and injured butterflies, boats tied securely to

the shore, in the broken wings of doves / Who, in leaping after an adolescent desire, forgets even his values").

60. The poems mentioned here can be found in *Beyond Belief*, a collection of Urdu poetry by Pakistani women poets originally published in 1990 by the feminist ASR Publications, and still the best collection of its kind available. The translations of the poems in this chapter are mine.

61. All official portraits depicted him as wearing the "Jinnah cap" and *achkan* (the long coat associated with the North Indian aristocracy) which Zia himself favored, even though Jinnah wore Savile Row suits for most of his adult public life.

62. For example, Faiz Ahmed Faiz, the bête noir of the *Jama'at*, was forced into exile in Beirut where he edited *Lotus*, the journal of the Afro-Asian Writers Union. Unable to stay away for too long, however, Faiz returned to his beloved Pakistan in 1982, where he died two years later. During the martial law regime, Faiz and his poetry was banned from the airwaves (as was progressive poetry in general, of course).

63. While there were a few brave dissidents who stood up to the regime, there were several who chose to cooperate. The tradition of the establishment intellectual institutionalized by Ayub continued under Zia. Many prominent intellectuals with formerly stellar progressive credentials such as Ahmed Nadeem Qasmi, past editor of the important PWA publication *Fanun* and one-time secretary of the Lahore chapter of the PWA, miraculously discovered their religious/mystical side under the benevolent shadow of Zia. Ashfaq Ahmed, whose collection of short stories dealing with the vicissitudes of contemporary heterosexual romance "*Ek Haqeeqat Sau Afsaane*" ("One Truth, A Hundred Stories") was turned into a successful television series during the Bhutto period, similarly morphed almost overnight into a mystical figure. Many well-known male artists simply abandoned the human figure, switching to calligraphy or landscapes; as Salima Hashmi notes, not a single woman artist did so (Hashmi, 2003).

64. The rise in a culture of conspicuous consumption and the obsession with consumer goods which characterized this period was reflected in the phenomenal popularity of the quiz-cum-game-show "*Neelaam Ghar*" (literally, "Auction House") in which both selected participants and members of the audience received much-coveted middle-class consumer items such as pressure cookers, refrigerators and motorcycles as prizes for correctly answering questions on various topics and for winning various challenges. Its host, Tariq Aziz, acquired iconic status as a national celebrity, and later became a politician himself.

65. The information on PTV is indebted to conversations with Tanvir Masood Khan, a producer at the Lahore station at the time.

66. For details, see Rashid and Gardezi (1983) and Siddiqa (2007).

67. The aid packages added to the military's assets while setting Pakistan up for the debt servitude which defines it today. Pakistan's first IMF agreement was signed in 1988, just before Zia's regime came to an abrupt end with his bizarre death.

68. Analysts have noted that Pakistan had—and continues to have—one of the worst records among developing countries when it comes to provision of social services. The result is an incredibly low score on the human development index, especially its gender components. The problem is not simply low social-sector allocations, which certainly fell during the Zia regime and have been falling ever since. It is that the commitment to human development is so low that even the abysmally small sums allocated are rarely spent in their entirety. For example,

education's share of the budget fell from 2.1 per cent of GNP in 1976–77 to 1.5 per cent of GNP in 1982–83, less than half of which was actually spent (Noman, 1988: 173). At the same time, religious parties and organizations were given both funds and *carte blanche* to establish *madrassas*, which were given full recognition; see Siddiqa (2007) and Ziring (1980).

69. Zia even acknowledged that actual deprivation in Sarhad and Baluchistan was behind the potential popularity of these reforms in these two provinces. The solution, of course, was not the redress of these grievances, but the defeat of the communist regime; see Sayeed (1980).

70. Rashid and Gardezi (1983: 15) noted that the Pakistan military had two divisions in Saudi Arabia, protecting the monarchy, and troops in 20 other countries.

71. Rashid and Gardezi (1983: 16) connect what they call this "militarization of the foreign service" to the mercenary role of the Pakistan Army in Asia.

72. Aside from the massive growth of the military as an institution under Zia, this congruence between economic and political power, and the secret nature of many of the "regimental funds" created by Zia to keep his senior generals happy (Siddiqa, 2007: 141) produced an environment in which corruption became endemic within the military.

73. The ISI played a major role within the political realm as well. Besides the surveillance of political activists (a responsibility it shared with the myriad other intelligence agencies which had increased in both number and size under Zia), the ISI was also responsible for creating political parties and groupings designed to undermine the PPP, such as the *Islami Jamhoori Ittehad* ("The Islamic Democratic Union") or IJI, and the MQM (Siddiqa, 2007: 87).

74. Guns also increasingly began to be used in domestic disputes during this time.

75. The regime and the Pakistani military establishment in general, took advantage of this refugee crisis in many other ways as well—it is worth recalling that the Taliban were the product of Afghan refugee camps.

76. See, for example, Mamdani (2004), Dreyfuss (2005), and Johnson (2010).

77. Of course, in a sense "Islam"—or at least being a "Muslim" army—had been part and parcel of the Pakistan military's identity from the very beginning. Within the logic of official nationalism, that is, the two-nation theory, India was the enemy because it was "Hindu." The defeat at the hands of the Indian Army in 1965 and in 1971 thus wasn't just humiliating; it also caused serious cognitive dissonance. The only way these two things—the idea that it was "God's army" and that it lost to the *kafirs* ("infidels")—could be reconciled was by finding scapegoats or by arguing that the reason for the defeat was that the army (and indeed the nation as a whole) had not been Muslim enough. Thus, as some have argued, Zia's coup and subsequent Islamization project can and should be seen as a delayed reaction to the crisis of 1971.

78. Both religious and secular.

6   THE LONG SHADOW OF ZIA: WOMEN, MINORITIES AND THE NATION-STATE

1. Violence against minorities was the result of widespread abuse of the Blasphemy Laws as amended by Zia. Recent estimates put the number of people charged under the Blasphemy Laws from 1986 to 2009 at 1,030, with over 30 being

killed extra-judicially (Asian Human Rights Commission, UAC-183-2010, December 21, 2010). Prior to the passage of Section 295-C, the clause which is at issue in almost all cases of blasphemy except those involving Ahmedis (for whom there was a separate set of Blasphemy Laws), a mere handful of cases of blasphemy had been filed. Of course, there is a whole set of Blasphemy Laws, but when referred to in the singular in mainstream discourse in Pakistan, Blasphemy Law generally refers to Section 295-C, and that is reflected in this chapter.

2. The Eighth Amendment to the Constitution gave the president the power to dissolve Parliament. It was introduced by Zia in 1985 as a precondition to declaring the end of martial law.

3. For example, she did not enter into an electoral alliance with the other parties of the MRD, in large part because she did not wish to be held accountable to the MRD's declaration of 1986 which emphasized federalism, limited the role of the Center to currency, communications, defense and foreign policy, placed curbs on the Center's ability to dissolve provincial governments, proposed a reorganization of the armed forces to reflect the federal structure, and laid out a six-month moratorium within which a referendum had to be called should the president need to declare a State of Emergency. Clearly, these conditions were unacceptable to the military establishment even as they would have given Benazir more popular legitimacy and strengthened her hand *vis-à-vis* the Opposition. However, in rejecting this alliance and thereby this politics, Benazir made it clear that she—like Nawaz Sharif—was cognizant of the true locus of power. Her other mistake was in not democratizing the PPP, which would have contributed towards the development of a democratic political culture and earned her respect from within the party as well as from outside it. Instead, she chose to follow her father's path and treated the PPP like a personal fiefdom. Much is made of her being the first female leader of a Muslim nation-state, and while it is true that there was a symbolic victory in having a young, foreign-educated woman be the head of state of the "Islamic Republic of Pakistan," and that this was indeed a perpetual thorn in the side of the religious Right, Benazir's concessions to social convention (such as an arranged marriage to someone she did not know, covering her head and wearing a *chaador* in public) undermined the progressive edge of her victory in many ways. Like her father before her, she did not appear to understand that this was a losing battle and that she would not only never manage to appease the religious Right, but that even attempting to do so would move Pakistani society further towards the right. The Taliban were also "created" and dispatched to Afghanistan under her administration.

4. The politics of patronage which had begun under Bhutto and accelerated under Zia had resulted in the politicization of already weak institutions of state, including the judiciary. An indication of the weakness of the political process and political leadership at this time was the fact that most legislation in this period was enacted through presidential decree, and thus under the control of the military establishment.

5. Zia's Sunnification drive and the rise of sectarian Sunni groups such as the *Anjuma-i Sipah Sahaba-i Islam* (SSP) must be seen in the context of these developments in neighboring Iran; in fact, sectarian Sunni groups and seminaries in Pakistan were funded by Saudi Arabia and Iraq in a bid to contain the influence of Iran (Nasr, 2000).

6. The ranks of this class were augmented by the return of large numbers of migrant workers to Pakistan in the late 1980s and 1990s. The influence of this migrant labor is significant for understanding, among other things, the rise of radical sectarianism in Pakistan in this period (Zaman, 1998).

7. Anti-Shia violence in Pakistan has its roots in the longer organized violence against the Ahmediyya community in Pakistan and specifically the Punjab. Many of the leading lights of the SSP, for example, cut their teeth in the earlier anti-Ahmedi mobilization of 1974 (Zaman, 1998).

8. Both Jahangir and her sister Jilani are Pakistan's best-known women's and human rights lawyers who became the *bêtes noir* of religious conservatives for their fearless work on behalf of the disenfranchised, and for their unremitting secularism. Both have been recognized internationally for their work—Jahangir has been the UN's Special Rapporteur on Extrajudicial, Arbitrary and Summary Executions and on Freedom of Religion or Belief, while Jilani has been the UN Special Representative of the Secretary-General on Human Rights Defenders, and a member of both the International Commission of Inquiry on Darfur and the UN Human Rights Council Fact Finding Mission on the Gaza Conflict.

9. It is important to note that this was done one month after Khan dismissed Benazir's administration in August 1990, that is, during the time when an interim government was in place. In November 1990, the Transport Workers Union organized a highly successful country-wide wheel-jam strike against the law, forcing the newly elected government of Nawaz Sharif to introduce amendments to it. Sharif's government could not get the ordinance passed by Parliament despite repeated attempts.

10. Amrita Chhacchi (1989) has, for example, argued that "whereas earlier the exercise of patriarchal authority rested only with particular men—fathers, brothers, husbands and extended family kin—what is significant about State-sponsored religious fundamentalism is that it not only reinforces this patriarchal control, but more importantly shifts the rights of control to all men."

11. Shahla Zia (2002) has documented case after case of the successful use of the "grave and sudden provocation" clause to justify men's use of violence against women whose behavior they found objectionable, even women they didn't know.

12. Conversely, the passage of the Women Protection Bill in 2006 under Musharraf resulted in a sharp decrease in the numbers of incarcerated women.

13. The vast majority of murders of women are committed by their male relatives, although their female relatives are often active enablers.

14. While Veena Hyat's case became the focus of media attention because of the high-profile nature of the victim, it was by no means the only case where sexual violence was used as a political weapon at this time; Khursheed Begum, the wife of a PPP activist, also alleged that she had been subjected to sexual assault by the police because of her husband's political affiliation. Thus Hyat's rape was part of a pattern of political intimidation against the PPP (Zia, 1995).

15. *Jirgas* are quintessentially patriarchal institutions, with women's status being mediated through their male relatives, kin-group, community, or tribe. Far from delivering justice to women, parallel customary legal systems such as *jirgas* in Pakistan expose them to violence in the name of "tradition" and "culture"— "honor killings" being a prime example. Another example is that of *vaani*, the gift of women (or even girls) as a means of settling disputes between individual

men or tribes. The mainstreaming of customary law and legal institutions has thus had a profoundly negative effect on the status of women in Pakistan.

16. As discussed earlier, Zia's "Islamic" laws relating to Zina as they were written and applied actually ended up subverting their original function within Islamic law (that is, the moral regulation of society through the sexual regulation of men *and* women), and turned them into instruments with which to punish women alone.

17. A First Information Report is the written documentation prepared by police in India and Pakistan after they receive information regarding a cognizable crime. Without the registration of an FIR, the police cannot begin a criminal investigation.

18. The *Pukhtoonwali* code is the honor code of the Pukhtoon people of Pakistan and Afghanistan.

19. This can hardly be a reference to Jahangir and Jilani, since they were neither girls nor did they dress in jeans; but "girls in jeans" was obviously code for agentic women who could thus instantly be dismissed as "westernized"—the chain of signification could then easily lead to "western agents" and "enemies of Islam."

20. According to Muslim family law as practiced in Pakistan, a woman can initiate divorce under certain prescribed conditions, which have nothing to do with her parents and certainly do not involve their consent.

21. Not all ANP members supported honor killings. Asfandyar Wali Khan, Khattak's protégé and the leader of the ANP at this time, strongly condemned such practices.

22. This is most obvious in cases involving property and inheritance. Under Islamic law, women have specific property and inheritance rights, which ironically becomes a liability for them within feudal and tribal contexts. See Toor (2011).

23. In the case of Sarwar, local *ulema* in Peshawar actually gave public statements to the effect that the murder had been carried out according to local tribal *and religious* tradition (Mullaly, 2007).

24. This issue comes up in the case of the Blasphemy Law as well. Under the Hanafi school of Islamic jurisprudence which prevails in Pakistan, blasphemy does not carry a death sentence for Muslims; blasphemy is not even applied to non-Muslim *dhimmis* in Hanafi law because the understanding is that being a non-Muslim is inherently blasphemous, and that *dhimmis* are protected communities.

25. The term is attributed to Stanley Cohen (1972: 9) who used it to define the situation in which a "condition, episode, person or group of persons emerges to become defined as a threat to societal values and interests."

26. This part of my essay is immeasurably indebted to Neelam Hussain's (1997) wonderful and complex analysis of the Saima Waheed case.

27. The "Saima Waheed case" also showed how state apparatuses, social institutions and the community colluded in maintaining both legal and social control over women's sexuality—from the discursive construction of Waheed's legal and religious right as an inexcusable transgression on her part to the police harassment of Ahmad's family and their refusal to take action against a member of the Ropri family found with a handgun inside the courtroom. For details, see Hussain (1997). See also the Human Rights Watch Report (1998) (section on Pakistan).

28. This strategy of dismissing or attacking feminists on the basis of the claim of "westernization" is not unique to Pakistan or even Muslim countries. Uma Narayan (1997) for example, describes the deployment of the same strategy in India.

29. Justice Chaudhry in his judgment presented such cases of "runaway marriages" as the literal manifestation of the clash of civilizations within Muslim societies, darkly hinting at the dastardly role played by "certain" Muslims who represented "vested interests from the west." See Hussain (1997: 226) for a more comprehensive analysis.

30. *Biradari*: literally, "brotherhood" or "fraternity," the *biradari* is a form of patrilineal kinship in South Asia.

31. It must be recalled that the conservative sections of the urban petit bourgeoisie, particularly the bazaar merchants, formed an important constituency for Zia, and that this class was one of the major beneficiaries of his policies. As Rouse (2004: 51) notes, "women's location within this middle class is essentially contradictory."

32. Shahnaz Khan's excellent ethnographic work with women jailed under the Zina Ordinance in Pakistan—who make up the vast majority of women prisoners—similarly illustrates the ways in which families use the law as a tool to punish and control non-compliant women. These women are almost entirely from the lower classes, showing that the need to control women and the use of the law to do so is not limited to any particular class. Needless to say, men are hardly ever accused of *zina* and if they are, they rarely end up in jail.

33. Paradoxical as it may seem, the caste system continues to structure social life in the (predominantly Muslim) Pakistani Punjab despite the fact that it is a Hindu institution. Since many of the subcontinent's poorer Christians were converts from the scheduled classes, Punjabi Muslim attitudes towards them reflect upper-caste Hindu ideas of "untouchability" (Sookhdeo, 2002).

34. Needless to say, minority women were doubly vulnerable. Abductions, forced conversions and marriages of Hindu and Christian women became commonplace in this period, with Christian women especially targeted because of stereotypes about their lax sexual morals (the result of the conflation of "Christian" with "western," and prevalent ideas about "western" women, often garnered from foreign films) (Sookhdeo, 2002).

35. The colonial laws were Section 295 (and later 298), while Zia added Sections 295-B, 295-C, and the specifically anti-Ahmedi Sections 298-A, 298-B and 298-C which essentially criminalized the Ahmediyya faith.

36. Nawaz Sharif's party at this time was the *Islami Jamhoori Ittehad*, the coalition of religious groups which the military establishment had cobbled together to oppose the PPP.

37. As mentioned previously, the issue is not as straightforward as the judgment implies; there are serious differences among the different Sunni schools as to what, if anything, the state needs to do about blasphemy.

38. It must be noted that when the government tabled the bill to change Section 295-C in accordance with the FSC's decision, the upper house or senate adopted it unanimously, but the lower house discussed it at length without passing it, citing its potential for abuse. In 1994, this potential was also noted by the Pakistan Law Commission, which is presided over by the chief justice of the Supreme Court and comprised of the minister for law, justice and parliamentary affairs, the chairman of the Council of Islamic Ideology and the chief justices of the four provincial courts.

39. As I write this (2011), Pakistan's Blasphemy Laws have once more become the focus of international attention, this time through the case of Aasia Bibi, a Christian woman and field hand who was sentenced to death on the charge of blasphemy by the Lahore High Court, and by the murders of Salman Taseer, a member of the PPP and governor of the Punjab, at the hands of his own security guard and most recently, the murder of Shahbaz Bhatti, the only Christian member of the National Assembly. Taseer's guard, Mumtaz Qadri, killed him because he believed that Taseer had committed blasphemy himself through his vocal critique of the Blasphemy Laws and his advocacy on behalf of Aasia Bibi. For weeks prior to the murder, religious parties and individuals had been denouncing Taseer and others with similar views, declaring them blasphemers and therefore the legitimate target of the wrath of all pious Muslims. These extremist views and their proponents were given prominent space on television and radio channels, often without being challenged. In addition, *maulvis* or leaders of religious groups and parties who openly advocated that Taseer be killed for blasphemy—including the cleric of one mosque in Peshawar who offered a monetary award to anyone who would do the deed—were pointedly not brought to task by the media or the government for incitement to violence and/or endangering the lives of Pakistani citizens. In fact, the government, after having initially endorsed Taseer's views that the Blasphemy Laws should be amended and Aasia pardoned by presidential decree, did a complete about-turn after the backlash from religious groups. Taseer's murder has yet to be openly condemned in the National Assembly. Meanwhile, the murderer has been hailed by certain sections of society (including many lawyers) and by the religious groups as a hero for protecting the honor of the Prophet. Those who are horrified by the murder and are attempting to intervene in some meaningful fashion find themselves facing a hostile public, a sensationalist media and a pusillanimous government.

40. Ahmedis are, of course, also specifically targeted by Sections 298-B and 298-C which explicitly criminalizes them for their religious beliefs, but this does not prevent them from coming under the mischief of Section 295-C.

41. One of the most dangerous fall-outs of Zia's "Islamization" project has been the phenomenal rise in the use of violence by private actors. This, combined with the official designation of Pakistan as an Islamic state which should be ruled by the *shariah* along with the increasingly intolerant and narrow version of Islam propagated by the state and its affiliated religious outfits contributed to an alarming rise in vigilantism in the name of Islam by individuals and religious/sectarian outfits from the 1990s onwards.

42. The targeting of religious minorities was connected to the rise in sectarian violence within Pakistan at this time, as can be seen by the prominent role played by the SSP in inciting violence against minorities and those who defend them.

43. Jahangir, for example, was the counsel for the defense in the Salamat Masih and Rehmat Masih case.

44. The Asian Human Rights Commission has reported an even more grim trend among the recent cases of alleged blasphemy which indicates that the laws are increasingly being used to facilitate land-grab through "a criminal collaboration among government organisations, in which the Muslim clergy, on receiving bribes from land-grabbers in the National and Provincial Assemblies, colluded with local police to expropriate land owned by minorities by bringing

allegations of blasphemy against them" (Asian Human Rights Commission, UAC-183-2010, December 21, 2010).

45. The bias of members of the judiciary is exacerbated by the fact that many of them appear ignorant of what the Pakistan Penal Code (PPC) actually says and doesn't say. For example, a sessions judge turned down a bail application for a Christian defendant (who was harassed in jail and later died while in custody under mysterious circumstances) who happened to be a recent convert from Islam, on the erroneous grounds that conversion was itself a cognizable offence under the PPC, which it is not.

46. Christians point out that the system of separate electorates has contributed to the rise in violence against Christians, whether through the Blasphemy Law or otherwise. Under separate electorates, Christian votes become useless to local (Muslim) politicians, who therefore have no incentive to look after their interests, or intervene on their behalf. Sookhdeo (2002) notes that in the absence of separate electorates, there was a good chance that the Blasphemy Law might not have been so easily and frequently used against Christians.

47. The liberalization of the broadcast media under Musharraf has only contributed to this right-ward drift as ratings-hungry commercial channels actively search for and feature the most extreme views.

EPILOGUE

1. One of the slogans raised by the *Anjuman-i Mazarin-i Punjab*.

2. Under the Punjab Tenancy Act, ownership rights could be granted to farmers if they made the land cultivable. The Act made a distinction between "simple" versus "occupancy" tenants—simple tenants could be easily evicted while the eviction of occupancy tenants required a court decree. The villagers on the military farms were occupancy tenants.

3. For details, see HRW (2004) and Saigol (2004).

4. Human Rights Watch references the "long and sordid history of human rights abuses against civilians" (HRW, 2004: 15).

5. "Everywhere you look, the army"; the second line of a verse from a well-known satirical poem by the late Progressive Punjabi poet Ustaad Daman. The full verse goes thus: "*Pakistan diyaañ maujaañ ee maujaañ, Jithe vekho faujaañ ee faujaañ*" ["Pakistan is so lucky, Everywhere you look, the army"].

6. This does not include the amount of land which is under the ownership of individual members of the military fraternity, especially officers (serving and retired).

7. Siddiqa (2007) details numerous examples of the brutal and rapacious way in which military and paramilitary forces have occupied land, evicting local communities, such as: (1) In 1977, the Rangers (a paramilitary border security force) took over four lakes in Sindh and leased out fishing rights to private interests in violation of provincial law, depriving the local fishing community of their livelihood; they later occupied 20 more lakes in Sindh. Within the same period, they also took over a significant stretch of the Sindh-Baluchistan coastline (purportedly to secure it from Indian threat), stopped local fisherfolk from fishing in the waters off the coast, and sold the permits to large contractors, resulting in a decimation of the local fishing communities. (2) In the village of Nawazabad in Bahawalpur, hundreds of landless peasants were threatened with dire consequences unless they vacated state land on which they had lived

for many years. (3) The land of the small and poor village of Mubarik, Sindh was completely taken over by the Pakistan Navy, and its residents evicted.

8. Siddiqa (2007: 205) reports a naval officer as saying "Why do landless peasants have greater rights over land? They do not deserve land just because they are poor," and quotes another military officer who believed that "there is no difference between allotment of land to poor people and the military. The armed forces personnel deserve to be given land as much as the poor landless peasants."

9. The effects of land concentration on impoverishment go beyond the issues of control of and access to assets; land distribution has repercussions in terms of the abuse and exploitation that the poor are subject to in rural Pakistan. A Planning Commission report on poverty showed that the poor see land as an important source of power. Improved land access is linked to poverty alleviation in both the short and the long term, and women's access to land is of special importance (Agarwal, 1994).

10. Under the provisions of the Corporate Farming Ordinance, foreign firms were allowed to lease land in Pakistan for 50 years, extendable for another 49 years; the minimum amount of land they could lease was set at 1,500 acres. This Ordinance, as well as follow-up efforts to woo foreign investors have been analyzed as part of the "global land grab" whereby rich countries lease or buy land in poor countries in order to secure their food supplies in the future. In Pakistan, the state has wooed mainly Gulf states. In May 2009, for example, the ministry of investment decided to offer 1 million hectares of farmland for long-term investment or sale to foreigners—specifically, the Emirates Investment Group (Toor, 2010). See, for example, "Buying Farmland Abroad: Outsourcing's Third Wave," *Economist*, May 21, 2009; "Land Deals in Africa and Asia: Cornering Foreign Fields," *Economist*, May 21, 2009; "Food Security Fuels Land Grab, Says Report," *Financial Times*, May 24, 2009.

11. Siddiqa (2007: 186–205) outlines the use of brute force by the military and paramilitary forces to occupy land at will, often without compensation.

12. Estimates of the number of the disappeared in Baluchistan ranges from 1,500 to over 4,000 ("MT," 2010b).

13. "MT" is a *nom de plume*.

14. This is saying something, given Pakistan's abysmal performance on human development indicators as a whole.

15. The military took advantage of the recent devastating floods to illegally occupy even more land in Baluchistan.

16. Siddiqa (2007: 18) states that "Since 9/11 US policymakers' generous statements endorsing Musharraf's apparent efforts to strengthen democracy were just one example of the mind-set that views non-western militaries as relatively more capable than civilian institutions."

17. Ironically, in its efforts to discredit the movement, the military establishment has taken the line that it is only an "NGO" initiative and not a genuine movement.

18. I speak from personal experience; from 1993 to 2000, I worked with various development, women's and human rights NGOs in Pakistan.

19. Rubina Saigol, personal communication with the author.

20. The recent murder of Salman Taseer at the hands of a zealot has mobilized the liberal elite, but its attempts at responding to the tide of Sunni sectarianism reflects all the drawbacks of elite politics. The very fact that this mobilization happened in response to Taseer's murder as opposed to the pogroms against

Christians and Ahmedis over the last few years is revealing. For critiques of liberal politics and analysis, see Zia (2011) and Akhter (2011).

21. At a press conference in December 1998, Binyamin claimed that "The Institute of Women's Studies Lahore headed by Nighat Said Khan, instigated people against the Shariah Bill and was promoting Jewish culture." N.S. Khan (2004: xviii) writes that "these comments were carried by all the newspapers, many on the front page. This was the beginning of a vicious campaign. On the 30th of December he went on to say 'The government will never allow these modern, westernized women to create a free society' and further, 'Strange organizations like the Women's Institute should not make him open his mouth because if he informs the nation about their activities, the people will burn down their bungalows and skin them alive where they teach their special studies.'"

22. Liberals were not the only ones to succumb to the charms of the general. Even the National Workers Party, led by veteran leftist intellectual Abid Hassan Manto, joined the military alliance.

23. In early 2002, the military launched an attack on the legendary "people's republic" of Hashtnagar, an area comprising eight villages ("hasht" means "eight," and "nagar" means "settlement") which had been freed from landlord control in the late 1960s under the leadership of Afzal Bangash of the Mazdoor Kissan Party. The struggle of the Hashtnagar peasants against landlord control goes back to before Partition. See Chughtai (2008) and Aziz (2010).

24. My critique of liberals for their obsession with religious extremists should not, under any circumstances, be taken as an apologia for the latter. There is no doubt that their agenda is retrogressive and reactionary in the extreme.

25. For example, see Siddiqi (2010) and Amirali (2010).

26. While Benazir Bhutto and Nawaz Sharif exhibited differing levels of enthusiasm for liberalization given their different constituencies, the IMF's program was most effectively implemented during the interim administrations in the 1990s; so obvious was this that they were openly referred to as "IMF administrations." The first of these was headed by Moeen Qureshi, an ex-vice-president of the World Bank (derisively referred to as the "imported Prime Minister" given that prior to becoming the PM he had been living abroad for 25 years), and in the second another ex-vice-president of the World Bank (Shahid Javed Burki) was the economic adviser to the caretaker prime minister. Scholars have also pointed to the "Punjabi-ization" of liberalization under Nawaz Sharif, as non-Punjabi business groups were cut out of deals (Talbot, 1998).

27. Needless to say, the military's budget and expenditure remained untouched.

28. According to Aasim Sajjad Akhter, over 160 PSEs were privatized in the 15 years prior to the PTCL strike, of which 130 had collapsed, leaving hundreds of thousands of workers in the lurch (Akhter, 2005).

29. This strike was only the latest event in a stand-off that began in 2001. For details, see Action for a Progressive Pakistan, 2010 and "M.T.," 2010a.

30. A tragic mark of the success of the LQM has been the violence—both from the state and from owners—that its leadership and its members confront on a daily basis. In June 2010, gunmen entered the office of the LQM in Faisalabad and killed two of its leading lights—Mustansar Randhawa and his brother. In response, Faisalabad was confronted with the largest strike it had witnessed in recent history, as 100,000 workers took to the streets in protest. See Memon, 2010 for more details regarding the struggle of the workers of Faisalabad.

References

Abbasi, Muhammad Yusuf.1992. *Pakistani Culture: A Profile*. Islamabad: National Institute of Historical and Cultural Research.

Action for a Progressive Pakistan. 2010. "PC Workers' Occupation." March 8. <http://progpak.wordpress.com/2010/03/08/pc-workers-occupation>.

Adhikari, Gangadhar M. 1943. *Pakistan and Indian National Unity*. London: Labour Monthly.

Agarwal, Beena. 1994. *A Field of One's Own: Gender and Land Rights in South Asia*. New York: Cambridge University Press.

Ahmad, Aijaz. 2000. *Lineages of the Present*. London: Verso.

Ahmad, Aijaz. 1993. *In the Mirror of Urdu: Recompositions of Nation and Community, 1947–65*. Shimla: Indian Institute of Advanced Study.

Ahmad, Aijaz. 1983. "Democracy and Dictatorship." In Hassan Gardezi and Jamil Rashid (eds.). *Pakistan, the Roots of Dictatorship: The Political Economy of a Praetorian State*. London: Zed Press, pp. 94–147.

Ahmad, Aziz. 1965. "Cultural and Intellectual Trends in Pakistan." *Middle East Journal*. Vol. 19, No. 1, Winter, pp. 35–44.

Ahmed, Ateeq. 1987. *"Taraqqi-Pasand Tehreek aur Karachi"* [The Progressive Movement and Karachi]. In Qamar Raees and Syed Ashoor Kazmi (eds.). *Taraqqi-Pasand Adab: Pachaas-saala Safar* [Progressive Literature: A Fifty-year Journey]. London: Institute of Third World Art & Literature, pp. 307–32.

Ahmed, Eqbal. 2004. *Between Past and Future: Selected Essays on South Asia*. Dohra Ahmed et al. (eds.). Karachi: Oxford University Press.

Ahmed, Sultan. 2003. "No land reforms any more!" *Dawn*. March 20.

Akhter, Aasim Sajjad. 2005. "Privatisation at Gunpoint." *Monthly Review*. October. <http://www.monthlyreview.org/1005akhtar.htm>.

Akhter, Aasim Sajjad. 2003. "The Lie Industry." <http://www.responsibleadventures.com/details.php?id=1084>.

Akhter, Hameed. 1987. *"Taraqqi-Pasand Tehreek aur Lahore"* [The Progressive Movement and Lahore]. In Qamar Raees and Syed Ashoor Kazmi (eds.). *Taraqqi-Pasand Adab: Pachaas-saala Safar* [Progressive Literature: A Fifty-year Journey]. London: Institute of Third World Art & Literature, pp. 333–50.

Alavi, Hamza. 2002. "Misreading Partition Road Signs." *Economic and Political Weekly*. Vol. 37, No. 44/45, November 2–15, pp. 4515–23.

Alavi, Hamza. 1997. "Marxism, Ex-colonial Societies and Strategies of the Left." Unpublished letter to a friend. <http://www.scribd.com/doc/19084216/Marxism-ExColonial-Societies>.

Alavi, Hamza. 1990. "Authoritarianism and Legitimation of State Power in Pakistan." In Subrata Mitra (ed.). *The Postcolonial State in South Asia*. New York: Harvester Wheatsheaf, pp. 19–71.

Alavi, Hamza. 1989. "Politics of Ethnicity in India and Pakistan." In Hamza Alavi and John Harriss (eds.). *Sociology of Developing Countries*. London: Macmillan Education Ltd., pp. 222–46.

Alavi, Hamza. 1988. "Pakistan and Islam: Ethnicity and Ideology." In Hamza Alavi and Fred Halliday (eds.). *State and Ideology in the Middle East and Pakistan.* New York: Monthly Review Press, pp. 65–111.

Alavi, Hamza. 1982. "State and Class under Peripheral Capitalism." In Hamza Alavi and Teodor Shanon (eds.). *Introduction to the Sociology of "Developing Societies."* New York: Monthly Review Press.

Alavi, Hamza. 1973. "The State in Postcolonial Societies: Pakistan and Bangladesh." In Kathleen Gough and Hari P. Sharma (eds.). *Imperialism and Revolution in South Asia.* New York: Monthly Review Press, pp. 145–73.

Ali, Ahmed. 1988. "The Progressive Writers' Movement and Creative Writers in Urdu." In Carlo Coppola (ed.). *Marxist Influences in South Asian Literature.* Delhi: Chanakya Publications, pp. 42–53.

Ali, Tariq. 2008. *The Duel: Pakistan on the Flight Path of American Power.* New York: Scribner.

Ali, Tariq. 2005 [1987]. *Street Fighting Years.* London: Verso.

Ali, Tariq. 1983. *Can Pakistan Survive? The Death of a State.* Harmondsworth: Penguin.

Ali, Tariq. 1970. *Pakistan: Military Rule or People's Power?* New York: W. Morrow.

Amin, Samir. 1989. *Eurocentrism.* New York: Monthly Review Press.

Amirali, Asha. 2010. "The New Left Revisited." *Dawn.* March 9 <http://archives.dawn.com/archives/26543>.

Amnesty International. 1994. *Pakistan: Use and Abuse of the Blasphemy Laws.* Index Number: ASA 33/008/1994 <http://www.amnesty.org/en/library/info/ASA33/008/1994>.

Asdar Ali, Kamran. 2005. "The Strength of the Street Meets the Strength of the State: The 1972 Labor Struggle in Karachi." *International Journal of Middle East Studies.* Vol. 37, No. 1., February, pp. 83–107.

Asian Human Rights Commission. 2010. *Pakistan: Appeal to Amend the Blasphemy Laws.* AHRC-UAC-183-2010 <http://www.ahrchk.net/ua/mainfile.php/2010/3614>.

Askari, Muhammad Hasan. 2001. *Maqalaat-i Muhammad Hasan Askari.* Shima Majid (ed.). Lahore: Ilm-o-Irfan Publishers.

Askari, Muhammad Hasan. 1952. *Hashiya Aarayi* (Border-making). In Sa'adat Hasan Manto, *Siyah Hashiye.* Lahore: Maktaba-i Jadid.

Aziz, Ammar. 2010. "Hashtnagar: A Land, Forgotten." <http://pakteahouse.net/2010/06/01/hashtnagar-a-land-forgotten>.

Aziz, Khursheed Kamal. 1993. *The Murder of History: A Critique of History Textbooks used in Pakistan.* Lahore: Vanguard Books.

Azmi, Khalil-ur Rahman. 1996. *Urdu Meiñ Taraqqi-Pasand Adabi Tehreek* [The Progressive Literary Movement in Urdu]. Aligarh: Educational Book House.

Babar, Zaheer. 1949. "*Ya Khuda aur is ka Dibaacha*" (Ya Khuda and its Preface). *Naqush,* No. 5.

Ballard, Roger. 1989. "Effects of Labour Migration from Pakistan." In Hamza Alavi and John Harris (eds.). *Sociology of Developing Societies: South Asia.* New York: Monthly Review Press, pp. 112–22.

Barlas, Asma. 1995. *Democracy, Nationalism and Communalism: The Colonial Legacy in South Asia.* Boulder, CO: Westview Press.

Bourdieu, Pierre and Jean Claude Passeron. 1977. *Reproduction in Education, Society and Culture.* SAGE Studies in Social and Educational Change. Vol. 5.

Brohi, Allahbuksh Karimbuksh. 1970. "Reflections on Islamic Socialism." In Haider Mehdi (ed.). *Essays on Pakistan*. Lahore: Progressive Publishers, pp. 63–75.

Brohi, Allahbuksh Karimbuksh. 1968. "Iqbalian Ijtehad and the Concept of Islamic Socialism." *Iqbal Review*. April.

Bukhari, Ahmad Shah (Patras). 1985. *Kuliyaat-i Patras*. Lahore: Maktaba-i Sher-o-Adab.

Burki, Shahid Javed. 1991. *Pakistan: The Continuing Search for Nationhood*. Boulder, CO: Westview Press.

Burney, Iqbal Hasan. 1996. *No Illusions, Some Hopes and No Fears: The Outlook Editorials of I.H. Burney, 1962–4, 1972–4*. Karachi: Oxford University Press.

Callard, Keith. 1957. *Pakistan: A Political Study*. London: Allen & Unwin.

Chatterji, Joya. 1994. *Bengal Divided: Hindu Communalism and Partition, 1932–1947*. Cambridge: Cambridge University Press.

Chhachhi, Amrita. 1989. "The State, Religious Fundamentalism and Women: Trends in South Asia." *Economic and Political Weekly*. Vol. 24, No. 11, March 18, pp. 567–78.

Chughtai, Mobeen. 2008. "Hashtnagar: A Revolutionary Struggle Forgotten." <http://redtribution.wordpress.com/2008/01/06/hashtnagar-a-revolutionary-struggle-forgotten-by-mobeen-chughtai/>.

Cohen, Stanley. 1972. *Folk Devils and Moral Panics*. London: MacGibbon and Klee.

Cohen, Stephen. 2004. *The Idea of Pakistan*. Washington, DC: Brookings Institution Press.

Cohen, Stephen. 1984. *The Pakistan Army*. Berkeley: University of California Press.

Coleman, Peter. 1989. *The Liberal Conspiracy: The Congress for Cultural Freedom and the Struggle for the Mind of Postwar Europe*. New York: Free Press.

Coppola, Carlo. 1981. "The *Angare* Group: The *Enfants Terribles* of Urdu Literature." *Annual of Urdu Studies*. Vol. 1, pp. 57–69.

Coppola, Carlo. 1975. "Urdu Poetry, 1935–1970: The Progressive Episode." Unpublished PhD dissertation, University of Chicago, IL.

Coppola, Carlo. 1974. "All India Progressive Writers Association: The European Phase." In Carlo Coppola (ed.). *Marxist Influences and South Asian Literatures*. South Asia Series Occasional Paper No. 23, Vol. I, East Lansing, Michigan: Michigan State University, pp. 1–34.

Corrigan, Philip and Derek Sayer. 1985. *The Great Arch: English State Formation as Cultural Revolution*. New York: Blackwell.

Debray, Regis. 1977. "Marxism and the National Question." *New Left Review*. I/105, September–October, pp. 20-41.

Dreyfuss, Robert. 2005. *Devil's Game: How the United States Helped Unleash Fundamentalist Islam*. New York: Metropolitan Books.

EBLC (East Bengal Language Committee). 1958. *Report of the East Bengal Language Committee, 1949*. Dacca: Officer on Special Duty (Home Dept.), East Pakistan Government Press.

Engerman, David, et al. (eds.). 2003. *Staging Growth: Modernization, Development, and the Global Cold War*. Amherst: University of Massachusetts Press.

Faiz, Faiz Ahmed. 1988. *Pakistani Kulchar aur Qaumi Tashakhkhus ki Talaash*. [In Search of Pakistani Culture and National Identity]. Lahore: Firozensons, Ltd.

Faiz, Faiz Ahmed. 1968. *Report of the Commission on Sports, Culture and the Arts*. Islamabad: Government of Pakistan.

Fatehpuri, Farman. 1987. *Pakistan Movement and Hindi-Urdu Conflict*. Lahore: Sang-e-Meel.

Feldman, Herbert. 1967. *Revolution in Pakistan: A Study of the Martial Law Administration*. London: Oxford University Press.

Fukuyama, Francis. 1992. *The End of History and the Last Man*. New York: Free Press.

Gardezi, Fauzia. 1997. "Nationalism and State-Formation: Women's Struggles and Islamization in Pakistan." In Neelam Hussain, Samiya Mumtaz, and Rubina Saigol (eds.). *Engendering the Nation State*. Vol. I. Lahore: Simorgh Publications, pp. 79–110.

Gilmartin, David. 1988. "Partition, Pakistan, and South Asian History: In Search of a Narrative." *Journal of Asian Studies*. Vol. 57, No. 4, pp. 1068–95.

Gilman, Nils. 2003. *Mandarins of the Future: Modernization Theory in Cold War America*. Baltimore, MD: Johns Hopkins University Press.

Gopal, Priyamvada. 2005. *Literary Radicalism in India: Gender, Nation and the Transition to Independence*. New York: Routledge.

Government of Pakistan. 1962. *The Emerging Society*. Karachi: Bureau of National Reconstruction.

Gramsci, Antonio. 1971. *Selections from the Prison Notebooks of Antonio Gramsci*. Hoare, Quintin and Nowell-Smith, Geoffrey (eds.). London: Lawrence & Wishart.

Grossberg, Lawrence. 1986. "On Postmodernism and Articulation: An Interview with Stuart Hall." *Journal of Communication Inquiry*. Vol. 10, No. 2, pp. 45–60.

Haider, Qurratulain. c. 1984. *Sarood-i Shabaana* [Song of the Night]. *Adab-i Latif, Faiz Number* [Special Issue on Faiz], pp. 99–117.

Haithcox, John Patrick. 1971. *Communism and Nationalism in India: M.N. Roy and Comintern Policy, 1920-1939*. Princeton, NJ: Princeton University Press.

Hall, Stuart. 1982. "The Re-Discovery of 'Ideology': Return of the Repressed in Media Studies." In Michael Gurevitch, et al (eds.). *Culture, Society and Media*. New York: Methuen, pp. 56–90.

Hall, Stuart. 1979. *Drifting into a Law and Order Society*. London: Cobden Trust.

Handler, Richard. 1988. *Nationalism and the Politics of Culture in Quebec*. Madison: University of Wisconsin Press.

Haq, Mahbub-ul. 1963. *The Strategy of Economic Planning: A Case Study of Pakistan*. Karachi: Oxford University Press.

Hasan, Arif. 2002. "The Roots of Elite Alienation." *Economic and Political Weekly*. Vol. 37, No. 44/45, pp. 4550–53.

Hasan, Mushirul. 1993. *India's Partition: Process, Strategy and Mobilization*. New York: Oxford University Press.

Hasan, Sibte. 1987. *Sukhn Dar Sukhn*. Karachi: Makataba-i Daniyaal.

Hasan, Sibte. 1986. *The Battle of Ideas in Pakistan*. Karachi: Pakistan Publishing House.

Hashmi, Salima. 2003. *Unveiling the Visible: Lives and Works of Women Artists of Pakistan*. Lahore: Sang-e-Meel Publications.

Hijazi, Naseem. 1978. *Saqaafat ki Talaash* [The Search for Culture]. Lahore: Qaumi Kutb Khana.

Human Rights Watch. 2004. *Soiled Hands: The Pakistan Army's Repression of the Punjab Farmers' Movement*. New York: Human Rights Watch.

Human Rights Watch. 1999. *Crime of Custom? Violence Against Women in Pakistan*. New York: Human Rights Watch.

Human Rights Watch. 1998. *World Report*. New York: Human Rights Watch.

Husain, Khurram. 2006. "The Political Origins of Economic Reform: Pakistan's Accession to the IMF Structural Adjustment Facility in 1988." Paper presented at the annual meeting of the American Sociological Association, Montreal Convention Center, Montreal, Quebec, Canada. <http://www.allacademic.com/meta/p105292_index.html>.

Hussain, Akmal. 1989. "Pakistan: Land Reforms Reconsidered." In Hamza Alavi and John Harris (eds.). *Introduction to the Sociology of "Developing Societies": South Asia*. New York: Monthly Review Press, pp. 59–69.

Hussain, Intizar. 1997. *Charaaghoñ ka Dhuaañ, Yaadon ke Pachaas Baras* [The Smoke of Lamps, Fifty Years of Memories]. Lahore: Sang-i Meel.

Hussain, Mazna. 2006. "'Take My Riches, Give Me Justice": A Contextual Analysis of Pakistan's Honor Crimes Legislation." *Harvard Journal of Law and Gender*. Vol. 29, pp. 223–46.

Hussain, Mumtaz. 1949. "*Ruja'atPasand Adab Kya Hai?*" [What is Reactionary Literature?]. In *Naye Tanqeedee Goshe* [New Critical Areas]. Delhi: Azad Kitab Ghar.

Hussain, Neelam. 1997. "The Narrative Appropriation of Saima: Coercion and Consent in Muslim Pakistan." In Neelam Hussain, Samiya Mumtaz, and Rubina Saigol (eds.). *Engendering the Nation-State*. Vol. I. Lahore: Simorgh Publications, pp. 199–241.

Ikramullah, Shaista. 1966. "The Writer and His Social Responsibility." *Orient Monthly*. January/February.

International Crisis Group. 2004. *Devolution in Pakistan: Reform or Regression?* Asia Report. No. 77, March 22. <http://www.crisisgroup.org/en/regions/asia/south-asia/pakistan/077-devolution-in-pakistan-reform-or-regression.aspx>.

Iqbal, Muhammad. 1930. *Presidential Address, All India Muslim League, Allahabad Session*. Lahore: Ripon Press.

Islam, Syed Manzoorul (ed.). 1994. *Essays on Ekushey: The Language Movement 1952*. Dhaka: Bangla Academy.

Jafri, Ali Sardar. c. 1956 [1955]. *Taraqqi Pasand Adab*. Lahore: Maktaba-i Pakistan.

Jafri, Ali Sardar. 1948. "*Daar-o Rasan*"[The Gallows]. *Naya Adab*. Vol. 10, No. 2, September, pp. 9–13.

Jafri, Amir H. 2008. *Honour Killing: Dilemma, Ritual, Understanding*. Karachi: Oxford University Press.

Jahan, Rounaq. 1972. *Pakistan: Failure in National Integration*. New York: Columbia University Press.

Jahangir, Asma and Hina Jilani. 1990. *The Hudood Ordinances: A Divine Sanction?* Lahore: Rhotas Books.

Jalal, Ayesha. 1996. "Secularists, Subalterns and the Stigma of 'Communalism': Partition Historiography Revisited." *Modern Asian Studies*. Vol. 30, No. 3, pp. 681–737.

Jalal, Ayesha. 1995. "Conjuring Pakistan: History as Official Imagining." *International Journal of Middle East Studies*. Vol. 27, No. 1, pp. 73–89.

Jalal, Ayesha. 1994. *The Sole Spokesman: Jinnah, the Muslim League, and the Demand for Pakistan*. Cambridge: Cambridge University Press.

Jalal, Ayesha. 1990. *The State of Martial Rule: The Origins of Pakistan's Political Economy of Defence*. Cambridge: Cambridge University Press.

Jalib, Habib. 1991. *Jalib-Naama*. Lahore: Jang Publications.

Jilani, Hina and Eman Ahmed. 2004. "Violence Against Women: The Legal System and Institutional Responses in Pakistan." In Savitri Goonesekere (ed.). *Violence, Law and Women's Rights in South Asia*. New Delhi: Sage Publications, pp. 148–206.

Jinnah, Mohammad Ali. 2004. *Quaid-e-Azam Mohammad Ali Jinnah: Speeches as Governor-General of Pakistan, 1947–1948*. Lahore: Sang-e Meel Publications.

Jinnah, Muhammad Ali. 1976. *Selected Speeches and Statements of the Quaid-i-Azam Mohammad Ali Jinnah, 1911–34 and 1947–48*. Islamabad: Research Society of Pakistan.

Johnson, Ian. 2010. *A Mosque in Munich: Nazis, the CIA, and the Muslim Brotherhood in the West*. Boston, MA: Houghton Mifflin Harcourt.

Jones, Rodney W. 1985. "The Military and Security in Pakistan." In Craig Baxter (ed.). *Zia's Pakistan: Politics and Stability in a Frontline State*. Boulder, CO: Westview Press, pp. 63–91.

Joshi, Puran Chandra. 1945 [1944]. *They Must Meet Again*. Bombay: People's Publishing House.

Kamal, Simi and Asma Khan. 1997. "Review of the Legal Status and Socio-Economic Context of Women in Pakistan (With Special Reference to Minorities)." Volume I of *Research Study on the Interplay of Formal and Customary Laws on Women in Pakistan*. Karachi: RAASTA Development Consultants.

Kashmiri, Zaheer. 1948. "*Idaariya*" [Editorial]. *Savera 5/6*.

Kausar, Zeenath. 2003. "A Philosophical Critique of Nationalism: Reflections of Iqbal." *The American Journal of Islamic Social Sciences*. Vol. 20, No. 2, pp. 1–25.

Khan, Nighat Said. 2004. Preface. In Nighat Said Khan (ed.). *Up Against the State*. Lahore: ASR Publications, pp. i–viii.

Khan, Nighat Said. 1985 [1988]. *Women in Pakistan: A New Era?* London: Change International Reports.

Khan, Nighat Said and Rubina Saigol. 2004. "Women's Action Forum: Debates and Contradictions." In Nighat Said Khan (ed.). *Up Against the State: Military Rule and People's Resistance*. Lahore: ASR Publications, pp. 146–208.

Khan, Shahnaz. 2006. *Zina, Transnational Feminism and the Moral Regulation of Pakistani Women*. Vancouver: University of British Columbia Press.

Khan, Shahrukh Rafi. 2004. *Pakistan Under Musharraf, 1999–2002*. Lahore: Vanguard.

Khattak, Saba Gul. 1997. "Gendered and Violent: Inscribing the Military on the Nation-State." In Neelam Hussain, Samiya Mumtaz and Rubina Saigol (eds.). *Engendering the Nation State*, Vol. I. Lahore: Simorgh Publications, pp. 38–52.

Kiernan, Victor. 1955. *Poems from Iqbal*. London: John Murray.

King, Christopher, R. 1994. *One Language, Two Scripts: The Hindi Movement in Nineteenth Century North India*. Delhi: Oxford University Press.

Kumar, Krishna. 1990. "Quest for Self-Identity: Cultural Consciousness and Education in Hindi Region, 1880–1950." *Economic and Political Weekly*. Vol. 25, No. 23, pp. 1247–55.

Laclau, Ernesto and Chantalle Mouffe. 1985. *Hegemony and Socialist Strategy: Towards a Radical Democratic Politics*. London: Verso.

Lakshman, Kanchan. 2008. "A Seething Fury." *Outlook India*. May 15.

Latham, Michael E. 2000. *Modernization as Ideology: American Social Science and 'Nation Building' in the Kennedy Era*. Chapel Hill: University of North Carolina Press.

Lerner, Daniel and Richard D. Robinson. 1960. "Swords and Ploughshares: The Turkish Army as a Modernizing Force." *World Politics*. Vol. 13, No. 1, pp. 19–44.

Lowy, Michael. 1976. "Marxists and the National Question." *New Left Review*. No. 96, pp. 81–100.

Mahmood, Khalid. 2010. "Labor Unions and the Left in Pakistan." Radical Film and Lecture Series, New York University. September 27.

Mahmud, Shabana. 1996. "*Angare* and the Founding of the Progressive Writers Association." *Modern Asian Studies*. Vol. 30, No. 2, pp. 447–67.

Malik, Abdullah. 1949. *Naqush, Azadi Number* ("Independence Issue").

Malik, Abdullah. 1949. *Mustaqbil Hamara Hai* ("The Future is Ours"). Pamphlet. No publication information.

Malik, Fateh Muhammad. 1991. *Ta'asubaat* [Prejudices]. Lahore: Sang-i Meel Publications.

Malik, Hafeez. 1967. "The Marxist Literary Movement in India and Pakistan." *Journal of Asian Studies*. Vol. 26, No. 4, pp. 649–64.

Malik, Hafeez. 1963. *Moslem Nationalism in India and Pakistan*. Washington, DC: Public Affairs Press.

Malik, Iftikhar Haider. 1997. *State and Civil Society in Pakistan: Politics of Authority, Ideology, and Ethnicity*. New York: St. Martin's Press.

Malik, S.K. 1979. *The Quranic Concept of War*. Lahore: Wajidalis.

Mamdani, Mahmood. 2004. *Good Muslim, Bad Muslim: America, the Cold War, and the Roots of Terror.* New York: Pantheon Books.

Mamdani, Mahmood. 1996. *Citizen and Subject: Contemporary Africa and the Legacy of Late Colonialism*. Princeton, NJ: Princeton University Press.

Mateen, Arif Abdul. 1948. "*Pakistan ke She'ri Rujhaanaat*" ["The poetic trends of Pakistan"]. *Savera*. 3/4.

Maududi, Abul ala. 1968. Interview. *Al-Muslimin*. June.

Maududi, Abul ala. c. 1939. *Mussalman aur Maujuda Siyasi Kashmakash* [Muslims and the Contemporary Political Struggle]. Lahore: Risalah Tarjumanulqur'an.

McMahon, Robert. 1994. *The Cold War on the Periphery: The United States, India, and Pakistan*. New York: Columbia University Press.

Memon, Qalandar Bux. 2010. "Blood on the Path of Love: The Striking Workers of Faisalabad, Pakistan." *Monthly Review*. Vol. 62, No. 7 <http://monthlyreview.org/101201memon.php>.

Metcalf, Barbara. 2007. "An Argumentative Indian: Maulana Husain Ahmad Madani, Islam and Nationalism in India." In Anthony Reid and Michael Gilsenan (eds.). *Islamic Legitimacy in a Plural Asia*. New York: Routledge, pp. 81–97.

Metcalf, Barbara. 2004. "Nationalism, Modernity, and Muslim Identity in India before 1947." In Barbara Metcalf (ed.). *Islamic Contentions: Essays on Muslims in India and Pakistan*. New Delhi: Oxford University Press.

Mir, Muhammad Safdar. 1998. *Modern Urdu Prose*. Lahore: Azad Enterprises.

Mir, Muhammad Safdar. 1997a. *Adab aur Siyaasat* [Literature and Politics]. Lahore: Classic.

Mir, Muhammad Safdar. 1997a. *Tasavvurat* [Reflections]. Lahore: Classic.

Mir, Muhammad Safdar. 1990. *Iqbal the Progressive*. Lahore: Book Traders.

Mir, Muhammad Safdar. 1969. *Maududiyyat aur Maujudah Siyaasi Kashmakash* [Maududi-ism and the Present Political Struggle]. Lahore: al-Bayan.

"MT." 2010a. "Hotel Workers' Stand in Karachi." *Socialist Worker*. March 22 <http://socialistworker.org/2010/03/22/karachi-hotel-workers-strike>.

"MT." 2010b. "What's Balochistan Got to Do with It?" January 25. <http://moband-multitude.com/2010/01/25/whats-balochistan-got-to-do-with-it>.

Muhammad, Ishaq. 1982. *Nazariya aur Amal* [Ideology and Practice]. Faisalabad: Ishaq Academy.

Mullaly, Siobhan. 2007. "Women, Islamization and Human Rights in Pakistan: Developing Strategies of Resistance." In Javaid Rehman and Susan C. Breau (eds.). *Religion, Human Rights and International Law: A Critical Examination of Islamic State Practices*. Boston, MA: Martinus Nijhoff Publishers, pp. 379–408.

Mumtaz, Khawar and Farida Shaheed. 1987. *Women of Pakistan: Two Steps Forward, One Step Back?* Lahore: Vanguard Books.

Narayan, Uma. 1997. *Dislocating Cultures: Identities, Traditions and Third World Feminisms*. New York: Routledge.

Nasr, Vali R. 2000. "International Politics, Domestic Imperatives, and Identity Mobilization: Sectarianism in Pakistan, 1979–1998." *Comparative Politics*. Vol. 32, No. 2, January, pp. 171–90.

Nasr, Seyyed Vali Reza. 1994. *The Vanguard of the Islamic Revolution: The Jama'at-i Islami of Pakistan*. Berkeley: University of California Press.

Niazi, Zamir. 1994. *Web of Censorship*. Karachi: Oxford University Press.

Niazi, Zamir. 1986. *Press in Chains*. Karachi: Karachi Press Club.

Noman, Omar. 1988. *The Political Economy of Pakistan 1947–85*. London: KPI.

Oldenberg, Philip. 1985. "'A Place Insufficiently Imagined': Language, Belief and the Pakistan Crisis of 1971." *Journal of Asian Studies*. Vol. 44, No. 4, August, pp. 711–33.

Overstreet, Gene and Marshall Windmiller. 1960. *Communism in India*. Berkeley: University of California Press.

Packenham, Robert. 1973. *Liberal America and the Third World*. Princeton, NJ: Princeton University Press.

Papanek, Gustav. 1967. *Pakistan's Development: Social Goals and Private Initiatives*. Cambridge, MA: Harvard University Press.

Pearce, Charles and Pearce, Kimber Charles. 2001. *Rostow, Kennedy, and the Rhetoric of Foreign Aid*. East Lansing: Michigan State University Press.

Polanyi, Karl. 1944. *The Great Transformation*. New York: Farrar & Rinehart, Inc.

Pradhan, Sudhi. 1985. *Marxist Cultural Movement in India: Chronicles and Documents*. Vol. I. Sudhi Pradhan, (compiler and ed.). Calcutta: Pustak Bipani.

Prakash, Shri. 1983. "CPI and the Pakistan Movement." In Bipan Chandra (ed.). *The Indian Left: Critical Appraisals*. New Delhi: Vikas.

Progressive Writers Golden Jubilee Conference Committee. 1986. *Taraqqi-Pasand Adab: Dastavezat* [Progressive Literature: Documents]. Karachi.

Puckle, Frederick. 1945. "The Gandhi-Jinnah Conversations." *Foreign Affairs*. Vol. 23, No. 2, January, pp. 318–23.

Qasmi, Ahmed Nadeem. 1948. Open letter to Manto. *Sang-i-Meel*. December 15. Peshawar.

Rahman, Sheikh Abdur. 1974. *Iqbal and Socialism: A Paper*. [With presidential remarks by A.K. Brohi]. Karachi: Hamdard National Foundation.

Rahman, Sheikh Abdur. 1970. "Ideology of Pakistan." In Haider Mehdi (ed.). *Essays on Pakistan*. Lahore: Progressive Publishers, pp. 1–13.

Rahman, Tariq. 1996. *Language and Politics in Pakistan*. Karachi: Oxford University Press.

Rai, Amrit. 1984. *A House Divided: The Origin and Development of Hindi/Hindavi*. New York: Oxford University Press.

Rashid, Ahmed. 2010. "Pakistan Floods: An Emergency for the West." *The Telegraph*. August 12 <http://www.telegraph.co.uk/news/worldnews/asia/pakistan/7941820/Pakistan-floods-an-emergency-for-the-West.html>.

Rashid, Jamil and Hassan Gardezi. 1983. "Independent Pakistan: Its Political Economy." In Jamil Rashid and Hassan Gardezi (eds.). *Pakistan: The Roots of Dictatorship*. London: Zed Press, pp. 4–18.

Raza, Rafi. 1997. *Zulfikar Ali Bhutto and Pakistan, 1967–1977*. New York: Oxford University Press.

Robin, Ron Theodore. 2001. *The Making of the Cold War Enemy: Culture and Politics in the Military-Intellectual Complex*. Princeton, NJ: Princeton University Press.

Robinson, Francis. 1974. *Separatism among Indian Muslims: The Politics of the United Provinces' Muslims, 1860-1923*. London: Cambridge University Press.

Rohde, Joy. 2009. "Gray Matters: Social Scientists, Military Patronage, and Democracy in the Cold War." *Journal of American History*. Vol. 96, No. 1, pp. 99–122.

Rohde, Joy. 2007. "'The Social Scientists' War': Expertise in a Cold War Nation." Unpublished PhD dissertation, University of Pennsylvania <http://repository. upenn.edu/dissertations/AAI3271806>.

Roots for Equity. 2006. "Agrarian Reform Research in Pakistan." In Ujjaini Halim (ed.). *Neoliberal Subversion of Agrarian Reform*. Quezon City, Philippines: Asia Pacific Research Network, pp. 363–99.

Rostow, Walt Whitman. 1960. *Stages of Economic Growth: A Non-Communist Manifesto*. Cambridge: Cambridge University Press.

Rouse, Shahnaz. 2004. "Gendered Struggles: The State, Religion and Civil Society." In Nighat Said Khan (ed.). *Up Against the State*. Lahore: ASR Publications, pp. 42–64.

Rouse, Shahnaz. 1998. "The Outsider(s) Within: Sovereignty and Citizenship in Pakistan." In Patricia Jeffrey and Amrita Basu (eds.). *Appropriating Gender: Women's Activism and Politicized Religion in South Asia*. New York: Routledge, pp. 53–70.

Rouse, Shahnaz. 1992. "Discourses on Gender in Pakistan: Convergence and Contradiction." In Douglas Allen (ed.). *Religion and Political Conflict in South Asia*. Westport, CT: Greenwood Press, pp. 87-112.

Rushdie, Salman. 2000. *Shame*. New York: Picador.

Saigol, Rubina. 2004. *Ownership or Death: Women and Tenant Struggles in Pakistani Punjab*. New Delhi: Rupa & Co.

Saigol, Rubina. 1995. *Knowledge and Identity: Articulation of Gender in Educational Discourse in Pakistan*. Lahore: ASR Publications.

Samad, Younus. 1995. *A Nation in Turmoil: Nationalism and Ethnicity in Pakistan, 1937–1958*. Thousand Oaks, CA: Sage Publications.

Saunders, Frances Stoner. 1999. *The Cultural Cold War: The CIA and the World of Arts and Letters*. New York: New Press.

Sayeed, Khalid bin. 1980. *Politics in Pakistan: The Nature and Direction of Change*. New York: Praeger.

Sayeed, Khalid bin. 1968. *Pakistan: The Formative Phase, 1857–1948*. London: Oxford University Press.

Scott-Smith, Giles. 2001. *The Politics of Apolitical Culture: The Congress for Cultural Freedom and Post-War US-European Relations*. London: Routledge.

Scott-Smith, Giles and Hans Krabbendam. 2003. *The Cultural Cold War in Western Europe, 1945–1960*. London: Frank Cass.

Seelye, Dorothy (ed.). 1951. *Islam in the Middle East*. Report of Conference on Middle Eastern Affairs. Washington, DC: Middle East Institute.

Shahab, Qudrutullah. 1948. *Ya Khuda*. Karachi: Lala Rukh Publications.

Shaikh, Farzana. 1989. *Community and Consensus in Islam: Muslim Representation in Colonial India, 1860–1947*. New York: Oxford University Press.

Shireen, Mumtaz. 1963. "*Fasaadat par Hamaare Afsaane*" ["Our Novels on the Riots"]. *Mi'yar* [Standard]. Lahore: Naya Idara.

Siddiqa, Ayesha. 2007. *Military, Inc.: Inside Pakistan's Military Economy*. London: Pluto Press.

Siddiqi, Muhammad Ali. 2010. "Pakistan's New Left." *Dawn*. March 3.

Sookhdeo, Patrick. 2002. *A People Betrayed: The Impact of Islamisation on the Christian Community in Pakistan*. Fearn, Scotland: Christian Focus Publications.

Stewart, Neil. 1999. "Honor Killings, Human Rights Defenders Face Death Threats While Killers Walk Free." *Tribune Des Droits Humains*. Vol. 6, No. 3, September.

Suleri, Abid. 2009. "The Social Dimensions of Food Insecurity in Pakistan." Talk given at "Hunger Pains: Pakistan's Food Insecurity" conference. Woodrow Wilson Center for International Scholars. Washington, DC. June 3.

Sumar, A.K. 1970. "Islam and Socialism." In Mehdi, Haider (ed.). *Essays on Pakistan*. Lahore: Progressive Publishers, pp. 44–62.

Tahir, Madiha. 2010. "Balochistan: Pakistan's Broken Mirror." *The National*. March 25 <http://www.thenational.ae/news/worldwide/balochistan-pakistans-broken-mirror>.

Talbot, Ian. 1998. *Pakistan: A Political History*. New York: St. Martin's Press.

Talpur, Mir Mohammad. 2010. "Luckless Gwadar." *Daily Times*. January 10 <http://www.dailytimes.com.pk/default.asp?page=2010\01\10\story_10-1-2010_pg3_4>.

Taseer, Muhammad Din. 1949. "*IshtiraakiyatPasandon ka Nazariyya-i Ilm-o Adab*" ["The Literary and Intellectual Ideology of Communists"]. *Chatan*. June 27.

Taseer, Muhammad Din. 1948. "*Pakistan Mein Kulchur ka Mustaqbil*" ["The Future of Culture in Pakistan"]. *Mah-i Nau. Khaas Number* [Special Issue].

Toor, Saadia. 2011. "How Not to Talk About Muslim Women: Patriarchy, Islam and the Sexual Regulation of Pakistani Women." In Steven Seidman, Nancy Fischer and Chet Meeks (eds.). *Introducing the New Sexuality Studies*. 2nd edn. New York: Routledge.

Toor, Saadia. 2010. "The Structural Dimensions of Food Insecurity in Pakistan. In Michael Kugelman and Robert Hathaway (eds.). *Hunger Pains: Pakistan's Food Insecurity*. Washington, DC: Woodrow Wilson International Center for Scholars, pp. 99–115.

Toor, Saadia. 2009a. "Behind the Nightmare in Swat." *Socialist Worker*. May 22. <http://socialistworker.org/2009/05/22/behind-the-nightmare-in-swat>.

Toor, Saadia. 2009b. "The Cynicism of the Liberal Elite is Hampering the Development of an Effective Democracy." *Herald*. April, pp. 46–9.

Toor, Saadia. 2005. "Culture/Nation/State: Cultural Nationalism and Moral Regulation in Pakistan, 1947–1971." Unpublished doctoral dissertation. Ithaca, NY: Cornell University.

Toor, Saadia. 2001. "Globalisation with a Human Face: The Role of Nongovernment Organisations in Pakistan." *Tarikh*, No. 11.

Umar, Badruddin. 2004. *The Emergence of Bangladesh: Class Struggles in East Pakistan, 1947–1958*. Karachi: Oxford University Press.

Usmani, Adaner. 2010. "Pakistan's Ship-breakers' Strike." *Socialist Worker*. July 6. <http://socialistworker.org/2010/07/06/pakistan-ship-breakers-strike>.

Waseem, Muhammad. 2007. *Politics and the State in Pakistan*. 3rd edn. Islamabad: National Institute of Historical and Cultural Research, Centre of Excellence, Quaid-i-Azam University.

Williams, Horatio. 2001. Hindsight After the Cold War: Samuel Huntington, the Social Sciences and Development Paradigms. *Dialectical Anthropology*. Vol. 26, Nos. 3-4, pp. 311-324.

Williams, Raymond. 1977. *Marxism and Literature*. New York: Oxford University Press.

WAF (Women's Action Forum). 2008. Press Release: "WAF Condemns Appointment of Zehri, Bijrani in Cabinet." *Dawn*. November 13 <http://archives.dawn.com/2008/11/13/top18.htm>.

Zaidi, Syed Akbar. 2005. *Issues in Pakistan's Economy*. 2nd edn. Karachi: Oxford University Press.

Zaidi, Zulqurnain S.M. 2003. *The Emergence of Ulema in the Politics of India and Pakistan 1918–1949*. New York: Writers Club Press.

Zaman, Muhammad Qasim. 1998. "Sectarianism in Pakistan: The Radicalization of Shi'i and Sunni Identities." *Modern Asian Studies*. Vol. 32, No. 3, pp. 689–716.

Zia, Afiya Shehrbano. 2011. "The Liberals' Dilemma." *Viewpoint*. January 11. <http://www.viewpointonline.net/the-liberals-dilemma.html>.

Zia, Afiya Shehrbano. 1995. "Women and Media: An Overview." In Nighat Said Khan, and Afiya S. Zia (eds.). *Unveiling the Issues*. Lahore: Asr Publications, pp. 83–91.

Zia, Afiya Shehrbano. 1994. *Sex Crime in the Islamic Context: Rape, Class and Gender in Pakistan*. Lahore: ASR Publications.

Zia, Shahla. 2002. *Violence Against Women and their Quest for Justice*. Lahore: Simorgh Publications.

Ziring, Lawrence. 2001. *Pakistan in the Twentieth Century: A Political History*. Karachi: Oxford University Press.

Ziring, Lawrence. 1980. *Pakistan: The Enigma of Political Development*. Boulder, CO: Westview Press.

Index

Compiled by Sue Carlton